# THE EXPLORATION OF THE PACIFIC

# THE EXPLORATION
## OF
# THE PACIFIC

BY

## J. C. BEAGLEHOLE

### THIRD EDITION

Danger hath honour! great designs, their fame!
Glory doth follow! Courage goes before!
And though th' event oft answers not the same,
Suffice that high attempts have never shame.
SAMUEL DANIEL

STANFORD UNIVERSITY PRESS
STANFORD, CALIFORNIA

TO
# ROBIN AND TIMOTHY
AND
# THEIR MOTHER

Stanford University Press
Stanford, California

© 1966 by John Cawte Beaglehole
First edition published by A. and C. Black Ltd, London, 1934
Third edition (first Stanford edition) 1966
Stanford edition printed in the United States of America

Cloth ISBN 0-8047-0310-8
Paper ISBN 0-8047-0311-6

Last figure below indicates year of this printing:

00  99  98  97  96  95  94  93  92  91

# PREFACE TO THE THIRD EDITION

IN the more than thirty years since this book was first written and published a great deal of work has been done on the history of Pacific exploration—enough to make the present writer, looking at some of the statements he made so long ago, feel exceedingly uncomfortable. The best of this work, indeed, has appeared since the second edition was prepared in 1945, and that edition is long out of print. Clearly, if the book were to have any continued usefulness, it needed much revision and re-writing. That revision and rewriting it has now had. No doubt it is still far from perfect. It should probably be made twice as long, for a start: to examine at greater length, for example, the ideas and plans of Magellan—or the observations of the Dutch (rather unjustly, perhaps, animadverted upon in the preface to the first edition), or the economic background to the voyage of Bougainville—would be interesting exercises. But there are objections.

The plan and proportions of this new version remain as before, though only a very few pages have survived without alteration. Apart from corrections of straight-out error, and some modifications of opinion, there are now more and better identifications of islands—though from obvious necessity I have had to refrain both from the controversial (on the whole) and from any attempt at comprehensiveness—and many of the quotations are from better texts. Questions of nomenclature, referred to in the preface to the first edition, no longer seem troublesome. A number of footnotes have been banished, and others brought in, though their total has still been kept to a minimum. The bibliography has been thoroughly overhauled and brought up to date: it is still highly selective, and almost all English. The maps also have had some revision.

To my publisher I owe a particular debt of thanks—and rejoice to pay it—for his determination to keep the book in print, and for his patience in waiting for the revised text. Three friends and co-workers in the field of Pacific history have helped me very much, from their printed pages and with critical notes: they are Dr Helen M. Wallis, Father Celsus Kelly, O.F.M., and Mr Andrew Sharp. To them also I record my great gratitude.

J.C.B.

Victoria University of Wellington
   *May* 1965

# PREFACE TO THE FIRST EDITION

THE aim of this book is to give an account of European exploration of the Pacific from Magellan to Cook—that is, of the long search for the imagined continent *Terra Australis incognita* and of the discovery of the main island groups of the ocean. It makes no pretence at describing the exploration of the continental shores of the Pacific, and the reference, for instance, to the work of Cook and Vancouver on the North American coast is of the slightest. Nor can it do what any final book on the subject must do, and discuss the story from the native standpoint as well as the European. The perfect Pacific historian, it might almost be said, should be in large measure ethnologist as well; for many things hard to explain in the contact of races are not to be understood from European sources only—especially when the Europeans involved were (like the Dutch) often bad observers. Geographical discovery is not a matter of geography alone, as the eighteenth century began to realize.

Prescribed limitations of space in addition have made it imperative to recount only what is actually known of the history of the subject; for that reason I have not engaged in speculation from early maps in regard, *e.g.*, to the first discovery of Australia —a sport as pleasant as it is indecisive; nor in identifying islands have I lost them again in an ocean of footnotes. Questions of nomenclature are somewhat troublesome: Guadalcanal or Guadalcanar? Tongatabu or Amsterdam? Anamocka or Nomuka? Paumotu or Tuamotu? For convenience I have generally used the modern form; in some cases, where the logic of the story seemed to lead to it, preferring the older word, *e.g.* Guadalcanal.

I have quoted freely, but so often from sources known to the student that I have given specific reference only where the argument seems to require it. A brief bibliography will be found at the end of the book.

Removed by so many thousands of miles from the British Museum and the Public Record Office, I have found some compensation in the Alexander Turnbull Library and the Library of the General Assembly, both in Wellington—to the staffs of which I owe thanks for their uniform benevolence. But I must particularly record my gratitude to Mr A. D. McIntosh, M.A., of the General Assembly Library, to D. E. B., and to my wife; while I am indebted to the editors for seeing the book through the press.

J. C. BEAGLEHOLE

Wellington, *October* 1933

# CONTENTS

# MAPS
## *Following page 346*

# THE EXPLORATION OF THE PACIFIC

# CHAPTER I

# THE PROBLEM STATED

IN every great discoverer there is a dual passion—the passion to see, the passion to report; and in the greatest this duality is fused into one—a passion to see and to report truly. But not only for this purest of motives do men travel. They wander by sea and by land; they feel the enchantment of strange skies, lit at midnight; they draw near an unknown coast with wonder ever renewed; they find fair prospect in freezing cold or burning heat; they endure exile and the rigours of privation, for curiosity or for pay, for the prospect of gold, to found a trade or extend a religion, for conquest or for settlement, as enthusiasts or in the plain course of professional duty. In the exploration of the Pacific Ocean all these motives have played due part; and though in different ages the guiding impulse has varied as widely as the interest of mankind, in none have voyages been directed with a single end in view. 'Geography', said Bougainville, that chivalrous and intrepid spirit, 'is a science of facts'; and it was the desire to make greater the harvest of facts fully and precisely known which urged the most decisive efforts of exploration in the Pacific. In the discoverers of the eighteenth century, to which Bougainville himself belonged, was first seen the organized pursuit of geographical knowledge for its own sake; and to science the reward was great. But statesmen were less disinterested; their devotion was sworn to commerce and to empire as much as to the expansion of the mind. This third and last great epoch of Pacific discovery, with its emphasis on knowledge, belonged to the English and the French; the first, the sixteenth century, was that of the Spanish, animated by a mingled zeal for religion and for gold; the second, the seventeenth century, that of the Dutch, the supporters of a prosaic and determined expansion of trade. Yet though pure discovery was not the only intention of these first voyagers, their discoveries were notable; among them were some alive with the compulsion to see and to report; positively or negatively they gave the geographer facts.

What, then, was the foundation of knowledge on which men built? Why was it not till the early sixteenth century that this exploration began? What difficulties made triumph so hardly won? Whence came the faith, the ambition, which drove men to seek that triumph? To answer those questions it is needful to have brief recourse to history.

Exploration of the Pacific, it is obvious, must be exploration by sea; and there were difficulties enough in that. But granted even the removal of such difficulties, before men could explore the ocean the fact of its existence must become patent to them; and when so much of their effort lay in the southern hemisphere they must at least believe in the southern hemisphere. One faces old controversy: the shape of the earth is in question. Among the thinkers of antiquity, the Greeks were well aware that the earth was round. Their solid knowledge was mingled with much improbable conjecture—Pomponius Mela, who wrote about A.D. 50, held that the unknown southern hemisphere was ocean, broken by a continent of which Ceylon possibly formed the northern tip; in this continent were the springs of the Nile, which flowed subterraneously to emerge in Africa—for between the two hemispheres lay the burning zone of the Tropic Seas, over which it was impossible for men to pass. Claudius Ptolemy, on the other hand, the second-century Egyptian astronomer in whom ancient geography came brilliantly to its climax, held that unknown land in the east swung round to the west and joined the southern part of Africa, making of the Indian Ocean a vast inland sea. Ptolemy's maps exercised persuasive influence on thinkers a thousand years later; and not till Diaz and Vasco da Gama, later still, was this conception finally disproved. Nevertheless, Ptolemy had proved the earth round by arguments known to every modern school-child; and for practical illustration, merchants of his time had sailed down the coast of Africa beyond Cape Guardafui, perhaps to Zanzibar, five degrees south of the equator.

Ptolemy was the last of a great line of sages. After him the boundaries of geographical knowledge contracted, as invaders closed in on the empire of Rome and the lamps of science went out. A Europe struggling for stability, with its learned men thinking and writing in Latin, not Greek, their intellectual energies centred on theological speculation, was no place for the enlargement of geographical theory. Travel itself—for we have always travellers—had a theological end. Men and women went on pilgrimage; and beyond the journeys of the pilgrims, little during the first few hundred years of the Christian era is recorded. For such centuries Pomponius Mela and Ptolemy pondered in vain. The world, it could be argued, was arranged symmetrically round Palestine: was it not written with clarity and emphasis in Scripture, 'thus saith the Lord, This is Jerusalem: I have set her in the midst of the nations and countries that are round about'? To this simple completion was geography brought; and a column erected in the sacred city marked the central point of the whole earth. Though some of the more sophisticated early Christian Fathers, indeed—a St Basil the Great, an English Bede—were driven to doubt the validity of this argument, they were in a minority. On the conception of antipodean hemisphere and antipodean inhabitants the generality of learned doctors poured out their wrath and scorn. God did not make rain fall upwards, trees grow backwards, men whose feet were higher than their heads.

There came upon the world the astonishing rise of Mahomet; the Tartars swept down over Asia; Islam solidified and became a civilization. The Arabs took up the scientific inheritance of Greece—including its geography—and through war and peace, through crusade and trade, intercourse with the West led to the transmission of learning, to a new enlightenment and sanity. And if an attitude of mind is important to discovery, so equally are the experienced facts of travel. The period of Tartar supremacy was a brief flowering-time of peace and of the intellect, and it was in the second half of the thirteenth century, when the great Khan Khubla reigned in China, that the Polo family reached Peking. The account, full and exact, which Marco Polo rendered of that enchanted kingdom was of tremendous importance to Europe—and in one particular direction to the future of discovery. For a universal misinterpretation of his narrative gave men to understand that there was south of Java a land which he had visited—the great and rich country of Locach. The name became corrupted into Beach, and round it clustered all the stories of an unknown southern continent. It was a good country and a rich, said Marco Polo, on the mainland, with a king of its own, and its people were idolaters. In it grew much brazil-wood; and there was found gold in incredible quantities, elephants and porcelain shells. It was a wild region, rarely visited, for the king did not desire the presence of strangers who might get knowledge of his treasures and resources. And this wild region, with its elephants and gold, the enlarged and misapplied vision of Polo's recollection of Siam or the Malay peninsula, crystallized in the tradition of geography into one of the chief articles of the faith which so often took the place of knowledge.

Nor was Marco Polo the only traveller to the East: merchants and monks followed the caravan routes across desert and mountain, and for fifty years, between 1290 and 1340, so well did Europeans know the East that it seemed that the ends of the world were in friendly contact. Then the Tartar empire fell; an anti-foreign dynasty rose up in China, Central Asia was plunged into its primal anarchy; Persia, where rival faiths had contended in difficult balance, went finally to Islam. Eastern trade sought the West now by devious and arduous routes, and the profits were to the infidel. But there was a difference in this second darkness from that first when Rome fell—it was as if a curtain had come down on a stage blazing with coloured jewels and magic lights, odorous with legendary incense, rustling with silks and fabled fabrics. The whole intent and effort of men was now to penetrate behind that curtain.

Such effort involved an alternative route to the East. Meanwhile the sphericity of the earth was matter of argument again, and to the educated later Middle Ages the idea was familiar. Lambert, Canon of St Omer, a popular author from about 1130, when he wrote, to the end of the fourteenth century, enunciated the old idea of a southern uninhabited clime, cut off from the north by a wide equatorial sea, heated past the endurance of men, beyond which was a southern land still unknown, temperate in climate, but 'having nothing which is related to our race'. The Schoolman, Albertus Magnus, on the contrary, believed that southern peoples must exist in great numbers, saved or unsaved. Roger Bacon had no doubts; his authority influenced the great Cardinal Pierre d'Ailly, at the beginning of the fifteenth century. D'Ailly was learned: he had read Ptolemy, he quoted Greek, Latin and Arab writers. 'Pliny tells us', he said, 'that ships from the Gulf of Arabia can arrive in a short time at Gades in the south of Spain.' Here was a conjecture of importance—could it be that Ptolemy was wrong and Pomponius Mela right, that the Indian Ocean was not a landlocked sea, that a passage was possible round Africa to Arabia, to India, to Marco Polo's Cathay and all its riches? These witnesses to knowledge are important: more indicative are the spurious *Travels* of the figure known as Sir John Mandeville, written about 1370, not for the savant, but for the entertainment of the average educated man. Mandeville was quite explicit that 'if a man found passages by ships that would go to search the world, men might go by ship all about the world and above and beneath'. And already eighty years before Mandeville the first expedition had set out to find a sea-way round Africa to the East—that of the Genoese Doria and Vivaldi in 1291. Of them we have no further record.

Such being the theories of men, such their knowledge, why did they not immediately and confidently set out to girdle this world? There were two reasons—the dangers of the deep and of strange lands, and the dangers of the greater deep of man's mind. The actual difficulties of the medieval sailor were sufficient, in all conscience; but not content with the shipwreck and sudden death of familiar experience, men must people the unknown with all imaginable terrors—darkness and fog, whirlpools and waterspouts, monstrous birds and basilisks and giants, unchained Leviathan in the sea, all the fantastic embodiments of hell by land. More attractive wonders there might be, islands of gold and silver and dolphins who leapt over the mainsails of ships; the discouragements remained too many. What tempestous and fatal sea had claimed Doria and Vivaldi?

Yet there comes a time when the terrors of the unknown are outweighed by its fascination, when experiment must be tried and scepticism urges it on, when sailors are moved not so much by legend as by a careful calculation of possibilities. To such motives, sometimes overtopping them, is added material interest. From the middle of the fourteenth century Europeans knew the East directly no more. Still the products of the East were vital to them. The Turks straddled across the caravan routes levying tribute, while in Europe the monopoly of Eastern trade lay with the merchants of Venice and the Hansa. Europe rebelled, and trade, religious proselytism and the ardour of discovery met in that fifteenth-century effort of exploration which broke into the full fervour of the Renaissance. The continuous tradition of European discovery, it may be said, began with the home-keeping Portuguese Prince Henry the Navigator, who died in 1460, the impulsion of whose spirit made certain the doubling of Africa, and so the whole course of exploration east of the Cape of Good Hope. In 1488 Diaz returned in jubilation from the Cape, and ten years later Vasco da Gama was in India. Meanwhile Columbus, taking his western route, had discovered America. In 1511 Albuquerque, the magnificent viceroy, conquered Malacca and founded Portuguese empire in the Far East; by 1542 his countrymen had reached Japan. Before then, in 1513, Balboa had stood on a 'peak in Darien' and had seen the Pacific. A new ocean lay presented to the mind of man.

So, by the middle of the sixteenth century, ancient and medieval conceptions put behind, the world was being mapped in something of its final shape. The Mediterranean was no longer the summary of men's voyaging—the Scottish islands were no longer Ultima Thule. The mass and outlines of Asia, Africa and the Atlantic side of America were approximately known, though assumption and guesswork were still to play their part; the seamen of Europe had sailed most of the great oceans of the world. The geographers of Europe—Mercator, Ortelius, Wytfliet—were busy with their maps and projections; and only the South remained to discover. Geography is a science of facts; but in the absence of known facts scientists reasoned by analogy. What could exist in that fabled South but another, the last great continent, the *Terra Australis incognita* of the ancients, the immense land which must at last be revealed to the amazed if expectant eyes of men? Symmetry demanded it; the balance of the earth demanded it—for in the absence of this tremendous mass of land what, asked Mercator, was there to prevent the world from toppling over to destruction amidst the stars? The great southern continent was to most thinkers of the time more than mere knowledge founded on discovery and experience— it was a feeling, a tradition, a logical and now even a theological necessity, a compelling and inescapable mathematical certitude. Its discovery must come. To most geographers the probability was that this continent adhered to the southern coast of New Guinea. Mercator, Ortelius and Wytfliet on the other hand all drew a strait between the two countries, while none gave any evidence either way. Mercator and Ortelius agreed that there was uncertainty, but Wytfliet entertained no doubt. All this may seem to imply some knowledge of Australia: but it was more than a mere Australia that these geographers envisaged— it was a land which in width might stretch from anywhere in the Indian Ocean to South America, and from the East Indies to the Pole. The problem of the Pacific and its solution is summed up in the attempt to find this *Terra Australis incognita*, growing scepticism as to its existence, the antagonism of two schools of thought, those who believed and those who disbelieved in the continental hypothesis, and the gradual revelation of the truth, voyage by voyage, till the extraordinary achievement of Cook left his successors (as a Frenchman said) with little to do but admire it.

It remains in this chapter to consider some of the difficulties, inherent in early discovery, against which captains and idealists struggled often in vain, and nearly always at great disadvantage to work long and eagerly planned; for without knowledge of difficulties, who shall estimate success or failure? There were those difficulties inherent in the nature of the ocean. There was its immense size: at its widest 10,000 miles from east to west, and 10,000 from north to south. There was the minute size of most of the islands that sprinkled its surface, apart from the larger groups (and most of those not really large) of its western side. There was a whole wind system to be learnt: the westerlies of the south and north, the south-east and north-east trades of the centre, and all the modifications of the months and seasons. There was the silent force of the currents, like the Humboldt current that combined with the westerly wind to keep ships from striking freely into the ocean from the southern coast of South America. Those were all factors in discovery as well as facts to be discovered. Independent of them were obstacles of a different kind.

These were obstacles especially to the sixteenth and seventeenth centuries; for the scientific genius did not come to its full fruit in navigation till the eighteenth. Even then the human factor was preponderant. The early conditions of exploration were adverse in the extreme—ships were, to the modern mind, ludicrously small and ill found. Not till the Portuguese invented the three-masted ocean-going ship, in place of the medieval oared galley or one-masted vessel of coastwise passages, were long voyages of any sort possible. The invention was developed in the fifteenth and sixteenth centuries. Sometimes good ships were provided, according to the lights of the time; but long afterwards still, where the most careful and stringent organization was a vital necessity, governments might fob off seamen with the last remnants of a worm-eaten navy. Yet somehow, sometimes, these vessels floated; somehow they resisted tide and tempest, and before they sank rendered their account of the unknown. In the eighteenth century, and not before then, could a great Pacific voyage be carried out with a reasonable margin of safety. The quality of the ships was not exceeded by that of their crews. The constancy of the trained sailor was the exception; none but the roughest of men would peril their lives and character under the prevalent conditions, and too often the expedition of discovery was manned from the dregs of piracy, prison and dockyard inn. The old voyages were one continual struggle against mutiny; it will be seen in the pages that follow how often a good pilot failed as a captain, and with what a regular and fatal persistence great aims were doomed utterly from the character of those who could be made worthy of their calling only by the most heroic genius of inspiration and organization. All men, good and bad alike, were at sea affected by scurvy, a greater obstacle to long-distance navigation than all other factors, human or technical. The absence of fresh food and the everlasting diet of salt meat and decaying biscuit made many a voyage simply a test of endurance, with death as the preordained end for the majority of a ship's company. Exploration not once or twice became a heart-breaking search for any shore where a ship could put in and refresh.

There were deficiencies in the technique of navigation. Maps and charts were rudimentary, but it was the very purpose of exploration to improve them. The greatest and for centuries the insuperable impediment to exactness was the absence of any method of determining longitude at sea. By means of primitive instruments, the cross-staff and the astrolabe, the latitude could be found with fair precision, and the compass was generally used from the beginning of the fifteenth century. The problem of longitude remained, seemingly, insoluble. It was impossible to tell with accuracy how far a ship had sailed or to steer by the shortest route for a known port. A captain made a landfall where he could and groped along a coast by traditional landmarks or rule of thumb. 'Now there be some that are very inquisitive to have a way to get the longitude,' said a writer of the time of the Armada, who was echoed through the seventeenth century, 'but that is too tedious for seamen, since it requireth the deep knowledge of astronomy, wherefore I would not have any man think that the longitude is to be found at sea by any instrument; so let no seamen trouble themselves with any such rule, but (according to their accustomed manner) let them keep a perfect account and reckoning of the way of their ship.' This 'perfect account and reckoning' could be kept only from a very rough estimate of the ship's speed.[1] Under these conditions errors of upwards of two thousand miles were not unknown in crossing the Pacific. Governments offered prizes for a successful solution of the problem; the prizes stood unclaimed. Greenwich Observatory was founded in 1675 for the benefit of navigation, with the calculation of longitude particularly in mind—for the position of the moon as it moved in relation to the heavenly bodies lying in its path had been found by expert hands to give some indication of position. In 1714 the English Government founded the Board of Longitude, the 'Commissioners for the discovery of longitude at sea', to stimulate meritorious work. Not till about 1730 did John Harrison begin to develop his capital invention of the chronometer. The sextant had been invented a few years earlier, and from this period modern navigation takes its birth. It is not hard to imagine the earlier difficulties of accurate discovery, nor to picture the tax on the ingenuity of the map-maker.

---

[1] Judged, *e.g.*, from the time taken by some floating object to pass the ship; for this purpose a small log of wood attached to a rope was used, while the time was judged from the repetition of stock sentences.

So much for the hindrances and inevitable error which faced any sailor. There are also things necessary and elemental to the great discoverer, which, though many men have had some of them in some measure, are found rarely in plenitude and combination. Of the three qualities of seamanship, leadership and knowledge, seamanship has been the commonest. It grew, of course, with the growth of scientific navigation and naval construction, but it was strong with the strength of an instinct when scientific navigation was yet unknown; it has been the tradition of countless pilots and captains and mates, from the time men first left their shores in ships. Leadership is a more uncommon quality; seamanship is its prerequisite, it involves knowledge of an end to be attained and fortitude in its attainment: not only fortitude, but the power of inspiring others with fortitude, and those others frequently the least likely to feel the breath of the heroic. It implies the ability to adapt insufficient means to great ends; and to constrain, more than to seek success. The great leader is a transforming man: he will give coherency and steadfastness and faith to his followers; he will go forward not doubting their loyalty because of that in him which makes loyalty certain. Thirdly, there is knowledge—knowledge of navigation, knowledge of self and of men, knowledge of the work to be done and how best to do it. And the knowledge necessary for exploration by sea was not confined to an acquired technique and the accumulation of facts, mastery of the ordinary details of seamanship and geography, of winds, tides and charts. It resided almost as much in a sense of the possibilities, in a sort of intuition, founded none the less on science and the scientific spirit—a spirit which had theories but no dogmas, which reckoned on all factors and all chances with a fair and equable mind, and yet divined when merely to calculate was to greet failure.

To few men has this supreme gift been given, that in them the three qualities meet and fuse. Seamanship is to be expected; a Quiros, a Dampier, for their ages, have a full measure of technical knowledge and idealism and scientific curiosity, but cannot command; the great buccaneers, the English heirs of the Elizabethan tradition, can command but never seek further; in those few elected spirits, such as Cook, is the complete equipment of genius, and fortune coincides with their appearance, and the face of the world is changed.

# CHAPTER II

## MAGELLAN

ON 25 September 1513 Vasco Nuñez de Balboa first of European men sighted the Pacific. With a chosen band of soldiers he toiled and fought his way across the Isthmus of Panama; and on that day from the summit of the Sierras he saw the ocean. He gave thanks to God and descended with his companions to the beach of the Gulf of San Miguel, which here bent round to the north. How natural it was therefore to call this new expanse the 'Great South Sea': and Balboa waded into the water and claimed it and all the continents and islands it washed and all it contained for his master the King of Spain. Such tremendous gestures did men make in those excited days. Beyond this ocean, they thought, China and Japan and the spices of the East at last must lie, could another Columbus but bridge it. But alas, what then: what would it profit Spain? For already the Papal Bull of 1493 had divided the world into two, the West for Spain and the East for Portugal; already, though they knew it not, Portuguese had entered the eastern gates of the ocean. The Tordesillas *Capitulacion* of 1494 had drawn the dividing line north and south 370 leagues west of the Cape Verde Islands: this had given Portugal part of Brazil, and Portuguese sailors had ventured down the seaboard of South America. How much Gonzalo Coelho and Christovaño Jacques saw of the coast of Patagonia we do not know; Juan de Solis indeed sailed south to 40 degrees of latitude and in the Rio de la Plata was killed and eaten by savages, with sixty of his companions. There seemed no break in all that land that Columbus had discovered through which men might penetrate to the east; and while they still disputed as to the longitude of Maluco—

the Moluccas or Spice Islands—ardent Spaniards even proposed to cut a canal through Panama. Others argued that a measure so heroic was unnecessary, for there must surely be a strait somewhere through the continent, or perhaps land itself came to an end, as Africa had done at her Cape of Good Hope. Juan de Solis, however, had passed farther south than the southernmost point of Africa; harbours and rivers there were, but no strait. The German geographer Schöner marked a strait on globes which he made in 1515 and 1520, the fruit of conjecture rather than of knowledge. Knowledge of the Pacific at the beginning of the sixteenth century was summed up in a strip of coastline and a blank. The man who first interpreted this blank, entering directly upon it from the Atlantic, was Fernão de Magalhães— a name Englished as Ferdinand Magellan.

Magellan was born in 1480, of a noble Portuguese family, at Sabrosa in the mountainous province of Traz-os-Montes. No man, it might be thought, would be less likely to find eminence on the sea, but it was Portugal's great age, and adventure might take a Portuguese anywhere in the world. Magellan's youth was spent at court, in the train of the queen, and after 1495, of Don Manoel, a king of curiously mixed character. A youth of that time in that court breathed influences from the uttermost parts of the earth. Portuguese captains had pushed north, south, east and west, to Labrador and the Congo, to Brazil and India: to the court they brought their tales and their scars, their harvest of gold and spices and strange men made slaves. Empire for the Portuguese lay east, and to a youth like Magellan in the East lay adventure and fame. Don Manoel was ambitious though mean; he it was who first determined to take what the Pope had given and make Portuguese might a reality. It was a task of conquest —a task for which in 1504 the greatest armada that had ever left Portugal was being prepared to sail under Francisco d'Almeida, one of the ablest, certainly the most stainless, of all Portuguese viceroys in India. The death-rate on expeditions to the East was nearly six out of every seven who went; the rewards of the survivor none the less might be enormous, and apart even from gold there was a stir in the blood still at the thought of fighting Moor and infidel on strange seas and coloured lands. So Magellan enlisted under Almeida as a volunteer, and in 1505 left his country for seven years. He was not a man of importance in the fleet, and in the histories of those extraordinary years is rarely mentioned by name. Yet it is known of him that he fought valiantly in engagements which made the Portuguese the acknowledged masters of commerce from the Red Sea to the East Indies; and here and there emerges evidence of the presence of mind, the decision and constancy which made Magellan's small body and restless spirit the key to the future in seas stranger yet. In 1509 he was in the abortive expedition to Malacca, where his bravery in the rescue of Portuguese attacked on shore led to fast friendship with one of them, Francisco Serrano. It was he who the next year, when two ships were wrecked near the Maldive Islands, stayed with the sailors while his fellow officers returned to port in a small boat for help. Malacca was taken in 1511; and then at the end of the year three ships set sail for the remoter East and the unvisited, the fabulous Spice Islands. The captain of one of these ships was Serrano: his vessel was wrecked, and in a junk he was wrecked again, finally to reach the small island of Ternate, with its neighbour Tidore the very heart of all the spices of the East. Here he stayed; and from here he wrote to his friend Magellan, 'giving him to understand that he had discovered yet another new world, larger and richer than that found by Vasco da Gama'.

By the middle of 1512 Magellan was back in Portugal and at court again. He did not stay at home longer than a year. In a punitive expedition against the Sultan of Azamor, in Morocco, he was wounded behind the knee and acquired a permanent limp; worse still, he was accused of selling cattle, part of the booty, to the Moors. He was declared innocent and returned once more to the court. But Don Manoel, who disliked him beyond reason, refused him promotion or further employment in the royal service, and granted him with insulting complacency the privilege of entering on any other service he chose.

Kings have sometimes lived to regret their insolence; it was so with Don Manoel.

For the ambitious scheme of Magellan must by this time have been very clearly defined in his mind. A while longer he lived in Portugal, 'always busied with pilots, charts and the question of longitude', acquiring all the geographical knowledge of his time, perfecting himself in the theories of navigation, and brooding over his letters from Francisco Serrano in Ternate. He met Ruy Faleiro, another student of maps and navigation and an astrologer of dark looks and uncertain temper, suspected of being in league with a devil. Faleiro, like many other Portuguese, had his grudge against Don Manoel; and like Magellan, he was possessed by the idea of a western passage to the East. The two men went into alliance. Among Serrano's papers after his death was found a letter from Magellan saying 'that he will be with him soon, if not by way of Portugal, by way of Spain, for to that issue his affairs seemed to be leading'. In 1517, at the age of thirty-seven, Magellan formally denaturalized himself and crossed the border. He arrived in Seville on 20 October, and on that day the conquest of the Pacific began.

Magellan had the good fortune to meet almost immediately a fellow Portuguese, Diogo Barbosa, who was alcalde of the Arsenal; with Barbosa he made his home, Barbosa's daughter Beatriz became his wife, and a nephew, Duarte Barbosa, a man of imperious temper and unhappy fate, one of his most trusted captains. He then applied for help in the proper quarter. This was the Casa de Contratacion at Seville, the 'India House' of Spain, where all colonial and naval affairs were centred, where pilots reported, and where geographical knowledge was most recent and organized. Now that the Spice Islands had been found it was disputed between Spain and Portugal in which half of the world they lay. Magellan offered to show the Spaniards a shorter route thereto than any already known, and, in addition, by so doing to prove that they lay within Spain's legal boundaries. Nevertheless at first the officials refused to consider his offer, for he had promised Ruy Faleiro not yet to disclose the exact details of their plan. But the chief of them, Juan Aranda, guessed what that plan was; he questioned Magellan closely, wrote to friends in Portugal to enquire into his reputation—wrote simultaneously to the Chancellor of Castile that there was come to Seville 'one who might do a great service to his Highness'. The report from Portugal was favourable, and Aranda forthwith set about all that was in his power to further the project. He was not, it appears, entirely disinterested. During a journey to Valladolid, where the court then lay, he proposed to Magellan and Faleiro that he should share in the profits of the voyage, and an agreement was actually made by which he was to receive one-eighth. He probably deserved some consideration; for he spent money generously on this mission, the outcome of the voyage was still highly speculative, and Faleiro, with his thin-skinned and self-centred moodiness growing on him, was a difficult man to deal with. He accused Magellan and Aranda alternately of betraying him, and as time went on seemed to become almost mad.

Within a very short time of their arrival at Valladolid, Aranda had arranged interviews with the principal counsellors of the young King Charles, the Emperor Charles V to be, and finally with the king himself. Magellan and Faleiro explained their plans and the arguments for the Spanish ownership of the Moluccas. A council divided in opinion was swayed favourably by its most powerful member, Juan de Fonseca, Bishop of Burgos, whose attitude towards other explorers of the New World had not been encouraging. The king acceded. An agreement was drawn up, whereby Charles promised to fit out five ships, with two years' provisioning (the organization was to be as complete as possible), under the command of Magellan as captain-general and Faleiro as joint leader. No other explorer was to be allowed to trespass on their route for ten years; no discoveries were to be made within the territories of the King of Portugal (he being thus in theory quite deprived of the Spice Islands), nor anything done prejudicial to his interests. Magellan and Faleiro were to receive a twentieth of the profits arising from their discoveries, a fifth of the profits of this first expedition, and if they discovered more than six islands a fifteenth of the profits of trade with any two they might choose. They were each to receive the title of *adelantado*, or governor; and all these profits and privileges were made hereditary. As a measure of supervision the king was to appoint to the fleet a treasurer and other financial officers.

All seemed to be going well; Charles bestowed the Order of Santiago on both leaders, and commanded the preparation of the fleet. Difficulties, however, were not at an end. Don Manoel, who had repulsed Magellan, now became thoroughly alarmed, and both the Portuguese ambassador at Valladolid and the Portuguese 'factor' at Seville were actively concerned in intrigues to stop the expedition. They recognized in Magellan the real moving spirit: 'As for the bachelor,' wrote the ambassador about Faleiro, 'I do not count him for much, for he is half crazy.' Sebastian Alvarez, the factor, held constant conversations with Magellan, endeavouring to shake his determination, either by flattery or by threats; he instigated a riot on board the *Trinidad*, one of the fleet, when in dock; and of the ships themselves he was contemptuous. 'They are very old and patched . . . and I would be sorry to sail even for the Canaries in them, for their ribs are as soft as butter', he wrote to his master. This did not stop preparations from going on steadily, and the vessels were made as seaworthy as possible. They were the *Santo Antonio*, 120 tons, the *Trinidad*, 110 tons, the *Conception*, 90 tons, the *Victoria*, 85 tons, and *Santiago*, 75 tons. As time went on the royal funds were exhausted, and Christopher de Haro, a member of a wealthy Antwerp firm trading with the East and West Indies, who had had seven ships sunk on the Guinea coast by the Portuguese, advanced a fifth of the whole cost; the merchants of Seville also made subscriptions. The Spice Islands were regarded as a good investment, even by way of a problematical western passage. It is evident also that there was in Magellan some quality which drew to him the confidence of shrewd men. It was harder to gather a crew. The ports of Spain were ransacked for volunteers, and the body assembled shows how really international was this Spanish effort: Spaniards, Portuguese, Basques, Genoese, Sicilians, French, Flemings, Germans, Greeks, Neapolitans, Corfiotes, Negros, Malays, even one Englishman—'Master Andrew of Bristol', a gunner. The king did not want more than five Portuguese; Magellan was driven to take thirty-seven, including several pilots and officers whom he could trust. Magellan himself, as captain-general, sailed in the *Trinidad*, the best though not the largest of the ships; to the *S. Antonio* was appointed Juan de Cartagena, to the *Concepcion* Gaspar de Quesada, to the *Victoria* Luis de Mendoza, the treasurer of the fleet. These three men were Spaniards, and from them was to come much trouble. The commander of the *Santiago* was João Serrano, another Spaniard, of great ability, a staunch supporter of Magellan, though unconnected with Francisco Serrano, now dealing vigorously in spices in Ternate.

As the time of departure came near the king drew up a most comprehensive manual of instructions, nautical, commercial and moral, which still exists, an index perhaps more to his intentions than to his sense of reality. Then Mendoza was insolent to Magellan, and was reduced to obedience only by royal command; then Faleiro's behaviour became more and more impossible, till finally he was ordered to stay behind and superintend the preparation of a second fleet; but it appears that he had already decided not to go. He gave Magellan his treatise on the finding of longitude, the fruit of his deepest studies, and the equipment must have seemed complete. In addition to the stores which Magellan had helped to pack with his own hands, and the looking-glasses, beads, knives, fish-hooks, red caps, stuffs, ivory, quicksilver, brass bracelets, and '20,000 bells' carried for trade, there were prepared for navigation twenty-three parchment charts, six pairs of compasses, twenty-one wooden quadrants, seven astrolabes, thirty-seven compass needles and eighteen hour-glasses. Such were the scientific resources which men used—over which, it might almost be said, they triumphed—in prosecuting what some have thought the greatest single voyage in history. When preparations were almost finished a solemn service was held at the church of Santa Maria de la Victoria at Seville, at which Magellan received the royal standard and his captains and men took oath of obedience to him. The ships sailed down the river and spent a month at San Lucar de Barrameda while the last details were completed. 'May God Almighty grant that they make a voyage like that of the Cortereals', wrote Alvarez to Don Manoel, with pious malevolence—the brothers Corte Real who with the true devotion of the Portuguese heroic age had perished in 1501 and 1502 on successive expeditions in search of a north-west passage. It remained to be seen how Providence would treat the explorers for a passage to the south-west. Magellan, so Don Manoel had been persuaded, was a boaster, a worthless adventurer; now, all intrigues, all persuasions, even the suggestion of poison, having failed to stop the braggart, the king's thought of his Spice Islands was touched with alarm. It might be that Magellan would indeed reach them, would indeed prove them to be legally Spanish: and Portuguese ships were ordered to the Cape of Good Hope, to the River Plate and to the Moluccas to waylay the traitor. But already Magellan had sailed. On 20 September 1519 his five ships crossed the bar of the Guadalquivir and stood southward.

Among Magellan's company was a gentleman volunteer, one Antonio Pigafetta of Vicenza, who had come to Seville in an ambassadorial train while the expedition was preparing, and being 'desirous of seeing the wonderful things of the ocean' had seized this opportunity, as tempting as it was unique. It was Pigafetta who wrote the best account of the voyage, though there are others shorter and sometimes differing in detail.

Of the voyage across the Atlantic little need be said. At Tenerife a caravel caught the ships up, bearing a message for the captain-general from Diogo Barbosa, 'to keep a good watch, since it had come to his knowledge that his captains had told their friends and relations that if they had any trouble with him

they would kill him'. Magellan was not dismayed: he sent back
the answer that 'be they good men or evil, he would do his
work as a servant of the Emperor; and to this end he had offered
his life'. Before the little fleet reached the equator, indeed, his
authority was challenged by Juan de Cartagena in the *S. Antonio*,
who questioned the course steered, and refused to salute
Magellan at evening as was the custom. After Tenerife there
was a fortnight's good weather, then twenty days of baffling
winds during which the ships advanced no more than three
leagues, then great storms in which the yard-arms dipped into
the waves and St Elmo's fire was seen to stand on the mast-
tops. The delay led to rationing of food, early in the voyage as
it was, and Juan de Cartagena thought the time had arrived to
upbraid Magellan openly. When he did so, at a council of
captains and pilots, he was arrested and confined in the *Victoria*
under the guard of Mendoza. There was no support for mutiny
as yet. All the while Pigafetta was industriously observing the
wonders of the ocean: the sixty days' rain round the line, sharks,
petrels—sea-birds which had no feet and whose life was one of
infinite skimming of the troubled waters, whose eggs were laid
and hatched on the backs of their males—and other marvels. On
29 November the coast of Brazil was sighted, and following it
south the fleet anchored in the Bay of Santa Lucia, where now
is Rio de Janeiro, on 13 December. Here there was trade with
the natives, who gave fowls and sweet potatoes and pineapples
in great quantities for fish-hooks and combs or little bells; for
an axe or a large knife they were prepared to barter their
children, if Magellan had permitted such commerce. It was
Portuguese territory; nor could extra mouths be fed. So after a
fortnight's refreshment they left that pleasant bay with its
amiable natives, so generous and so greatly impressed with the
service of the Mass, and pushed on through constant storms
down a coast steadily more unknown into seas of ever-
increasing cold. At the beginning of February 1520 they
arrived in the estuary of the Rio de la Plata and examined it
carefully for a passage to the west; it was an immense river and

no strait. As they went on there were more storms and the *Victoria* hit on a shoal; so Magellan sailed out to sea for two days, and then back to the Gulf of San Mathias, to examine what coast had been missed, again without finding the passage he sought. The cold became intense. Peculiar 'ducks' and 'sea-wolves' were met with—penguins and seals; in another violent gale all the cables of the *Trinidad* parted except one, and her crew gave themselves up for lost. Calm next day was succeeded by a second night of terror, relieved only by the appearance at the mast-heads of the three saints, Anselmo, Nicholas and Clara, by which the mariners knew that they were safe. A few days afterwards the narrow entrance of the 'Bay of Toil' seemed to give them hope of shelter, but once inside they had six days of the worst storms they had yet experienced. They emerged with difficulty, still making south, and on 31 March, having come to good anchorage and shelter in Port St Julian, in latitude 49° 20', Magellan decided there to make his winter quarters. With fish abundant, once again he reduced the rations from the ships' stores.

There was more discontent. It is rarely that a hero is followed by heroes, and few men were like Magellan himself, prepared to go on as far as latitude 75°, until either he found a strait or the land ended altogether; for he was convinced that passage must exist. It was argued plaintively that ships and men were more valuable than spices, that the land went down to the Pole without a break, that humanity could not endure such privations. Magellan answered as one proud to endure all. He marvelled that Castilians, under the king's orders, should be guilty of such weakness. Would not their privations be a measure of their future glory? There were wood and water in plenty, fish and birds for the catching; he himself was determined to die rather than shamefully turn back. The men were temporarily silenced; it was the officers who spread treason. Magellan was a Portuguese, it was whispered; what greater service could he render to his own king than to destroy this fleet of Spain in these icy solitudes? Was it not a duty to circumvent him? So discussion went on, till at Easter mutiny flared out. On Easter Day Magellan ordered general attendance at mass, and asked all his captains to breakfast with him. Quesada and Mendoza did not attend mass; Alvaro de Mesquita, Magellan's kinsman, who now had the command of the *S. Antonio*, alone came to eat. That night the blow fell. In the middle watch Quesada, Juan de Cartagena and Sebastian del Cano, a good pilot but a faithless man, silently boarded the *S. Antonio* with thirty armed followers. Alvaro de Mesquita was imprisoned in a cabin; the ship's master, who courageously ordered the invaders off, was stabbed by Quesada. Sebastian del Cano was put in command of the ship, the decks were cleared for action, and the stores were pillaged in the name of hunger. The *Victoria* was in the plot; the *Santiago*, its crew only half Spaniards, was untampered with. This was the situation to which Magellan awoke in the morning of 2 April 1520.

He discovered the revolt on sending a boat to the *S. Antonio* to pick up men for a watering party. The ship, was the reply, was under the orders of Gaspar Quesada, not Magellan. Each captain then being asked for whom he declared, answered 'For the king and for myself'; except Serrano in the *Santiago*. Magellan was brought to the testing-point; he acted with decision and with speed. A boat brought a letter from Quesada: if Magellan would accede to the demands of the mutineers, they would agree to acknowledge his authority again. Magellan invited them on board the *Trinidad* for consultation; they warily refused. He seized the boat and the men who brought their message. The next step was the crisis. Among the *Victoria*'s crew was a large proportion of foreigners, likely to be loyal to the captain-general; a dangerous manoeuvre therefore might succeed. A skiff was sent bearing six men with concealed arms and a letter to Mendoza ordering him immediately to the flag-ship. He smiled scornfully as he read it, shook his head, and fell dead, stabbed in the throat. Simultaneously a boat with fifteen picked men led by Duarte Barbosa leapt from the *Trinidad* to the support of the six on the deck of the *Victoria*, and with hardly a stroke of resistance the ship was theirs. Three of the ships, the majority, were now in Magellan's hands, and these three were ranged across the entrance to the harbour; for it was thought the mutineers would attempt to steal out under cover of night. The *Trinidad* cleared for action, and shortly after midnight the form of the *S. Antonio* loomed up. She had dragged her anchors, as if fate were on Magellan's side. The *Trinidad* poured in a broadside, grappled her and boarded; and the crew, half-hearted and without leadership, surrendered at once. Not a life was sacrificed. Juan de Cartagena in the *Concepcion*, seeing that all was lost, also surrendered, to join his fellow conspirators in irons. The mutiny was over.

The punishment which Magellan meted out can hardly be called excessive, unpleasant though some of the details may be. On the following day the body of Mendoza, who alone had lost his life (for the master of the *S. Antonio* did not die of his wounds till July), was brought ashore and drawn and quartered. Forty men were found guilty of treason and condemned to death, but pardoned under penalty of working in chains till the fleet left the harbour. Quesada, however, could receive no mercy, and the life of his servant Molino, who had been a very active mutineer, was spared on condition that he beheaded his master. The headless trunk was also drawn and quartered. Juan de Cartagena and a priest were sentenced to be marooned; and before the fleet set sail, at the end of August, they were put ashore with a store of biscuit and wine. They were never heard of again.[1]

Inaction spelt discontent, as Magellan well knew; and perhaps to guard against this he sent the *Santiago* at the end of April on a reconnaissance to the south. On 22 May, seventy miles from Port St Julian, she was wrecked, though no lives were lost; and it was only after extreme privation that a rescue party, sent overland through the snow and ice, returned with

[1] A different view of the mutiny as well as of the voyage as a whole, critical of Magellan and stressing the services of Sebastian del Cano, will be found in Markham, *Early Spanish Voyages to the Strait of Magellan*, pp. 4–12.

the famished crew. A small party was despatched into the interior as well, returning with the report that it was unpeopled and without resources. No inhabitants had been seen indeed for many weeks, when one day a man appeared dancing and singing on the beach, so tall that the voyagers were to report a race of giants. He was followed by others, with their wives, and Pigafetta devoted several paragraphs to their extraordinary habits—they could force arrows half-way down their throats, they ate rats without even skinning them. Two of this interesting race—Patagonians, as they were called, from the size of their feet[1]—Magellan captured for the information and entertainment of his master the emperor, and one was successfully converted to Christianity, though he said his prayers in a rather loud voice. All this lent interest to Port St Julian, but Magellan, perhaps oppressed by thoughts of the mutiny, determined to spend the rest of the winter in the Rio de la Cruz, just north of where the *Santiago* had met destruction. After the wreck the command of the ships had been rearranged—Serrano took the *Concepcion*, Duarte Barbosa the *Victoria*, while the largest ship, the *S. Antonio*, remained under the not very effectual Alvaro de Mesquita. These men, two of them Portuguese, were all firmly loyal to Magellan. In the Rio de la Cruz the fleet remained for nearly two months longer without great incident, catching and drying fish; and on 18 October, with the coming of warmer weather, Magellan sailed south again, closely examining the shore.

For two days he had head winds and bad weather, then the wind went round to the north. The fleet ran south-west two days more and on 21 October a cape was sighted, and an opening like a bay. It was St Ursula's Day, and in celebration of that unfortunate princess the headland was named the Cape of the Eleven Thousand Virgins; but what of the bay? Other bays had been explored fruitlessly; was it possible that here would be better fortune? The *Concepcion* and the *S. Antonio*, sent on to investigate, were swallowed in storm. Days passed, and just as

[1] *pata gones*, big feet.

Magellan had given up hope of their safety they were descried hastening back, with all flags flying and guns booming, excited beyond measure. They had sailed up the bay for three days, and saw no end to it. The soundings were deep and in some places there was no bottom, while the flood tide was stronger than the ebb—there must be a passage at last! They had indeed passed the first narrows of the Strait of Magellan, and were jubilant in the prospect of success, 'upon which', says Pigafetta, 'we united our shouts to theirs, and thanking God and the Blessed Virgin Mary, resumed our journey'.

The navigation of the Strait of Magellan, or of Todos los Santos—All Saints' Strait, as the discoverer himself called it—is difficult beyond most tasks of a like nature. Yet for once Magellan had high luck. It was spring, the weather was good, he did not go astray into the numerous sounds and channels which make the strait a maze, and the thirty-eight days he spent there might easily have been reduced had it not been for necessary exploration and a period of search after a missing ship. The ship was the largest one, the *S. Antonio*, with a great part of the stores, that now deserted and sailed back the way it had come. We have no exact itinerary or time-table of the remarkable passage. At its beginning Magellan called a council of captains and pilots to ask their opinions as to the further prosecution of the voyage, though he had no doubts himself. All were in favour of pressing on except Estevão Gomes, the pilot of the *S. Antonio*, who urged that with only three months' provisions left the reasonable thing was to return to Spain, report success, and equip a new fleet to follow it up. The argument was plausible, but Magellan was not to be moved. 'If they had to eat the leather on the ship's yards', he said, 'he would still go on, and discover what he had promised to the Emperor, and he trusted that God would aid them and give them good fortune.' To clinch the decision he ordered that no one should discuss the difficulties or the shortness of provisions under pain of death. Next day, having passed the Narrows, they sailed down a wide reach. At its end they came to a point where three channels diverged and here the fleet split up—the *Concepcion* and *S. Antonio* were sent to investigate to the southeast, while Magellan with the other two ships sailed up what proved to be the right channel and anchored at the 'River of Sardines', taking in wood and water, and sending a small boat ahead to explore. The boat was away for three days; when it came back it had news to move every heart—it had seen ahead a long cape and beyond that the expanse of the open sea. Then indeed Magellan put away all reserve and wept openly: 'at the joy which the captain-general had at this', says Pigafetta, 'he began to cry, and he gave the name of Cape of Desire to this cape, as a thing which had been much desired for a long time.'

The only thing which remained was to put back as quickly as possible for the *Concepcion* and the *S. Antonio*. The *Concepcion* was soon met with, but of the *S. Antonio* there was no trace, either of men or of wreckage. Right to the entrance of the strait was the search carried, but in vain. Estevão Gomes and his party had overpowered Alvaro de Mesquita, and the *S. Antonio* was once more on the Atlantic turned towards Spain, bearing a cargo of falsehood against Magellan and leaving the three surviving ships sadly depleted in resources. Such was the reading of a horoscope cast by an astrologer with the fleet; and such was the truth. So once more Magellan retraced his course through that strait of bay and precipice and snow-covered mountain, with the fires of Tierra del Fuego on his left hand and in his ears the sound of ocean beating on a farther shore, which persuaded him there must be islands and no continent to the south. Another council was held, at which he reiterated his decision to go forward and his trust in God; and a week later, on the evening of 28 November, the three ships passed by the Cabo Deseado and entered the Great South Sea.

Magellan's conduct of the voyage had thus far been masterly. The discovery of the strait was in itself a shining achievement; the voyage that followed was one of astonishing endurance and persistence, though indeed to turn back once the fleet was in mid-ocean would have been impossible. To some in those three vessels as they passed the Cape of Desire the Spice Islands seemed already within their reach: no man had an inkling of the size of the ocean—'a sea so vast that the human mind can scarcely grasp it', said one historian of the voyage. And Magellan went long without sight of land; for many as are the islands of the Pacific, the course followed by the fleet took it right round the skirt of the main archipelagos. Magellan steered always for the Moluccas, the position of which he approximately knew, and many an island which would have given the weary crews refreshment was passed by over the rim of the horizon. Day after day, week after week, the fleet sailed on. Till 16 December Magellan made north up the western coast of Patagonia, not a great distance from land—a pleasant period enlivened by the observation of the *colondrini*, sea-swallows or flying-fish, and then struck out to the north-west to sail steadily for two months. No storm troubled all that placid voyage, and it seemed that the *Mar del Sur* might well be renamed the *Mare Pacifico*—the Great South Sea become truly the Pacific Ocean. But there was a peril worse than tempest. Two years' provisions, it was supposed, had been shipped; already in the Atlantic they had begun to run short, and then there was the cruel defection of the *S. Antonio*. Water became little more than a liquid stench and men held their noses as they drank it. Worms had reduced the biscuit to powder, and that powder the rats had befouled; but it was eaten, and sawdust was eaten. Half a ducat was paid for a rat. Magellan had said he would go forward if he were reduced to eating the hides which kept the rigging from chafing on the yards, and the moment of compulsion came; for the hides, hardened by wind and weather, rain and sun, were dragged overboard four or five days to soften them, and then broiled on the embers, and so eaten. Yet there was no land. Disease, especially scurvy, attacked the crews, and their gums swelled so that they could not eat even what fare there was; pains racked their arms and legs. Few remained healthy, many died, and, wrote Pigafetta, 'if our Lord and his Mother had not aided us in giving us good weather . . . we should all have died of hunger in this very vast sea, and I think that never man will undertake to perform such a voyage'.

On 24 January 1521 they sighted an islet covered with trees; it was uninhabited, and the anchors reached no bottom. They sailed on; eleven days more brought them to another island, where was neither fruit nor water. The first was named *San Pablo*, the second *Los Tiburones* or Shark Island, from the number of sharks found there, and though these two were so far apart Magellan included them both as a group under the name *Desadventuradas*—the Unfortunate Islands.[1] Still he steered north-west, allowing so far as he could for the variation of the compass, which his pilots would have ignored; and at last, on 6 March, after ninety-eight days of solitude and endurance, the strained eyes of that sick and starving company saw land and the outriggers of savages. They were savages, but they were men; and their islands harboured fruit and refreshment. The long crossing was over.

The stay at these islands was short. Their inhabitants did not impress the voyagers favourably. They stole the skiff of the *Trinidad* and everything else they could; hence the name given to the group, the Ladrones, or Thieves.[2] Magellan was much irritated, as after such a voyage was perhaps natural; he took forty armed men on shore, burned forty or fifty houses and several boats, killed seven men and recovered his skiff—vengeance which may be called ample. As he went the sick asked for the entrails of any savages who were killed, for such things were potent to cure. The natives continued to barter fruit despite this cruel punishment, and the Spaniards to display interest in the spears tipped with fish-bones, and the outrigger canoes

[1] Identifications are not quite easy. San Pablo was one of the north-eastern Tuamotu atolls, Pukapuka or Fangahina or Fangatau. Los Tiburones was one of the Line islands in the central Pacific, farther north-west: Caroline or perhaps Vostok or Flint, the three points of a rather widely spaced triangle.

[2] They were Guam and Rota, the two most southerly of the group now more commonly known as the Marianas.

which were so fast that as the fleet departed in full sail they dashed in and out under the ropes by which the ships towed their boats. On 9 March, the day the fleet left, its only Englishman, the gunner Master Andrew of Bristol, died of the hardships of the Pacific passage. Magellan was now north-east of the Moluccas; he did not make for them immediately, but westward, hoping for speedier refreshment, and after a week once more met with land. He had come to Samar in the Philippines, a group he called the Islands of St Lazarus; not till 1542 were they named after the emperor's son, Prince Philip. Here the fleet tarried for nine days. The sick were taken to a camp ashore and given coconut milk and other healing juices, while natives came from the neighbouring islet of Suluan with 'figs a foot long and two cocchi'—bananas and coconuts—and fish and palm wine to exchange for the red caps and trinkets of Spain. One chief had gold rings in his ears and about his arms gold bracelets. At last, it seemed to the sailors, they were within measurable distance of the tangible wealth of the Indies. Here, too, the career of the diarist Pigafetta and his history of the voyage were nearly cut short, for while fishing over the side of the ship he slipped on a wet spar, and only the benevolence of the Virgin put a saving rope within his grasp.

On 28 March, the sick being nearly recovered, the ships moved to the small island Limasawa. Here the Malay spoken by a Moluccan slave of Magellan, Enrique, was understood and dealings were much freer. Although at first the natives seemed shy, and presents had to be floated to them on a plank, soon their king allowed them to board the *Trinidad*, and even offered Magellan a large bar of solid gold, which, however, was refused. Next day was Good Friday, and as if to celebrate that anniversary the king and Magellan went through the rite of blood-brotherhood, and the king was presented with a red cap and a Turkish robe of red and yellow. He was amazed at Magellan's account of the size of the sea the ships had crossed, at the sword-play of two sailors, and at the Spanish armour which could be struck by swords and daggers and yet preserve

its wearer unharmed. The last day of March was Easter Day—
but how different from that mutiny-shadowed day of the year
before! The officers and sailors in full panoply went on shore
to where an altar had been raised and there was held the service
of the Church, while the ships discharged their broadsides, and
native kings knelt and kissed the cross. Afterwards a cross was
taken to the summit of the highest hill near by and raised for a
memorial of the power of Christ and the presence of Christian
men. Magellan did not wish to stay longer, in spite of native
gratification at such events, and on his asking which ports were
best for trade in provisions and spices and gold, the king
offered himself to pilot the fleet to Cebu, the largest. There
Magellan decided to go, 'for thus his unlucky fate willed it should
be'. So after a day occupied by the natives in sleeping off the
drunkenness of the preceding celebrations, and two more days
in which the Spaniards helped them to get in their harvest, the
fleet weighed anchor; and on 7 April it entered the port of
Cebu.

Here, and at another island a short distance away, were en-
acted the last scenes of Magellan's varied, active and much-
enduring life. That they were the last scenes must be attributed
to a sort of Christian arrogance in him—the sum of his own
profound religious feeling and a too great confidence in himself, the resources of western civilization, and the support
which God would continue to give him—together with the
sense of his duty to establish in this archipelago the power of the
emperor who sent him. Yet no man is master of his own fate,
and sometimes too much is asked of God. Meanwhile all went
well. Cebu was a rich district, and its rajah was accustomed to
receive tribute from those who entered his port. This Magellan
refused, for there was no greater king on earth than his emperor,
and it was not fitting that the servant of such majesty should
concede the dues of any lesser monarch; and the rajah, advised
by a Siamese trader who knew the terrors of western armament, decided that friendship was best. He waived the payment

of tribute and visited Magellan on board the *Trinidad*. There the captain-general spoke of the power of Spain and the greater power of God and his Mother, and the duties of Christian men; this rajah, too, became his blood-brother, and they settled a treaty. Presents were given, arrangements made for Christian burial in the town's open space of two sailors who had died, and a market started for barter.

The week was full of coming and going, of trade and piety. The rajah professed himself sincerely desirous of baptism; the following Sunday he and his queen were received into the Church with their principal followers and ladies; and in eight days between two and three thousand people had done like-wise. A prince, grievously sick, was restored to health through faith in the new god and the destruction of old idols, and Magellan was jubilant at this success of his expedition, so much more valuable even than trade in the richest spices of Maluco. Then he took a false step. All the surrounding chiefs did not pay to the rajah the obedience and respect he considered his right, and principal among these rebels was Silapulapu of Mactan, a little island off the Cebu coast. Magellan decided to bear further witness to the omnipotence of God, and to con-solidate the power of his ally, and hence the power of Spain, in this neighbourhood by the reduction of Mactan to a proper respect; and to do so by Spanish might alone. He rejected the contrary advice of his friend Juan Serrano, he rejected the rajah's offer of men—he refused even the ardent request of his own men not to lead the expedition in person. At midnight on Friday, 26 April, the Spaniards crossed to Mactan in three boats, which were too large to approach through the shoals close to the shore. Magellan, plunging into the water as dawn was breaking, led his fifty men to the beach, where they were met by a great host of natives. The rajah with his men had strict orders to keep off-shore and witness Christian valour. Valour there was, of little avail against such odds, and it was not dis-played by all the Spaniards. The natives were infuriated by the firing of their houses, and though the armour of Magellan's men protected their bodies their limbs were vulnerable to stones and spears. Magellan received an arrow in the leg and seeing that the day was lost ordered a gradual retreat. But his men broke and fled, except a few devoted friends who fought round him till they were separated. They fought for an hour or more, Magellan glancing round from time to time as if to see that his men were safe, while they moved slowly back to the boats, where their craven companions were threatening to row off and leave them. Pigafetta, wounded himself, saw the captain-general struck in the face with a bamboo spear. Magellan plunged his lance into his assailant's breast, and then tried in vain to draw his sword, for he had been wounded in the arm. The enemy rushed on him and felled him with a savage blow on the leg, and as he lay on his face in the water stabbed him through and through with every weapon they had, and so he died.

With the death of Magellan the element of the great and heroic departs from this voyage, though ardours and endurances were still required from the survivors. The fact remained, that the Pacific had been crossed; what was left to do was comparatively simple. It was not done without a melancholy train of distrust and betrayal. Enrique, Magellan's slave, was slightly wounded and after his master's death refused to work. He was roughly spoken to and threatened; in revenge he went on shore, told the rajah that the Spaniards were preparing to attack the town and advised him to strike the first blow. The rajah believed; twenty-seven Spaniards, including Juan Serrano and Duarte Barbosa, who were invited on shore to receive a gift of jewels for the emperor, were cut down; and Serrano, brought wounded to the shore on the chance of ransom by his shipmates, was left in cold blood to his death as they sailed away. There being by this time not enough hands to man all three ships, the *Concepcion* was sunk, and for over seven months the *Trinidad* and *Victoria* blundered about the eastern archipelago on a semi-piratical voyage of no more glory than technical distinction. They came finally to Tidore, their goal, in the centre of the Moluccas, on 8 November 1521. They discharged all their artillery in joy, giving thanks to God: for they had passed twenty-seven months 'always in search of Maluco, wandering for that object among the immense number of islands'; and the story spread by the Portuguese was found to be untrue, that Maluco was situated in seas that could not be navigated on account of shoals and the dark and foggy atmosphere. Alas, Francisco Serrano like his friend was dead, as Juan Serrano was dead and Duarte Barbosa was dead, and it seemed that no man noble in spirit was left. Yes: there was Pigafetta, of valour unquenchable and unquenchable curiosity, and he tells us how after six weeks of trading for cloves the two ships set sail for home, and how the *Trinidad* sprang a leak and they put back. The *Victoria* sailed again, down through the Indian Ocean and round the Cape of Good Hope and north through the Atlantic and so reached San Lucar once more, and cast anchor at Seville on 8 September 1522. And next day the survivors of that voyage, the first men to circumnavigate the globe, went under their commander, the one-time mutineer Sebastian del Cano, to the Church of Our Lady of Victory, where three years before Magellan had taken in his hand the royal standard and accepted their oaths of obedience; and there they rendered thanks that they had been preserved. The *Trinidad*, after striking off to the north-east from Tidore in a muddled attempt to sail to Mexico, returned and surrendered to the Portuguese. Only four men of her forty-four ultimately reached Spain; in the *Victoria* thirty-one came back. Nearly one hundred and seventy had perished. Such was the price of circumnavigation.

The world was amazed, and the passage of centuries makes Magellan's achievement no less amazing. It is indeed among the principal navigations of all history: the difficulties and dangers of Columbus's discovery of America pale before it, nor can Vasco da Gama be set by Magellan's side either in achievement or in the technical skill of the navigator. No Spaniard was able to follow triumphantly in his wake. The expedition of Loaysa and del Cano over the same route in 1525 reached the Moluccas horribly wasted by disease, but otherwise failed, as two others failed; and when later Spanish ships explored the Pacific they did so from the ports of Mexico and Peru. Drake and Cavendish paralleled the circumnavigation, true; yet in originality of conception, as in the constancy and endurance with which he realized the conception, Magellan stands single in that century. His character, too, was singularly little stained by the faults of the admirals of the time, though the proud reserve that was so strong in him, perhaps a hint of asceticism, made him little liked by those who found no equal quality in themselves. Nevertheless he could inspire faith and devotion, even if his friends were few; asking much of others, he sacrificed himself to the end; and when he died, wrote Pigafetta, there was deprived of life 'our mirror, light, comfort and true guide'. As an explorer his principal aim—or the aim that he set in the front to win support—was crowned with irony; for under the Tordesillas *Capitulacion* the Moluccas were, in fact, within Portuguese limits, and in 1529 the emperor abandoned whatever shadowy rights Spain had to their trade for a payment of 350,000 ducats. What other possible aims Magellan had, what golden Cattigara, what Tarshish or Ophir, is matter for deduction and argument—and perhaps of their own irony, measured against his fate, of a rather different sort. Such fabulous speculations were not absent from future thoughts on Pacific discovery.

There was no irony about the discovery and passage of the strait; nor about the revelation of the true size of that enormous sea to which it led. As for the very attempt to find a strait, 'the thing seemed almost impossible and useless', said Maximilian Transylvanus, a secretary to the court of Charles V, 'not because it was thought a difficult thing to go from the west right to the east under the hemisphere, but because it was uncertain whether ingenious nature, which has done nothing without the greatest foresight, had not so dissevered the east from the west, partly by sea and partly by land, as to make it impossible to arrive there by either land or sea travelling'. In that uncertainty as to the intentions of ingenious nature, Magellan, like other great discoverers, found an irresistible call. And the voyage displayed not less the immensity of the spirit of man than that of the South Sea. There was still no correct calculation of its size; pilots, said Pigafetta, at that time were so proud that they would not hear speak of longitude—one of Magellan's pilots was in error in his calculations at the Philippines by no less than 52° 55'—and yet men would sail for months on seas uncharted and unknown.[1] It was for other navigators, of a later day, with science gradually added to aptitude and the steeled mind, to fill in the multifarious details of the Pacific: Magellan had driven a memorable, if unrewarded, track across the ocean from corner to corner. One ray of light pierced original darkness.

[1] To get anything like an accurate notion of the size of the Pacific, east to west, the world had to wait for the observations of Pierre Antoine Véron, the astronomer with Bougainville on his circumnavigation (1766–9), nearly two and a half centuries after Magellan.

# CHAPTER III

# MENDAÑA AND THE SOLOMON ISLANDS

MAGELLAN had spanned the Pacific and discovered the Philippines for his grave, but Portugal retained the Spice Islands. Nevertheless there were Spanish minds not less eager than the Portuguese for Eastern empire, and one of these was Cortes, the restless conqueror of Mexico. He built ships, founded ports, despatched expeditions. In 1525 Loaysa and del Cano left Spain to follow Magellan's route and claim the Moluccas. Both died at sea, their followers met disaster, and to the help of the survivors Cortes in 1527 sent from Mexico three ships under Alvaro de Saavedra. Two of these parted company 1000 leagues from port and were never seen again—one, just possibly, may have been the wreck of which the people of Hawaii are said to have had a tradition from that time. Saavedra himself reached the Moluccas, could there do nothing, and turned to sail back to Mexico. The way was harder than any man thought: twice he set out and twice, after many months, his ships were driven back by contrary winds, the second time without their captain, who had 'died by the way'. But he had coasted along the north of New Guinea, discovered two years before by Meneses, a Portuguese—the land of the Papuas, 'black people with frizzled hair, who are cannibals, and the devil walks with them'; and he had discovered some of the Admiralty, Caroline and Marshall islands. Cortes continued to send out expeditions; two vessels under Grijalva and Alvarado set out in 1537 to search in the equatorial ocean for islands believed to abound in gold, and met new disaster; for after seeing a number of islands north and south of the line, the crew mutinied and slew Grijalva, and were finally wrecked near New Guinea. The seven survivors of disease and hardship were enslaved by the natives, till they were finally ransomed by the governor of the Moluccas. Truly the hazards of exploration were tremendous. It was not till 1565 that the Spaniards actually settled in the East: in that year Miguel Lopez de Legaspi crossed the ocean, passing through the Marshalls, and founded the colony of the Philippines. And a technical discovery of the utmost importance was that of his principal pilot, the friar-seaman Fray Andres de Urdaneta, who succeeded in returning eastwards to Mexico, after winds and currents had defeated other pilots. Urdaneta solved the problem by sailing in a wide northward sweep, to almost 40° latitude, where he picked up westerly winds like those of the North Atlantic.[1] After his discovery a ship, if it left Manila in June, could sail to Acapulco in Mexico in five or six months—twice the time occupied in sailing the route westwards; nevertheless it could be done, and a regular service of ships began, the annual galleons of a fabulous trade.

There was thus at last a settled highway over the Pacific, though in a part severely limited, and no man knew what lay south or even north of the regular course. Doubtless the great southern continent remained to discover, and in the discussion of such a possibility not Mexican but Peruvian myth began to play a part. There were tales among the Indians and the seamen of the ports. Long years before, it was said, the Inca Tupac Yupanqui had made a voyage to the west and found two marvellously rich islands, whence he had brought back gold and silver, a copper throne, black slaves and the skin of an animal like a horse. Perhaps, if the legends were at bottom true, these islands were the Galapagos, lying alone 600 miles off the Peruvian coast. True or not they excited the mind of a Spaniard of great ability and energy, Pedro Sarmiento de Gamboa, whose studies in Inca tradition and history led him

[1] Alonso de Arellano, another of Legaspi's captains, had preceded Urdaneta in the return crossing by a few months, but Urdaneta is usually credited with having deduced that the best course would be in high latitudes.

to the conviction that these islands were the outposts of a great continent stretching from Tierra del Fuego northwards to within fifteen degrees of the equator, where it was about 600 leagues from Peru. Pedro Sarmiento was a good mathematician and astronomer; he also dabbled in magic, which attracted the notice of the Inquisition. His friendship with the viceroy of Peru saved him from banishment; though possibly his eagerness to remove himself from the range of ecclesiastical enquiry was another motive behind his plan of a new voyage of exploration. His arguments—according to himself—prevailed, and an expedition was authorized in 1567. But we must notice that there had for many years been reports that the land of Ophir, whence came the gold of King Solomon, were islands in the Pacific, in the direction of the Spice Islands. Sarmiento was not given the command of the expedition; there was a new viceroy, who preferred to appoint his nephew Alvaro de Mendaña, a young man of twenty-five. Two ships were fitted out, *Los Reyes* of 250 tons, and the *Todos Santos* of 107 tons, furnished with a company of one hundred and fifty, seventy of whom were soldiers, with four Franciscan friars, and a number of slaves. These ships, which were about to cross and recross the ocean over more than 7000 miles, were provisioned for only 600 leagues, they were built for the perpetual fine weather of the Peruvian coast, and when they set out the hurricane season was just approaching. Yet in spite of disagreement among the leaders and threatened mutiny among the crew, in spite of storms and starvation, after nearly two years, and long given up for lost, they both appeared again in the port of Callao with more than two-thirds of their company still alive.

The declared aim of the expedition was 'to convert all infidels to Christianity'—*conquista espiritual*: a sort of conquest that has too often proceeded in company with one more violent. Its orders, so far as we know them, were to steer for the rich islands and the continent of Pedro Sarmiento's theory, form a settlement and send back the ships for reinforcements. Its leaders varied in experience and character. Of the earlier life

of the young Mendaña we are ignorant. His bearing on the
two voyages which he commanded shows him to have been
rather an idealist than a skilled navigator. Yet, if he was no
seaman, neither was he of the company of the great adventurers,
ruthless and unswerving in determination, the *conquistadores*
who had carved out Spanish empire in the West; there was in
him a gentleness and humanity, a feeling for the rights even of
savages and heathen, alien from the character of most Pacific
explorers of whatever age; and he took seriously the counsels
of his Franciscan advisers. Nor had he the genius of command;
on matters of navigation he took the advice of his pilots; on
critical issues he generally accepted the vote of the majority.
Nevertheless at one crisis, towards the end of the long voyage,
his uncompromising will saved the expedition from self-
destruction. He survives as a winning though not very effectual
figure in the history of the time. His chief pilot, Hernan
Gallego, was of a character widely different. In his fifties, with
all the repute of skill and long experience, a master of his art,
he knew the Pacific coast of America from California to the
Strait of Magellan. He was quick in decision and resource; to
him more than to any other man was due the salvation and
success of the expedition. Sarmiento sailed as captain of *Los
Reyes*; his capacity was great, and his deeds made him famous
in later years; but his character was not an attractive one. He
was a remorseless enemy, cruel in revenge, a bad subordinate
and a difficult commander, and he brooded furiously over the
elevation of Mendaña. The other leading officers had something
of Mendaña's moderation and humanity; and to Gomez
Catoira, the chief purser, we owe the fullest and most vivid
narrative of the expedition.

The ships sailed from Callao on 19 November 1567, and for
twenty-six days steered west-south-west till they arrived at a
latitude of 15° 30′ S. No land was seen. There were few alarming events—the day after the start *Los Reyes* struck a sleeping
whale, and later on a man who fell overboard at night was
rescued with the aid of a heavenly light which the Virgin

caused to shine over him. Already Sarmiento had quarrelled with Mendaña, who would neither investigate a cloudbank nor admit a duty to consult Sarmiento in the navigation; and now, to add to such injuries, Mendaña took Gallego's advice and turned the ships north-west. Hot discussions arose among the pilots, about the direction of land argued from the flight of sea-birds; yet where birds flew both north and south, might they not merely be in pursuit of flying-fish? The ships passed between the Marquesas and the Tuamotu or Low Archipelago without sighting land, and by the end of December the subordinate pilots had lost patience. They were pacified only by Gallego's promise to bring them to land before the end of January, and a north-west course was steered to latitude 6° S. Aided by the western current, they sailed along the parallel, and on 15 January an island was indeed sighted—probably one of the most northerly of the Ellice Islands, which the Spaniards called the Isle of Jesus. They had been sixty-two days at sea and their water was tainted, but Gallego, thinking the island uninhabited, at first ignored Mendaña's order to approach nearer and anchor. To leeward of it, however, canoes came out with numerous 'Indians' and Mendaña reiterated his order. In vain; the ships were carried away in a strong current, and all hope of a landing quickly faded. To the infuriated sailors and soldiers poor Gallego could merely promise more land than they could people. Nineteen days later they narrowly escaped disaster on a line of reefs right across their course, which Mendaña called Baxos de la Candelaria—Candlemas Banks: perhaps the reef of the atoll Ontong Java, perhaps the Roncador reef, forty miles farther southward. Here they ran into the outer edge of a cyclone, and for six days were unconsciously drifting south. Then at last they came upon indubitable land. It was Saturday, 7 February 1568, eighty days after leaving Callao. In the morning Gallego thought he saw something in the south, and ordered a sailor to the maintop. 'And the sailor reported land, and presently it was visible to us. And we hoisted a flag . . . and everybody received the news with great joy and gratitude for the grace that God had vouchsafed to us through the intercession of the Virgin of Good Fortune, the Glorious Mother of God, whom we all worshipped, to whom we all prayed, singing the *Te Deum laudamus*.'

The land, sighted from a distance of fifteen leagues, seemed so large and high that all thought it must be a continent. The ships were two days coming up with it, and as soon as they were seen from the shore, small canoes sped out, manned by natives who carried bows and arrows and lances of palm-wood. After some persuasion they climbed on board, and being presented with beads, red caps and bells, quickly made themselves at home, appropriating whatever they could lay their hands on; and one of them went up the rigging as lightly as the most practised sailor. They pronounced Spanish words with great ease, parrot-fashion, and even repeated the Lord's Prayer to admiration. Mendaña admired their canoes, crescent-shaped, well made and very light, and paddled with marvellous speed. Danger nevertheless there was still: as the ships drew nearer to the land they were entangled in the cruel intricacies of a barrier-reef, from which they emerged only through Gallego's skill and presence of mind. The voyagers had recourse to prayers and petitions 'according to the custom of navigators when they are in danger such as we were in at that moment'; the wind shifted a little, and over the maintop (it was ten o'clock in the morning) shone a resplendent star, which guided them to safety—surely the Star in the East appearing once again to men! It was, in fact, the planet Venus, which frequently shines in daylight in those latitudes; but the Spaniards, confident of miracle, straightway on landing raised a cross, before which the Franciscans chanted the *Vexilla Regis*; and the wide bay which was their harbour they called Bahia de la Estrella—the 'Bay of the Star'. And the new land they called Santa Ysabel, because they had sailed from Peru on the feast of that saint, and she had been their patron throughout the long voyage. Straightway also a party under Gallego began to fell trees, with which, together with timbers they had brought with them, they might build a brigantine for further exploration.

The day after they anchored a chief named Bilebanara came on board, magnificent in a head-dress of white and coloured plumes and armlets of shell, his face bedaubed with paint. He made signs of peace and some of his followers danced in strange fashion to the music of a flute a negro sailor was playing. The natives had small reed pipes themselves, and admired the Spanish trumpet, drum and fife, and the guitar to which the soldiers sang. Bilebanara, as was fitting, exchanged names with Mendaña, and promised supplies of food; and the Spaniards rejoiced greatly in the prospect of so many conversions to the Catholic Faith. Several times more the chief came while his visitors explored the bay, waiting on every hour to bring them fresh supplies of food; then for two days he did not come, nor did a driblet of coconuts satisfy the hungry men. Bilebanara, it seems, was a relatively hospitable savage, but somewhat taken aback at the request for immediate food for two ships' companies: and thus embarrassed, he retired unostentatiously into seclusion. After two days Mendaña's patience gave way, and he sent Pedro de Ortega, the camp master, to find and interview the chief. Ortega, though not attacked, was not received with any warmth, and returned without venturing into the interior. But there was still no food. A conference was therefore held with the friars. The need was admittedly urgent; supplies had been promised, none had appeared—what, then, was to be done? The decision was thus made: an expedition might be sent to search for food, and if the natives would not trade a moderate amount might be taken, but not so much as might denude a village; nothing should be taken but food, for this proper exchange must be given, and every care must be exerted to avoid conflict. The interesting thing is how closely exploring parties adhered to these instructions of the Church, though the first expedition was not encouraging.

Pedro Sarmiento was put in command, with orders to scale the range of hills that rose some leagues inland and see what lay behind. He was to trade if he could, though not to take by force. He failed both to trade and to maintain peace, but he found Bilebanara. The party spent a wet night at the foot of the range, firing arquebuses periodically to ward off danger; and in the morning, without further progress, they set off back to the beach with Bilebanara and his uncle, Havi, as guides, followed by an increasing number of people shouting the Spanish '*Afuera!*'—Away!—and fitting arrows to their bowstrings. Sarmiento seized Bilebanara and Havi as hostages. The agile chief slipped from his captors, but the action provoked a serious attack, in which a soldier was shot through the hand with an arrow and the arquebuses wounded several natives, one of whom Sarmiento despatched with his sword. He reached the beach, however, without loss and presented Havi and some other trophies to Mendaña, who was much annoyed. Havi was restored to his people, with their property, amid great rejoicing, and they brought food at last, though they set it down and retreated without coming within arquebus range.

It seemed as if relations might improve, and expeditions were despatched to explore the coast for a short distance east and west. In the west the country was precipitous and neither settled nor good for settlement; eastward there was a dense population. Then another attempt was made on the main range. At the beginning of March Ortega set out with sixty men, accompanied by two of the friars. Although Bilebanara's people were friendly, as the Spaniards began to climb they found the inland tribes hostile. At a village on a high ridge the chief was seized as a hostage, and the people fleeing, the party spent the night in their huts. Next day hard climbing and some fighting brought them to the top of the range, whence they saw, not the spreading hinterland of a great continent, filled with temples and gold, but the sea; and the captive chief, drawing a map in the sand, confirmed their discovery: Santa Ysabel was an island. In the night he escaped and when the Spaniards began their return they were heavily attacked. They fired in the air, and to delay their assailants set fire to the villages they met, as a less serious measure than bloodshed. The natives were checked only when one of them fell dead from an arquebus shot; on the Spanish side, two soldiers were wounded by arrows, one to die later from tetanus. Some of Bilebanara's people had been recognized in the attack, but as the party passed his village they were offered more food and found no opposition. The friars were much pleased with Ortega's moderation.

A few days later there was a motion of friendship made. A fleet of war canoes paddled into the bay as the men worked on the brigantine, and to the scandalized Spaniards was held out the quarter of a boy, garnished with taro roots. 'We were all struck with great wonder and pity', says Catoira, 'to see so much cruelty and so strange a thing'; for no one had ever heard of human flesh being offered to Europeans. A negro waded out and took the gift, which was buried with many expressions of disapproval, on which the natives paddled away, surprised and somewhat disgusted, to a small island near by where a large fire a little later heralded a cannibal feast. This visit was followed by advances from Bilebanara. Hostages were exchanged and well treated, and Mendaña agreed to prove Spanish friendship by aiding Bilebanara against his enemy, the chief Meta. When the time for action came, however, Bilebanara failed to appear, and Pedro de Ortega with a party of Spaniards alone captured Meta's son and three others for interpreters. Bilebanara himself then came out to the ships with great formality, plates of shell decorating him, and bracelets of shells and boars' teeth round his arms and legs, to suggest that the prisoners should be handed over to him. In spite of an unsympathetic refusal, the chief presented Mendaña with some of his finery, and professing his allegiance to the King of Castile, seemed 'very well contented and joyful' at the friendship shown him.

Meanwhile the building of the brigantine had been steadily continued, and on 4 April, after fifty-four days' work, she was launched—a little undecked vessel of four or five tons, called the *Santiago* and holding about thirty men, with all their stores. This brigantine, piloted by Gallego, was of the utmost use to the Spaniards, for she could venture without danger among reefs which would have destroyed the clumsy ships; and so good were the reports made that her movements can be traced almost league by league on the modern map. Her first voyage began on 7 April. Ortega was in command, with instructions to steer east for Sarmiento's continent, now suspected to lie south of the Isle of Jesus. Gallego decided that the vessel, small, and built of green timber, was not equal to the chances of the open sea, so they coasted down the side of Ysabel, and then by way of several small islands to a harbour on the northern side of a large one, Guadalcanal. From the southernmost point of Ysabel they had sighted to the eastward another large island, the Isla de Ramos, or Malaita. At Guadalcanal the natives dragged the brigantine inshore crying *'Mate! Mate!'* (Danger!) and showered stones on the crew. The Spaniards fired, and killed two, on which the rest fled. Here the brigantine could be victualled, and the island was annexed for the King of Spain; and thence a return to Ysabel was made, by way of a large 'bay'—St George's or New Georgia Sound—at its south-western end, where Ortega seized four canoes to ransom for pigs; and so, circumnavigating the island, once again to Estrella Bay. They reached the ships on 5 May.

It was then decided to move to Guadalcanal, to the harbour the brigantine had discovered, the Puerto de la Cruz. Here the ships anchored on 12 May, and a cross was raised on a high hill. This provoked a flight of arrows from the natives, two more of whom were killed. One was a chief, and the natives, according to their custom, stripped in his honour the coconut plantation which had belonged to him. No objection was made to the Spaniards' taking of the nuts, except from certain trees which were *tabu*. Coconuts meant a certain amount of fresh food, and some native fowls were brought back by the next expedition which went inland. The object of this expedition was not food, however—it was to prospect for gold in the streams which rushed down to the shore; for there were in the expedition several experienced miners. But though there was little opposition from the natives, and the miners declared that the country showed signs of gold, the current was too strong for the washing-dish, and these efforts resulted in little more than three deaths from fever. Meanwhile, on 19 May, the brigantine had sailed east along the coast on further exploration, and Mendaña himself with a small party had gone inland several miles, amazed at the number of small villages spreading over hillside and plain, and a whole country which seemed to be under cultivation.

While the brigantine was away the crisis of this period of exploration took place. Food was extremely short, and the daily ration was cut down to eight ounces of meat and eight of biscuit, with whatever native food the men could get. The 'Indians' of Guadalcanal were not friendly and only two had come on board. The native point of view is comprehensible. They were head-hunters by profession and hostile to strangers on principle. These strangers came with weapons new and deadly, and were for ever demanding food. Although cultivation was widespread, the number of the islanders was great, while the requirements of the Spaniards were not small; and though pigs were plentiful, they were wild and could not be supplied immediately to order. Curiosity could not allay suspicion and fear, fear created hostility; and in face of this situation, all Mendaña's good intentions proved inevitably abortive. Persuasion having failed to get supplies, Sarmiento, expert in force, was sent on shore and emptied a village of its stores, returning to the beach just in time to avert the massacre of his boat's crew. 'There was one Indian', it is said, 'who actually came to feel the legs of a soldier who stood there, by way of testing whether he were tender for eating, as he would be his share in the distribution which they had made.' Again Sarmiento had exceeded his orders and aroused Mendaña's anger by the treacherous capture of natives. Retaliation came quickly: Ascension Day was marked by the massacre of a watering party and its escort. Nine men were killed—only a negro slave escaped by swimming, wounded, to a small island and defending himself desperately with a cutlass; and as Mendaña hurried on shore their dismembered limbs were waved at him in triumph. Revenge followed in its turn, once again with Sarmiento as its instrument. Unable to provoke an open fight, he set on fire every village within reach. When a canoe approached full of natives, bearing with them a pig, it was at once assumed that they came to waylay sailors who were out cutting a mast, though it seems possible that they were on a mission of peace. Not one escaped, and their quartered bodies were laid grimly on the scene of the massacre of the watering party. Then, as the brigantine had returned with news of another harbour where the ships could be careened, the last village was fired, and Guadalcanal was left to its ashes and its memories of blood.

The brigantine had coasted the shore of Guadalcanal eastward, provisioning with food and water at the larger villages, and sometimes, when there was none forthcoming, seizing canoes for ransom. Hospitality, as always, was qualified by fear; in one place, unable on the spur of the moment to supply the Spaniards' demands, the natives tried to impose on them a dummy pig stuffed with straw, carried down with due solemnity to the beach. At another a single warrior in a canoe displayed his wild ceremonial defiance, 'making grimaces and contortions like a devil', to which an interpreter brought from Ysabel retaliated in kind. Then, when honour had been satisfied to their joint satisfaction, they parted without injury. It was always as the brigantine was departing from the shore that the natives became most threatening; yet it was the policy of Don Hernando Henriquez, who was in command, both to leave payment for the provisions that were taken and to refrain from firing till arrows were discharged—a policy which exasperated the downright Gallego. Nevertheless there was more than one skirmish, made fatal by the arquebuses. From the eastern end of Guadalcanal the brigantine crossed to Malaita, where the soldiers were much excited by metal in the native clubs—short weapons, ending in a heavy knob. They thought that here was gold, and joyfully exchanged red caps for them, till Henriquez knocked two together and broke them—and showed a glitter indeed, but only of iron pyrites mixed in the stone. Thence Gallego made for the small island of Ulawa, where the natives were peaceful at first, and all night sang songs to the Spaniards, but pursued them when they left, so that they were forced to fire and killed twelve men and a woman, besides taking canoes. They then sailed by way of small islands to the larger one of San Cristobal; and here their exploration was stopped by such severe ague and fever that they had to return to the ships.

It was to San Cristobal that the ships then sailed, a short journey lengthened by contrary winds and currents to seventeen days. There was the usual sequence of events. The Spaniards were peacefully received, food was not produced, and when they took it by force there came the clash. Enough was collected finally to load a vessel. The brigantine was sent on a third voyage to the eastern end of the island in search of a better harbour for careening, and there were continual hostilities. Once a foraging party was ambushed by natives streaked with paint, their heads covered over with boughs, who wounded three Spaniards and a negro; as reprisal their village was burnt. From others the Spaniards heard of land in the south-east, but when a sailor climbed a high palm to look for it he saw only the heavy swell of the open sea.[1] So, with enemies all along the coast, the brigantine returned unsuccessful, and Mendaña decided to careen where he was. The entire company dis-embarked and during three weeks camped on shore while the vessels were cleaned and scraped. Round them the natives formed a hostile semicircle; behind them was the sea. Strict orders were given that no Spaniard should wander beyond the camp; one who did was killed, for here again the natives were experts in ambush, concealed under broad leaves and invisible in the bush till they moved. They were attacked with dogs, but

[1] The nearest land to the south-east is that of the Santa Cruz islands, 150 miles away.

could not be drawn into the open, nor could Mendaña's men be more active in defence. Meanwhile all the natives they had captured escaped but two.

On 7 August, work on the ships being finished, Mendaña called a meeting of all his officers and men to discuss their next step. He was no autocrat, and opinions were freely given. His instructions had been to find the southern continent and settle there. No continent had been found; of settlement the prospects were extremely dubious. There was provision of biscuit and roots for five months. Mendaña himself was resolved, he said, to sail to latitude 20° or 22°, where it was understood there was land, 'and they must labour and expose themselves to every danger till they found it'. He also put the question whether, if this land was not found in spite of all labours and dangers, 'it would be befitting the service of Our Lord God and His Majesty, and the general good', to return and settle on one of the islands already discovered. To this the pilots had a decisive reply. The ships were worn and leaky and the rigging in bad repair, provisions were still short, and they might barely hope to reach Peru alive. The country was hostile; the arquebuses, in which lay the sole hope of salvation if they stayed, were damaged, and ammunition was very low. Most of the soldiers agreed: there were many sick, they were far from Peru, and succour could not come speedily. Ortega and the friars advised making for New Guinea, and so to Manila. Some soldiers, who believed in the presence of gold, wished to remain; so also, it appears, did Sarmiento, who had no fear of 'Indians' and was generally opposed to counsels of prudence. The final decision was to return. Mendaña wished to sail south-east towards the coast of Chile, still in search of Sarmiento's continent, and the pilots agreed so far as it might be possible. Four more natives were captured one night to take back as trophies to Peru; Mass was celebrated, the water-vessels filled; and on 11 August, in the early morning before dawn, they sailed. The wind was dead against them, and they were seven days coasting the island, a distance of thirty leagues. On the afternoon of the 17th they got a better wind, and next morning, when day broke, they had lost sight of land. And from that morning for two centuries the Solomon Islands remained lost to the sight of men.

The ships stood to the north-east, and in the heavy seas the brigantine, towing behind *Los Reyes*, had to be cut adrift for fear of damage. Before leaving San Cristobal it had been decided to steer south-east for 700 leagues, but the pilots were determined in their own minds not to allow Mendaña to override their professional judgment. The dispute was about the prevailing wind. Mendaña believed, wrongly, that it would change with the equinox and blow them steadily to the coast of Chile if Sarmiento's continent should prove illusory. He had even been prepared to wait at San Cristobal another month for the change. Gallego, however, had no faith in amateur theorizing, and with his fellow pilots persuaded the crews that the only safe course was to make for Mexico or California. An unsatisfactory compromise was reached; Mendaña let the pilots have their way while the wind favoured them, and whenever it allowed the course was to be changed to south-east. Gallego in his turn, near the Isle of Jesus, was not allowed to go on a supplementary voyage of discovery to the east in search of a land 'very prosperous and rich' which for no very apparent reason he felt convinced must be there. But of its goodness, he says, 'I did not wish to speak at this time, because all, being despondent, desired to return to Peru.' There was then, in fact, no land to the east within six hundred miles.

By 2 September they were three leagues from the equator and a few miles west of the Gilbert Islands; the burnt logs and other signs of land they encountered were thought by Gallego to have drifted from New Guinea. Two days later the pilots protested formally against the intermittent south-east course they were steering: 'the landsman reasons but the seaman navigates', they said. They were supported by both ships' companies, for water was already short as they crossed the line. Mendaña at last agreed, and they laid a course for California in daily expectation of sighting land, utterly ignorant of the terrors that lay before them. They were within easy distance of the Philippines, safety on which they hopefully turned their backs. On 17 September they sighted land—the Namu atoll of the Marshall Islands. Here they landed, but found no water; the islanders, who fled, obtained theirs from holes scooped out of palm-stems. They did find a chisel made from a nail, and some pieces of rope, presumably obtained from one or other of the Spanish voyagers who had previously traversed these islands. It was impossible to anchor, for there was no bottom even close inshore. A fortnight later they came to a small island destitute of water and bare of every living thing except sea-birds and a few stunted shrubs—it is now known as Wake Island, a minute speck in a waste of waters. The Spaniards called it San Francisco and passed on in bitter disappointment. More than 4000 miles still lay before them, and already they were rationed to one pint of water and twelve ounces of bread a day. Every day the pilots compared notes, *Los Reyes* waiting on the *Todos Santos*, which was slower; until on 16 October the latter fell behind and parted company altogether. The leaders on the flagship were alarmed and angry, persuaded that Sarmiento, now captain of the other ship, must deliberately have altered course. At the same time they began to doubt their own survival, for there arose the greatest storm of all that long voyage.

The hurricane came on them as they lay in the trough of a wave and suddenly threw the ship on her beam ends. Good as *Los Reyes* was in smooth waters, said Gallego, with a little sea she 'would pitch everybody overboard; and for these seas and gulfs she was only fit to drown us all'. She lay on her beam ends for a half-hour and more, while the sailors and soldiers swam about inside her, and below the friars exhorted the men to forgiveness and resignation, for now the hour of their death was come. With great trouble the mainmast and its rigging was cut away, and the ship slowly righted herself. Gallego ordered the sailors to set the foresail: they had hardly begun to do so when it was blown into a thousand fragments, while the ship laboured and plunged in the tremendous seas. They at last made a sail of a blanket and a piece of canvas, and for a day and a night ran to the south, the weather gradually clearing, with interludes so frightful that it seemed as if the world were coming to an end. Gallego had known storms enough, but never such a storm as this. Besides the mast, the ship's boat had gone overboard, and the seas had carried away the stern cabin.

With finer weather came hunger and thirst. The water was putrid and cockroach-ridden, the biscuit was rotten; but on this, a few black beans and a little oil the crew had to exist. For three months the daily allowance was six ounces of biscuit and half a pint of water, Mendaña having no more than the others. Scurvy tortured them, as it had tortured Magellan's men; their gums swelled till the flesh covered their teeth, they were weakened by fever, and the greater number were blind from disease and sheer weakness. 'Even when we had a little help and comfort', says the pitiful Mendaña, 'we threw a man overboard every day; their chief consolation was to call me to see them die; and not only did I feel great sorrow and compassion when I saw this, but even now, whenever I call to mind how I looked upon their death, it touches me to the soul and overcomes me.' There was talk of mutiny and of sailing the ship to the Philippines, so utter was the confusion as to longitude and distances. Mendaña faced the crisis: he spoke as one whose will had been disregarded before, with consequences that they were now suffering; this time he would have his way and they must continue their eastern course—for land could not be far off and to sail west would be to sail to destruction. A few days later they came on a pine-log floating in the sea, new and clean of barnacles; it was hailed with joy as a sign of land and the men made crosses from it to hang on the mast and round their necks. Rain fell, too, and was soaked up in sheets. On 19 December in the evening, a week after picking up the log, Gallego sighted land. It was the coast of Lower California, and safety. Thirty men had died on the homeward passage. The natives had outlived the journey and their conversion to the Catholic faith.

Within a few months nearly all of them were dead in a strange land.

As the ship lay in Colima harbour, watering and taking in wood, her company were startled to see the *Todos Santos*. Whatever the reason for her disappearance, it seemed impossible that she could have survived that October tempest; and now, strangely enough, utterly ignorant of her whereabouts on the American coast, she laboured into the same harbour as her consort, after the same bitter experiences, with boat, mast and rigging gone. Nine months more were to pass before the vessels anchored again at Callao, their progress down the coast being so slow. Sarmiento was arrested, it is uncertain why—perhaps to prevent his bringing false charges against Mendaña—and then released, though he did not return to Peru until Mendaña's uncle the viceroy had relinquished office. Californian and Mexican officials and people were suspicious: fortunately fishermen recognized Gallego. There was much provincial jealousy in the Spanish dominions in America; and the people of Mexico, raided two years earlier on the Atlantic coast by Hawkins's Englishmen, took the unknown sailors for 'strange Scottish people'. It was impossible to obtain credit for repairing the ships, royal ships though they were, and Mendaña and Gallego had to pledge their own resources. They finally reached Callao on 11 September 1569, twenty-two and a half months from the day on which they had set out, and nearly thirteen months after leaving San Cristobal.

Mendaña had completed a great voyage, but the official view of its results was not encouraging. The continent of Sarmiento and Peruvian legend might exist. It did not exist where it ought to; and certainly the expedition, of which it was the principal quest, had not succeeded in finding it. Mendaña was pleased with the appearance of the islands he had discovered, and it may be that in retrospect they seemed even more enticing. To the king a functionary of New Spain wrote otherwise: 'In my opinion, according to the report that I have received, they were of little importance, although they say that they heard of better lands; for in the course of these discoveries they found no specimens of spices, nor of gold and silver, nor of merchandise, nor of any other source of profit, and all the people were naked savages. . . . The advantage that might be derived from exploring these islands would be to make slaves of the people, or to found a settlement in some port in one of them, where provisions could be collected for the discovery of the mainland, where it is reported there is gold and silver, and that the people are clothed.' Thus, without sublimity and without illusion, spoke the voice of the office, a voice that for the next twenty years was continually sounding in Mendaña's ears. Meanwhile, about the quays and taverns of Callao, the Port of the City of the Kings, and up and down the Pacific seaboard of South America, rumours began to pass from ear to ear; and stories of the gold clubs of Ramos, and of the golden river-beds of Guadalcanal, became the common talk of sailors and of those who listened to their tales. Although Mendaña and Gallego had been obliged to repair the ships by pledging their own property, it was related that the Spaniards had returned from the islands with 40,000 pesos of gold. Tupac Yupanqui, it seemed, was a legend justified. Or perhaps it was the other tale that was justified, the tale of the land of Ophir, more likely to appeal to those who had not studied the legends of Peru. It was not Mendaña or his journal-keepers who spoke so; but what Gallego the chief pilot knew as the Western Islands became to imaginative minds in vivid detail the Isles of Solomon.[1] And so in history they remained, rich like those fabled treasuries and as inaccessible.

[1] The name Solomon Islands certainly occurs in the document quoted above, written just after the ships reached Mexico—as it had occurred in documents written before the voyage. On whose suggestion it was now used remains unknown.

# CHAPTER IV

# MENDAÑA AND QUIROS

MENDAÑA could not rest. He had made a great voyage and discovered an archipelago that stretched across the ocean for 600 miles—surely if not a continent the outposts of one. He had spent six months there and brought back an account so accurate that his descriptions were identified centuries later; and to the foundation of a fitting colony his life was thenceforth devoted. From his countrymen he met with little encouragement; his uncle the viceroy, Castro, was recalled, the new viceroy was not sympathetic, and Mendaña at the end of 1569 returned to Spain with Castro to plead his cause at court. Castro became a member of the Council of the Indies, and, helped no doubt by this circumstance, Mendaña in 1574 obtained sanction for his plan. He was authorized by royal decree to take five hundred men—fifty of whom were to be married with families—cattle, horses, goats, sheep and pigs for breeding, and within six years to found three fortified cities. For security he was to give 10,000 ducats; in return, he was granted the absolute government of his colony for two generations, a number of slaves, ten years' exemption from customs duties, the right to coin gold and silver, and the title of Marquis. The way seemed plain: he immediately began to enrol men, embarked at Seville in the middle of 1576, and reached Panama early in 1577. Here his uncle's enemies were in the ascendant. Just as he was leaving for Peru he was arrested and thrown into jail as a common prisoner, and when at last he arrived there he was twice prevented from sailing by the action of the viceroy, Toledo. How he spent the next fifteen years we do not know. His dream seemed to be decisively shattered; for Drake had come into the Pacific.

Drake's circumnavigation does not present the appearance of a voyage of exploration, though plainly it was conceived as something much more inclusive than the plunder of the Pacific coast of South America—well planned and executed as that work was. There were in Mexico English merchants, one at least of whom, Henry Hawks, sent news home in 1572 of Mendaña's discovery. English geographers thought the theories of Mercator and Ortelius, the leaders in their science, thus stood confirmed; and English patriots began in their turn to plan an empire not in America but in the South Sea. As early as 1530 or 1531, indeed, Englishmen had begun to erect vast schemes of expansion. About those years Robert Thorne and Roger Barlow composed their *Declaration of the Indies*, in which they urged a voyage northwards from England over the Pole and thence south through the Strait of Anian, the undiscovered passage supposed to divide America from Asia. If the voyagers then made down to the tropics, they might discover the richest islands and kingdoms of the world, filled with all precious things, 'that we here esteem most, which come out of strange countries'. The *Declaration* was presented to Henry VIII in 1540: not till nearly forty years later, in the reign of his daughter, had the English thoroughly assimilated its argument. Then pride, ambition and dreams of wealth at once began to move them. Spain might claim America, but, they held, in the words of Drake's nephew, the historian of his voyage, 'the maine Ocean by right is the Lord's alone, and by nature left free for all men to deale withall, as very sufficient for all mens use, and large enough for all mens industry'. Into the South Sea, thus free and sufficient, it was believed there were four possible ways—round the Cape of Good Hope, through the Strait of Magellan, by a north-east passage round Asia or a north-west passage round America. The Cape route was thought too long. Of the others, all received the support of ardent parties and famous names, and finally a project was evolved which seemed to combine the advantages of the north-west passage and the strait. The continent of *Terra Australis incognita* certainly existed, stretching perhaps through thirty degrees of latitude; let therefore Englishmen sail through the strait into the South Sea, discover its beautiful shores, and trade with the docile and civilized natives for their gold and precious stones. Then let them turn northward and annex whatever islands seemed useful as bases for future enterprise, sell English cloth in China and Japan, and waiting till the arctic ice was melted, pass through the Strait of Anian, and make their way home round North America. Such was the scheme projected by Sir Richard Grenville. None, in the late sixteenth century, could have appeared more logical or more neatly concluded. In essentials it seems to have been adopted, and the captain chosen to carry it out was Francis Drake.

The instructions actually drafted for Drake ordered him both to enter and to return from the Pacific by way of Magellan's strait; they were later amended to enable him either to push on to the Moluccas or to pass home through the Strait of Anian. Once in the Pacific, he was to explore unknown shores not in the possession of any Christian prince, as far as latitude 30°— that is, the coast of Terra Australis, or Beach, which was laid down in the popular atlas of Ortelius as running north-west from the strait. Here he was to spend five months, making friends of the country's rulers, choosing headquarters for the sale of English cloth, and investigating the chances of obtaining gold, silver, drugs and spices; and he was then to return. It was a proposal which, granting the existence of Beach, would have effectually forestalled the frustrated efforts of Mendaña. Drake, with the silent connivance of his queen, had in mind an alternative not of hypothetical but of certain profit: and even before he entered the Pacific he had altered his plans accordingly. He sailed on 13 December 1577 with five ships, the *Pelican*, of 100 tons, the *Elizabeth*, 80 tons, the *Marigold*, 30 tons, and two victuallers, their crews enlisted ostensibly and not very plausibly for a voyage to Alexandria. The disclosure of his change of plan to his officers occasioned opposition: and possibly it was this that lay behind the execution of one who had been Drake's friend, Thomas Doughty—a deed which has never been satisfactorily explained. Doughty was beheaded in Magellan's Port St Julian; and the English sailors, wandering on the shore, found the remains of a gibbet and beneath it the bones of the mutineers who had perished in that fatal bay fifty-eight years before. Drake, destroying the two victuallers and changing his ship's name to the *Golden Hind*, passed through the strait in seventeen days. But on entering the Pacific he met with a series of storms that put the expedition in dire peril. They raged from 7 September to 28 October 1578; the *Marigold* sank with all hands, and the *Elizabeth*, commanded by John Winter, was driven back into the strait. The master of the *Elizabeth* refused point-blank to steer west towards Beach, contrary winds prevented a course to Peru, and Winter was reluctantly forced to turn homeward. It was evident that a belt of strong westerly winds made it impossible to reach the Moluccas by way of the coast of Terra Australis.

To this conclusion Drake also came. But before he continued his voyage, now alone 'as a pellican alone in the wildernesse', he had made a discovery very damning to one part of the continental theory. For driven south-east by the tempest, he had come to what he thought must be the extremity of South America, and land ceased. 'The uttermost cape or hedland of all these Ilands', says Drake's admiring relative, 'stands neere in 56 deg., without which there is no maine nor Iland to be seene to the Southwards, but that the Atlanticke Ocean and the South Sea, meete in a most large and free scope.' Upon this uttermost point Drake cast himself down, reaching his body over it; and so jubilantly told his people that he had been upon the southernmost known land in the world.[1] Now, faced with winds that destroyed the possibility of following his original instructions,

---

[1] We do not know that this romantic gesture really belongs to Cape Horn. It seems more likely that Drake was on Henderson Island, part of the coast of Tierra del Fuego, about fifty miles to the west-north-west of the cape. Off that island there was still plenty of scope for the oceans to mix. Felix Riesenberg, *Cape Horn* (London, 1941), has a more radical theory, of an island that has since disappeared.

he had no difficulty in turning his attention to the ships and towns of the Peruvian coast, with a success that seemed to his own and later ages dazzling and complete. Then, with a richer lading than any English ship had ever borne before, he turned his course for the west coast of North America, presumably in search of the Strait of Anian—which was supposed to enter the Pacific in latitude 40° N—and a homeward passage to the east. But even as far north as 48° there was no sign of a strait, and from that latitude contrary winds and cold made it prudent to return. He spent a month on the Californian coast refitting, among friendly natives—a region where there seemed, to sixteenth-century eyes, signs of gold and silver in any common earth that was taken up. Drake had some idea that a colony might be founded here, and for this reason and because of the white cliffs that fronted the sea annexed the country under the name of New Albion. His problem then was how to return to England: the Strait of Anian either did not exist or was too far north; to attempt Magellan's strait must mean capture by the Spaniards, now thoroughly aroused; the solution appeared to be to cross the Pacific to the Moluccas, and so to round the Cape of Good Hope. This he did, leaving the coast of New Albion in July 1579, sailing south of the Marshalls to the Philippines; entering into very friendly negotiations with the Sultan of Ternate, on which the English later based their claims to a share in the spice trade; narrowly escaping disaster on a reef in those perilous East Indian seas, where the ship stuck fast for twenty hours; and arriving at Plymouth, amid excitement such as rarely met a ship returning from a foreign voyage, on 26 September 1580.

Although the booty was great, from the point of view of discovery Drake's voyage had not been so profitable; and though he might have stood upon the 'uttermost cape' of America and map-makers after 1580 sometimes drew only small islands below the Strait of Magellan, others remained fast in their continental faith, and forty years later Dutch voyagers were to report once more the existence of Terra Australis in those waters. But the fortunes of the *Golden Hind* and her sister ships had given denial to one other common report of the age— stimulated perhaps, as was suggested, by the Spanish in order to discourage other seamen from voyaging into the Pacific: the report that a perpetual easterly current and easterly winds, though they carried ships easily into that ocean, as effectually barred their return. The belief in the Strait of Anian and a north-west passage was not destroyed—the Spanish in Peru at first thought Drake to have sailed home that way; nevertheless the opening of the strait, it was evident, must be farther north than had been conjectured. The Californian coast was made known as a place of refreshment for Pacific voyagers, both Spanish and English. And the success of the raid on the riches of Peru deterred further search for *Terra Australis incognita* on the part of the English for upwards of two centuries. When Cavendish came into the Pacific in 1586 and Richard Hawkins in 1594 the gold immediately available rendered superfluous the pains of exploration. Nor was Spain more eager in the quest, over a period discouraging to enthusiasts. Against foreign invasion there was in 1581 an attempt to fortify the straits, led by the redoubtable Pedro Sarmiento, to which starvation and the rigours of the winter put an effectual end; while colonization by Spaniards themselves, it seemed, would merely provide future havens for the advancement of the enemy.

Against that final argument, against the refusal to tolerate any conceivable partition of the Pacific, Mendaña for long beat in vain. Yet at last a new viceroy of Peru was appointed, the Marquis of Cañete, and once more he began his preparations, this time without disappointment. 'Many years having passed in silence since the first voyage of Alvaro Mendaña,' writes the chronicler, 'God was served that in the city of Kings, residence of the Viceroys of Peru, the enterprise should be proclaimed which His Majesty had ordered the Adelantado to undertake to the Isles of Solomon.'

When Mendaña had first set out to discover the Southern

Continent he was barely more than a youth. He was now a man of fifty-three, married and with children, mature but in essential character unaltered. Only in one respect does he appear to have changed—his solicitude for the interests of native peoples, it seems, had lessened, or his control over his men, never strong, had weakened even more; for in no greater degree than in its relations with the 'Indians' did his second expedition fail. With him on this new voyage went his wife, Doña Isabel Barreto, a lady with a sense of her own merits and of the importance of her position as wife of the Adelantado, or governor. She herself, with part of her dowry, bought one of the ships for the expedition. There also went Doña Isabel's three brothers, a family party that helped to destroy what little harmony might otherwise have existed. There were four ships, the flagship, *San Jeronimo*, being captained by Don Lorenzo Barreto, Mendaña's brother-in-law, and two of the others being small—a frigate, the *Santa Catalina*, and a galiot, the *San Felipe*. In these sailed a company of 378, seamen and soldiers and their wives and children. Among them were some put on board simply to get rid of them, as a menace to good order at home. The camp master was an old soldier, brave, capable and zealous, but no less overbearing and quarrelsome. The Church was represented by a vicar and a second secular priest, and one Franciscan. The most important person, however, because of his position, ability and character alike, proved to be the chief pilot, Pedro Fernandez de Quiros. This man attained fame. Of its earliest foundations we know little. He was a Portuguese born in 1565, and when in 1580 Spain and Portugal were dynastically united became a subject of Philip II. We learn from a writer who has little good to say of him that he was brought up in one of the worst parts of Lisbon and became a supercargo on merchant ships. Certainly he grew to be an excellent sailor and pilot, and was only thirty when Mendaña prevailed on him, against his better judgment, to sail with the fleet in the position that was next to the leader's the most responsible. More than once, before the expedition left the South American coast, Quiros determined to abandon it as impossible, for already there was incipient mutiny, and the rival wills of family clique, camp master, soldiers and sailors threatened to stultify Mendaña's plans. Only the passionate pleadings of Mendaña persuaded him to remain. It is from Quiros's account, dictated later to his secretary, that we can trace the course of events.

Mendaña's first expedition had cost much; at least it had resulted in comparative success. Quiros tells a story of utter and disastrous failure. The fleet sailed from Callao on 9 April 1595, and spent some time on the coast provisioning, one of the ships behaving more like a pirate than a king's vessel; and at the port of Cherrepe, the least good of them, that bought by Mendaña's wife, was forcibly exchanged for a better one, the *Santa Ysabel*. Expeditions without a royal purse, says Quiros, could not, it seemed, be set forth without some mischief being done. Mendaña nevertheless wished to take only respectable persons with him, and here put ashore certain men and women who did not attain his standard. Quiros drew five charts for the leader and the pilots—whereon, at Mendaña's orders, appeared only the coast of Peru from Arica to Payta, and in the west two points 1500 leagues from Lima, one in 7° and the other in 12° S latitude, lest if more were shown some ship might desert to it. The longitude of the Solomons was reckoned by Mendaña to be within 1450 leagues from Lima, so that there was thus, he thought, ample margin. Provisions were inadequate in quantity and quality, and the soldiers and others bought supplies of their own. Finally, with Mendaña himself 'very uncertain what would be the end, when the beginning was so disorderly', they made sail from Payta on 16 June, displaying banners, playing upon the clarion and feasting.

There was little incident during the early part of the voyage. They sailed south-west, west-by-south, and west-by-north, marriages taking place nearly every day and the company regaling themselves with high hopes and many stories, of which none envisaged the good of the natives. On 21 July an island was sighted, Magdalena or Fatuhiva, and later others. Mendaña, for no very good reason, was immediately convinced that these were the Solomons, and with great joy ordered the *Te Deum* to be sung. The first island seemed uninhabited, but as they sailed near its southern coast many outrigger canoes shot from it, with about 400 natives, some swimming and some hanging on to the sides. They were clear-skinned, gracefully and robustly built, quite naked and tattooed in patterns of blue, with long loose hair. They had much cause to praise their Creator, says the pious chief pilot. Among so many beautiful youths came a boy about ten years old, with a face like that of an angel, 'so that I never in my life felt such pain as when I thought that so fair a creature should be left to go to perdition'. The natives brought coconuts, plantains and water in bamboo-joints. One the Spaniards dressed in a shirt and hat, to the immense amusement of his comrades; and at that about forty came on board the *San Jeronimo* and walked about boldly, much puzzled by the Spanish clothes till they discovered the natural skin and flesh beneath. Finally their curiosity became so free that Mendaña was annoyed and ordered a gun to be fired; they leapt into the sea in terror, but tried to tow the ship to the shore by a rope from the bowsprit. One who was slow in going was cut in the hand with a sword, at which, urged on by a chief to battle, they threw stones and brandished lances threateningly. Arquebuses were fired, seven or eight were killed and the rest displayed green branches as emblems of peace. By this time Mendaña realized the islands were a new discovery, and to the group, so thickly inhabited, so beautiful with their groves of trees, their plains and mountains, he gave the name of Las Marquesas de Mendoza, after his friend the viceroy. The Marquesas they remain.

Next day the camp master was sent with twenty soldiers to seek a port or a watering place on the island called Santa Cristina—which we know as Tahuata. The Spaniards, surrounded with canoes, by way of precaution, and with reckless cruelty, opened fire. One native jumped into the sea with a child in his arms—a soldier sent them both to the bottom with a single shot, lest he should lose his reputation as a good marks-man. Alas! asked Quiros, what would it serve him with such fame to enter into hell? No port or water was found, and the expedition had to be repeated the following day. This time the natives proved very friendly and brought fruit and water, but attempting to run off with four jars, they were once again shot down. It is hard to exaggerate the patience of these Marquesans, their idyllic peace so rudely shattered; though certainly they were allowed to attend the celebration of mass on shore. The Spaniards themselves were in danger, for the *San Jeronimo* narrowly escaped striking a rock; and only Quiros's insistence on the necessity of supplies kept Mendaña from departing im-mediately, disgusted as he was at the continual complaints that assailed his ears. In the end, however, he went on shore to take possession of the four islands he had discovered, walking through the nearest village and sowing maize, and returned to the ship in peace and goodwill. But further hostilities broke out. The camp master for a time stayed on shore with all the soldiers, who began to quarrel among themselves; at this the natives threw stones and lances, and when fired on fled to the summits of three high hills, whence their shouts of defiance came echoing all day through the ravines. The empty village and beach were guarded, while the women rested and the sailors got wood and water, and there was an interval of peace. Food was brought to the guards by natives, who seemed to ask when the invaders would go; one was taught to make the sign of the Cross and to say 'Jesu Maria', and many made friends among the soldiers and exchanged odd native words for Spanish. Yet when two canoes came to the ship with strings of coconuts, half their crews were shot and killed, and the camp master hung up three bodies for a warning to traitorous Mar-quesans. Four armed ships, felt Quiros, had little to fear from unarmed natives in canoes: but with men such as the soldier who declared it his 'diligence to kill, because he liked to kill' his protestations had little effect.

In the middle of this chronicle of murder Quiros gives a

description of the island of Santa Cristina and its harbour of
Madre de Dios where the fleet had anchored—its excellent
water and woods and climate, the houses of timber and cane
roofed with leaves, the great canoes carved from a single tree,
holding thirty or forty paddlers, the adzes of fish-bones and
shell, the native men, darker than those of Magdalena, the
women graceful and nearly white, some of them more beautiful than the women of Lima, who were famed for their beauty.
Grace and beauty availed nothing against the shot of arquebusiers. For natives and Spaniards did not understand one
another, Quiros says, and hence the evil things that happened.
Mendaña, who had not wanted to stay, before he left wished
to leave thirty men, some married, to colonize the islands; the
soldiers complained and he thereupon abandoned the idea. The
galiot was repaired, three crosses were raised and another cut
on a tree with the date, and on 5 August the fleet sailed again.
The symbols of religion did not, to Quiros, compensate for the
two hundred (so he reckoned) Marquesans left dead, killed both
under orders and casually by the soldiers. Such evil deeds, he
says sadly, 'are not things to do, nor to praise, nor to allow, nor
to maintain, nor to refrain from punishing if the occasion
permits'.

After a few days Mendaña recovered his good spirits; one
day he was certain they would sight the Solomons. At the news
everybody ate and drank extravagantly, and food and water
became short, for there was nothing but the ocean visible. The
soldiers became restive again, and slackness and suspicion
spread through the ships. On 20 August they passed four small
and low sandy islands, covered with palms, called then col-
lectively San Bernardo—the islands of the atoll Pukapuka, in
the northern Cooks;[1] and nine days later another, lying alone in
the expanse of sea, the island Solitaria—Nurakita, the southernmost of the Ellice group. A reef made it impossible to land and
there was much murmuring. The camp master became very

[1] A quite different Pukapuka from that in the Tuamotus, possibly discovered by Magellan.

quarrelsome. Impatience grew, some saying that the Isles of Solomon had fled away, or that the sea had risen and covered them, or that the Adelantado had forgotten where they were; others that 'to call himself a Marquis and advance his own relations, he had taken them, with 400 pounds of biscuit, to perish in that great gulf, to go to the bottom and fish for those wonderful pearls he had talked about'; others that they had sailed right past them and would come at last to Great Tartary. Mendaña, sensitive as he was, suffered greatly from these complaints, and he ordered public prayers to be said and the soldiers to be put to various employments. Then the captain of the *Santa Ysabel*, very despondent, reported that he was short of wood and water and was burning the upper works of the ship for fuel; she was crowded with people, carried little ballast, was very cranky, and would not bear much sail. Mendaña, disbelieving in the shortage of water, refused him supplies, but remained apprehensive about the ship. So they sailed on till 7 September, when they ran into thick fog. The galiot and the frigate were sent on ahead, and the ships navigated with great caution, communicating by lights when night fell. An hour before midnight a deeper darkness to port became perceptible; then the fog raised its curtain, and land stood out clearly, less than a league away. All the ships showed lights except the *Santa Ysabel*. The night was passed in praying to God to send the day. When it came the land was visible in truth; but of the *Santa Ysabel* there was no sign.

The land was a point, rather dark and rounded, covered with trees and very beautiful. In the west a bare conical hill stood out of the sea, flaming from the top more than ten ordinary volcanoes. A few days later it blew off its crown, with a mighty thundering that shook the ship, ten leagues away, and a smoke that covered the whole sky. The frigate was sent to sail round this volcano, in search of the missing ship, and Mendaña ordered all to confess, himself setting the example; for, he said, they were about to visit an unknown land, where enemies and dangers would not be wanting. As they neared the island a large canoe sailed to meet them, with a fleet of fifty smaller outriggers, full of natives shouting and waving their hands. The Spaniards hailed them doubtfully in return. These natives were different from the Marquesans, and so much more like the Solomon Islanders that Mendaña was once again deceived. They were black or tawny, partly clad in woven stuff, with frizzled hair dyed red and white, and red-coloured teeth, adorned with beads of fish's teeth and bone and plates of mother-of-pearl. They were armed with bows, darts and heavy wooden clubs. But they did not understand Mendaña when he spoke to them in the Solomon Islands tongue, and he had to bear disappointment once more.

Towards this people the Spaniards behaved as they had towards those of the Marquesas, with some variations. The humane Mendaña of 1565 is there: now hesitating, indecisive, almost bereft of authority. Only Quiros and one or two more, at the peril of their lives, protest against a butchery indiscriminate and objectless—unless it be an object to make oneself fearful in treacherous cruelty. At first the natives paddled chattering round the ships, nervous of venturing further; then after some consultation they took up their bows and shot arrows into the sails and rigging, without doing harm. In reply, the arquebusiers fired—some men were killed, others fell wounded, and the whole fleet of canoes fled in terror. The ships stood off and on, looking for a port, and the frigate returned from her mission unsuccessful; and anchoring on a dangerous bottom, they had some difficulty in getting out to sea. Next morning Quiros found a small port, where the natives were hostile; the following day Mendaña found a better one, in a sheltered bay, near to a river and several villages. All night the Spaniards heard the noise of music and dancing, and the villagers proved friendly as well as festive. For four days numbers of them came off to inspect the ships, with red flowers in their hair and nostrils, amazed at the mystery of looking-glasses, scissors and razors; delighted with the feathers, little bells, glass beads, bits of cloth and playing cards which the Spaniards gave them; learning to say 'friends' in Spanish and making the sign of the cross as they were taught. Among the first to come was a chief of fine presence and tawny-coloured skin, with blue, yellow and red plumes on his head, one Malope; Mendaña received him in a very friendly manner, they exchanged names, and Malope thenceforth insisted on being called Mendaña. After the fourth day fifty canoes approached with concealed arms, but when the natives saw a soldier take up an arquebus all fled. They were followed and had a consultation with their fellows on the beach, after which they returned to their village. The soldiers were disappointed at such signs of peace, says Quiros, because they would have preferred to slaughter.

At night there were great fires on the other side of the bay, and canoes hastened from village to village. Next morning, apparently as a result, a watering party from the galiot was ambushed and three men wounded. Mendaña at once ordered the camp master to land with thirty men and do all the harm he could. Natives were killed in spite of a stout resistance, huts and canoes were burnt at Malope's village, palm-trees were cut down, and pigs were taken for food. The following day the operation was repeated, though the natives again defended themselves bravely—'in order that, by means of the chastise-ment inflicted on them, it might have the effect of preventing greater evils'. In the afternoon Malope arrived at the beach in great distress: the authors of the ambush were not his suffering people, they were enemies from the other side of the bay, and he naturally would not come out to the ship to get Mendaña's explanations. Curiously enough, friendship was restored later. Meanwhile, Mendaña's brother-in-law Don Lorenzo, in the frigate, had made a second unsuccessful search for the *Santa Ysabel*, finding, however, a very populous bay and many small islands.

The ships now moved to a better port, not far from their first one; and here an attack by the natives led to another bloody foray. It was followed by dissension. The camp master was annoyed because Don Lorenzo followed up the victory without authority; Doña Isabel took her brother's part and the camp master spent the night on shore in dudgeon. Next day he proposed to the soldiers to found a settlement and to clear a space for this purpose near a large stream. There was dispute as to the healthiness of the site, and Mendaña was not pleased. It is difficult to read his irresolute mind: apparently he also was inclined to settlement, and had selected a bare point near the entrance to the bay. The soldiers, however, took things into their own hands and began to fell trees with the enthusiasm of men who have at last found something to do. Even then, we learn, the devil kept some in mind of the delights of Lima, and their enthusiasm was of brief passage. They complained of an order from Mendaña to ensure good treatment of the natives and their property—did not all belong to them, those who came as conquerors? Foraging parties had no difficulty in collecting pigs, coconuts and plantains, and the peaceful natives brought supplies both to the camp and to the ships. They were not allowed into the camp lest they should see how few were the Spaniards, but an agreement was made with them to help put up houses; for they not unnaturally showed much feeling when their own were pulled down to provide building materials. And the vicar presented them with a large cross.

This island, where settlement was now to take place, Mendaña called Santa Cruz. It was Ndeni in the group still known by this name. The flaming hill was Tinakula, another island fifteen miles to the north. Santa Cruz seemed about a hundred leagues round, not very high, and covered with trees. The ground was fertile; there were many birds and fish, fruits and edible roots, and no reptiles save black lizards. The bay, which retains its Spanish name Graciosa, provided good anchorage, the beaches were clean sand, the water of the streams was clear and good. The natives were numerous all along the sea-shore; they were skilful in weaving and in the making of canoes; their temper was on the whole peaceable. Their houses were well built, and around them, in small pots, or trained over low trees, they grew red flowers of several kinds, of which they were very fond. Each village had its well, its communal meeting-house, and its 'oracle' or place of tribal worship.

Though such surroundings might be considered agreeable, discontent began to reach a climax. The soldiers, who had insisted on settlement, were dissatisfied with everything. The land was now very wretched and poor, there was nothing in it, and the settlement was in a bad position. At last a petition to Mendaña was prepared, asking him to take them to a better country, or to the 'islands he had talked about'—the Solomons. Men who remained loyal were threatened. In the midst of these troubles a church was built, where every day a priest said mass. Religious exercises, however, seem to have been of minor effect: natives were shot and stabbed to death simply to provoke a war which would make it impossible to remain; rumours of mutiny and assault went round the camp and the ships; the soldiers were terrified of being left on the island and rebelled even at Quiros's going to sea on his proper business. Mendaña, apparently to placate them, had the sails unbent and put under guard. 'The camp master is my cock', said some. Then the sailors wanted to depart. Not a month had passed since their arrival. 'How can there be so little firmness in honourable men?' lamented Quiros. Mendaña fell sick from worry. Quiros obtained permission to go on shore and harangue the malcontents, which he did with elaborate sarcasm and complete lack of success. They complained that the land was bad, he said; did they expect to enter a house ready furnished, with the tables spread? To find mountains, valleys and plains of emeralds and diamonds, ready to be loaded and taken away? All the provinces in the world had their beginnings—was some new land to be the exception? They would be looked upon as the enemies of God and the king, of their general's honour and their own, if they abandoned such an enterprise and such a land. This eloquence earned merely a threat of death, while the audience went back to their 'old song', that they wanted to go to Manila, which was a land of Christians.

The prime mover in this discontent, thought those in the *San Jeronimo* at least, was the camp master, though his particular guilt is not clear from the narrative. 'He knew how to think much, but he could not be silent', says Quiros. When he came on board one day to speak to Mendaña, Doña Isabel was urgent to have him killed, and finally the resolution was taken. It heralded a day of blood. Quiros, on a foraging expedition a short time later, and in danger from hostile natives, received great help from Malope. Returning to the ship, he learnt that some days earlier soldiers had gone to kill the chief; and a message was sent to the camp to acquaint them with his services, and to order that no harm should be done him. That night Mendaña, from his sick-bed, with great caution told Quiros that next morning he was going on shore with four men in whom he had confidence, and with the royal standard, 'to do justice on the camp master', and that he would proclaim the will of the king at the proper time. When day came a squadron of soldiers was seen marching from the camp. Mendaña went on shore and found that they were sent by the camp master to Malope's village to get food. He warned them against harming Malope or his property, but received for answer only a laugh. He then walked to the camp with Don Lorenzo and his brothers. The camp master came out from his breakfast unarmed; finding himself among enemies, he called for his dagger and sword, but at a signal from Mendaña he was immediately stabbed dead; on which a drummer, coveting his clothes, stripped and left him naked. Then Don Lorenzo and his brother stabbed and killed a soldier, a friend of the dead man, and would have gone on had not Quiros stoutly protested. At the noise of arms the women ran from their huts in alarm, wringing their hands and praying for their husbands, while Mendaña's men went about with drawn swords like lunatics, shouting 'Long live the king! Death to traitors!' It seemed a day for avenging injuries; it was also, thought Quiros, a day of licence.

The heads of the two dead men were set up on posts outside

the camp, while the vicar and the sailors from the ship, all armed, with Doña Isabel and her sister, hurried on shore and in great excitement rallied round Mendaña and the royal standard. Mendaña ordered the whole company to church to hear mass, where the vicar recommended them to be quiet and obedient, and not scandalized at the deaths, which were ordained. In the afternoon a soldier came back and reported the murder of Malope while he was regaling the party with food in his house. The excuse for this deed was that Malope had intended to commit treason. 'He is well dead', said the murderer when he was surrendered. He was put in the stocks for judgment. An ensign who went with the party was seized and beheaded, his wife's tears availing nothing, and his head set up with the other two. There was a general intercession in favour of other prisoners, and even the murderer of Malope, in spite of Mendaña's abhorrence, was merely kept a prisoner; Quiros urging that the three heads should be shown to the natives as payment for the death of their chief—the Spaniards could ill spare more lives. The murderer was unhappy in this clemency; he was upbraided by some of his comrades and grew despondent. 'At last it seemed to him that it would be better to die than to live. He left off caring for himself, and died very suddenly after a few days. . . . With this', says Quiros, 'ended the tragedy of the islands where Solomon was wanting.' With this, rather, the tragedy entered on a new stage.

There was great mourning for Malope among the natives, and the head of the ensign was given them in expiation. But soon the Spaniards had cause to mourn also. Sickness which seemed incurable fell on them, a punishment from heaven, some thought, for their treacheries and disorder. Mendaña, already sick, daily grew weaker, and the supreme command was given to Don Lorenzo. Three times on the same day the Spaniards were driven back in skirmishes by the natives, so emboldened that they hurled stones and shot arrows into the camp, to the defence of which warfare was now restricted. The second priest died, and Mendaña, feeling his own end near, gave orders about his will, nominating Doña Isabel governess, as his heir, and Don Lorenzo captain-general. Next day, 18 October 1595, he, too, died; and in the afternoon, given what meagre pageantry was possible, he was buried, to the sound of muffled drums, a black cloth over his coffin, escorted by arquebusiers carrying their arms reversed. With this, says Quiros, the chronicler of so much failure, 'there ended his enterprise, so much and for so long a time desired. He was a person zealous for the honour of God and the service of the king, to whom the things ill done did not appear well, nor did those well done appear evil. He was very plain-spoken, not diffuse in giving his reasons, and he himself said that he did not want arguments but deeds. It seemed that he saw clearly those matters which touched his conscience. It seemed to me that he might say with reason that he knew more than he performed, yet he saw nothing that passed by stealth.' So perished one dream, not mean or little in its substance, of a continent colonized and converted; Mendaña's grave held a purpose greater than the man himself.

Men died every day, and the vicar began to perambulate the camp calling on all to confess. Those there were who had not confessed for many years, seven or fourteen or thirty; one man had done so only once in his life; another did not know whether he was a Christian or a Moor; others had murders on their souls. Among this sickness, war, discord, and famine—for there were now no native supplies—the good vicar went about giving the sacrament and burying the dead. The natives renewed their attacks, shooting from the shelter of the trees; but a sortie resulted in the burning of Malope's village and a parley which secured a fresh supply of food. Mendaña's death was concealed, lest it should encourage further onslaughts. Meanwhile the frigate had been sent on a third unsuccessful search for the *Santa Ysabel*, returning only with some native youths and pearl shell.

A petition was now drawn up by the vicar for the abandonment of the settlement. Quiros was still in favour of remaining, but, as before, his ardour merely brought him threats of violence. He thought the land healthy, for there were no sudden deaths, and the sick lived many days; rather it was the complete change of diet and custom, sleeping on wet ground and similar lack of care, which caused the sickness, and there were no doctors. Then the vicar fell sick, and Don Lorenzo was wounded in the leg and took to his bed. He became rapidly worse, while the camp did not hold fifteen healthy men. One soldier, at least, 'received death with such a cheerful countenance that in the words he spoke, and what he did, he seemed to be a pilgrim on the road to heaven.' Of the fate of the women and children the record has singularly little. Don Lorenzo died on 2 November; the vicar, five days later. By that time ten determined natives could have wiped out the settlement, and all the sick were embarked in the ships, leaving on shore only watering and wood-cutting parties, and a number of abandoned dogs, which ran barking desolately along the beach. There were two further forays, to get food and incidentally destroy native stores. The second was led by Quiros, who alone seems to have commanded his men to fire in the air to frighten, and not to kill, the natives. These natives, he said, were well ordered; they kept faith; and peace was broken with them, wilfully, even while the invaders were starving for need of their help. But this was the story of the expedition.

So, at last, on 18 November, leaving Santa Cruz 'in the claws of the devil', they sailed from the bay of Graciosa, and the sick and the dying men on board called it a corner of hell.

The Governess proposed to the pilots to search first for San Cristobal, to see if the *Santa Ysabel* were there, and if she were not found to go to Manila to enlist priests and people, with whom to return and complete the discovery. Quiros undertook to return also if this were done. He wished in the general interest to abandon the frigate and the galiot, which were in bad repair and needed thirty of the best men to work, while the pilot of the frigate neither had a chart nor knew how to use one. He was overborne. He even had difficulty in keeping those

in the *San Jeronimo* from jettisoning their sick into the frigate.
Mendaña's body was taken on board the frigate to be buried
at Manila.

Quiros, on whose shoulders now fell the whole responsibility for the expedition, knew nothing about these seas, and this
guideless voyage to the Philippines against contrary winds, in
rotten ships with a starving and dying company, must rank as
one of the greatest feats in the record of Pacific journeyings.
Forty-seven men had died at the island in a month; and now a
body was thrown overboard every day, on some days three or
four. They steered west-south-west two days; no land came in
sight, so the decision was taken to turn towards Manila. They
sailed north-west to avoid New Guinea, which was thought to
be near; and the explorer is manifest even under those conditions in Quiros, who laments the wretched condition of his
ship, which forbade the coasting of that island, to 'find out what
it was'. Great waves from the north-west knocked the ship
about, yet even these were preferred to calms or light winds.

By 10 December they were half a degree from the equator,
where an almost unbearable sun alternated with bitterly cold
nights. That night the galiot, after being reprimanded over
parting company, disappeared altogether. Incessant repairs to
the rigging were necessary; sometimes a sail would flap three
days together in the waist of the *San Jeronimo*, because no one
cared to attempt to hoist it with a rope that had been spliced
thirty or forty times. Only the beams of her hull kept the ship
above water; they were made of hardwood from Guayaquil,
in Peru, called *guatchapeli*, which never seemed to decay. When
she sailed on a bowline the water ran in and out, so open was it
in the dead wood. The sailors became tired of life. There was
little good fellowship; daily rations were cut down to a half-
pound of flour, mixed with salt water and baked in ashes, and a
half-pint of stinking water; the starving could hardly carry the
dead up from the 'tween-decks. Men, and women with children
at their breasts, prayed for a single drop of water. One soul
shines brilliantly out of that hell, that of an old soldier and

hospital worker, Juan Leal. Day after day he tended the sick and helped them to die, gentle and compassionate in his hermit's sackcloth and long hair, until at last he died also. Doña Isabel had her private store of wine, oil and vinegar, which she steadfastly refused to give up to the common use: when Quiros brought the complaints of her people to her she recommended hanging two of them as an example. Finally he prevailed on her to serve out two jars of oil. The water which he was carefully husbanding she took to wash her clothes. 'Cannot I do what I please with my own property?' she said angrily to his remonstrances. The soldiers might say, rejoined Quiros, that she washed her clothes with their life's blood. At which Doña Isabel took the keys of the store-room from the steward and gave them to her own servants; while with incredible levity she and her brothers plotted the chief pilot's death. So at least Quiros. Nevertheless Quiros refused to impose his own will where he thought his loyalty was due.

By 19 December, when they were in latitude 3° 30′ N, those in the frigate were utterly worn out by the pumps, but Quiros was not allowed to take them into the *San Jeronimo* and abandon the vessel. At last she was lost sight of and seen no more. On 23 December an island was sighted, Ponape, the largest of the Carolines, but the ship, now alone, got among reefs and it was impossible to land, though beyond could be seen the clearings of a cultivated countryside, and trees and flowers. On 1 January 1596 they were in sight of Guam and Rota in the Ladrones, but here again there was no seeking a port without the gear to manage a boat. At last, at daybreak on 12 January, they sighted land which must be the Philippines. Still they were not out of danger, on this unfamiliar coast. Even Doña Isabel, that pious lady, then appeared to be contemplating death, a book of devotions in her hand and suitable ejaculations on her lips. The ship made into a bay, however, where a Spanish-speaking native came on board, with a companion who had piloted Cavendish among these channels. And now there was food in plenty, which the natives sold for silver and knives and glass beads. For three days and nights the galley fire was never out, and eating went on continuously—with fatal results to several more of the sick.

Gratitude to Quiros at last overflowed. In the dangerous navigation which yet lay before him, nevertheless, he was not aided by the careless and foolish Doña Isabel, tenacious of her rights to the end. Had not her husband spent his fortune on the expedition? The natives fled before the strange ship, warned by the governor of the islands to beware of marauding Englishmen. But Doña Isabel's two brothers made their way by a convenient channel straight to Manila, and as the *San Jeronimo* drew nearer to the haven a boat came out to meet it with four Spaniards. 'They seemed', said Quiros, 'like four thousand angels.' Doña Isabel had still two pigs alive. 'Is this a time for courtesy with pigs?' asked one of the four, and the animals were slain. The ship anchored finally at Manila on 11 February 1596. Since leaving Santa Cruz fifty of her company had died, and within a few days ten more perished from their privations. Of the remainder Doña Isabel complained bitterly to the local magistrate. The galiot reached port at Mindanao; the frigate was never heard of again, beyond a vague report that she had been seen run on some shore unspecified, with all her sails set and her crew rotting.

The survivors were well tended in Manila. They arrived in time to help to celebrate the coming of a new governor; after which Doña Isabel, having buried Mendaña once again, married Don Fernando de Castro, a relative of his predecessor. Their combined resources enabled the ship to be refitted and revictualled, and on the day of St Lawrence, 10 August 1596, she sailed for Mexico. Of this voyage we know nothing beyond the lateness of its start, which resulted in 'incredible hardships and troubles'. On 11 December 1596 she arrived at Acapulco, whence Quiros left for Peru.

# CHAPTER V

## AUSTRIALIA DEL ESPIRITU SANTO

ONE more great voyage the Spanish were to make before the fading of their heroic age, a voyage that indeed holds the secret of all their success and all their failure. As the last voyage had proved the shining qualities of Quiros, his mastery of navigation and pilotage, his patience and devotion, so this final one displayed not only that ideal strain in him which was almost mysticism, but also his closely related weaknesses. For where action was required, a will to be obeyed, a sort of passionate but irresolute humanity stepped in, and the honours of achievement belong largely to his subordinate captain, Luis Vaez de Torres, a man from (probably) the province of Galicia. Of Torres we know little apart from this achievement, signal and for so long hidden. Then Spanish seamanship in those waters became a thing for history to brood over.

Quiros's virtues we have seen; his story from the time he arrived again in Peru from Manila is that of a man fired with a single religious ambition. Towards the end of his narrative of Mendaña's unhappy voyage he discussed the reasons for the failure to find the Solomon Islands. From an examination of Gallego's report and the other available evidence he concluded that the Solomons, New Guinea and Santa Cruz must be all fairly close together; and now, it seems, he drew the further conclusion that the great southern continent could not be far away. To the discovery of this continent he henceforth dedicated himself, an enthusiast appalled, but never finally discouraged, by the opposition or listlessness of the men upon whom he depended for support. Quiros had a vision of a greater empire than Spain had ever known; his heart yearned over an innumerable multitude of heathen who seemed before his eyes to perish everlastingly, to bring whom in peace to the bosom of the Church seemed the single end of life, the culminating mission of the servants of a Christian king. Santa Cruz had souls to save; yet its discovery had its dangers, 'for man does not know what time brings'; and, wrote Quiros to the governor of the Philippines, the islands called the Marquesas having a middle position between the Philippines, Mexico and Peru, the English might settle there if they heard of them, and so 'do much mischief in this sea'; therefore their existence should remain concealed till the king decided on some course of action.

He first offered his services to the viceroy of Peru, proposing to take a vessel of 60 tons and forty sailors, and return to discover those lands and many others which he suspected to exist and felt certain he should find. The viceroy would be responsible for no such voyage, but was willing to recommend Quiros to the court of Spain if he should go personally to seek support. Quiros agreed gladly enough. His passage across the Atlantic was delayed by tempests, and it was not till February 1600 that he landed in Spain. It was a year of Christian jubilee, and he decided to inaugurate his mission by going to Rome. He had little property and sold it all for the dress and staff of a pilgrim, took ship to Italy, and went on foot to the Holy City. Here he made himself known to the Spanish ambassador, the Duke of Sesa, who had him examined by a committee of pilots, mathematicians and geographers: Quiros was in his element and his examiners were deeply impressed. He was brought before the Pope, and successfully stressed the importance of saving such an infinity of souls. Finally, after about eighteen months' residence in Rome he set off for Madrid with a portion of the True Cross, together with letters from the Pope and the Duke of Sesa to the King of Spain and important officials at court. He arrived early in June 1602; his reception was mixed. Some of the notables were favourably inclined, others thought that sufficient lands had been discovered and now ought to be settled and made useful; others that Quiros was not a great enough personage to be put in charge of such a voyage. Nevertheless, by April 1603 his pertinacity had triumphed; royal orders directed the viceroy of Peru to give him two good ships well fitted out with naval stores and barter, and with all costs defrayed from the royal revenues. Some Franciscan friars were to be taken; Quiros was to have absolute authority and a wide discretion as to his course of action; and the Spanish officials abroad were to render promptly every help in their power. For some reason the business was managed through the Council of State, and not the Council of the Indies, the properly competent body; and as jealousy between the two was not unknown, enemies were made for the idealist from the outset.

Quiros took his departure. Shipwrecked in the West Indies, he was then constrained to spend eight months at Guayra, on the mainland, in what is now Venezuela. Here he discovered two orphan nephews, who accompanied him when he left, and on his voyage. In spite of peremptory royal orders, he could get no help from officials; he arrived in Panama without money, and was sued by his muleteer and his other creditors. Misfortunes accumulated. In Panama he went to see a religious festival at the hospital; the upper storey of the building collapsing, he was compelled to spend ten weeks in bed recovering from his injuries. Barely convalescent, he went on to Peru without water or provisions, arrived at Callao on 6 March 1605, owing for his passage and food, and entering Lima by night could find no lodging till a charitable potter gave him shelter.

But when finally he reached the viceroy's court that great man was impressed with his credentials and his story. There was inevitable delay, inevitable opposition. Don Fernando de Castro objected on behalf of the Mendaña claim to the Solomons, and it was not till the end of the year that every obstacle was overcome and a small fleet actually equipped and provisioned. Quiros was given three ships, the *San Pedro y Paulo*, of 60 tons, the *San Pedrico*, of 40 tons, and a small launch or *zabra*, very strong and a good sailer, called *Los Tres Reyes Magos*, which was intended to bring back news if the south land was discovered. These carried nearly three hundred sailors and soldiers, Spaniards and Portuguese and Flemings, biscuit and other provisions for a year, many hundred jars of water, iron implements, animals and fruits to stock any settlement that was formed, and goods for barter. Among the company were six Franciscan friars, and four nursing brothers of the order of John of God. Quiros was in general command; Luis Vaez de Torres was captain of the *San Pedrico*, and Bernal Cermeño captain of the launch. The chief pilot, Juan Ochoa de Bilbao, thrust on a very unwilling Quiros, was a source of trouble rather than of help. All decisions in navigation were taken by Quiros himself; on which fact Diego de Prado, one of his officers and his bitter enemy, casts the blame for its lack of success. Alas! apostles invariably make enemies, and the apostolic character was one which Quiros more and more assumed. He desired a special religious festival ere the ships departed; it was not allowed him, but at least he could dedicate his fleet to Our Lady of Loreto and dress himself and his officers in the habits of Franciscan friars. He sailed with pomp, and all Callao saw him go. The beach, the roofs, the galleries, the ships in port were crowded with onlookers as the three vessels shook out their banners and fired their guns, and Quiros, this once, must have been a happy man. It was 21 December 1605; and, said one of his pilots, Gonzalez de Leza, 'with our good will and desire to serve God and spread our Holy Catholic Faith, and aggrandise the royal crown of the King our Lord, all seemed easy to us'.

The outward voyage was marked by the personality of Quiros. His purpose was to sail west-south-west to latitude 30°; if no land were seen, north-west to 10°; if still there was no land, south-west to 20°, north-west to 10° 15', and then west along that parallel to Santa Cruz. After three days he fell ill, but recovered, 'for whom God wishes will live'. He seems to have been suffering ill health, however, at important crises of the expedition, and here at least must be found one of the reasons why it took the course it did. A few days later he had all gaming-tables thrown overboard, and on 8 January 1606 he issued to the other two ships voluminous orders, embracing piety, morality, rationing and the treatment of native peoples, hints on navigation and the recognition of signs of land. Cards, dicing, cursing and blasphemy were prohibited. Natives were not to be ill used, nor their property injured: nor were they to be despised in case of warfare. 'Our position should be as fathers to children, but they must be watched as if they were known enemies. . . . Our part is to be always in the right, with open and honest intentions.' Admirable as many of these instructions were, however, they had little chance of acceptance in those days of lax discipline, and Quiros had continually to be making ordinances against quarrelling and 'giving the lie', on pain of deprivation of life and goods—a threat which he could never bring himself to carry out. More to the point were directions on independent voyaging. If one ship reached Santa Cruz before the others, it was to wait three months; and if they had not then appeared, to sail in search of the south land south-west to latitude 20°, then north-west to 4°, thence west along the north coast of New Guinea and so to Manila, and home to Spain round the Cape of Good Hope.

They sailed on the planned course over a sea truly pacific, though the wind changed frequently, till by 22 January, in latitude 26°, the weather turned squally, with a great swell from the south. 'Whither are they taking us in this great gulf, in the winter season?' asked the discontented. The strength of the wind and sea was great, the crew mutinous, Quiros was sick. He decided to change his course and steer west-north-west despite the protests of Torres. 'It was not a thing obvious that we ought to diminish our latitude, if the season would allow, till we got beyond 30 degrees,' he said, but in vain. On the new course they sighted a succession of uninhabited atolls, looking always for anchorage, for they were in need of water and fuel. As January passed the weather grew stormier and their need greater. The water ration was reduced drastically, and a 'machine' for distilling fresh water from salt was brought into use—fifty jars of good sweet water were obtained, when lack of fuel brought its operation to an end. Then, on 10 February, land was seen ahead—then smoke, then people on the beach. It was the island called by Quiros Conversion de San Pablo—that, most probably, now known by its native name, Hao.[1]

The natives on the beach were armed with clubs and lances, but they did not oppose a landing, which high waves made difficult. Four men who swam ashore were felt all over, in surprise at such whiteness of skin. Next day a boat's crew landed in a different place to try to find water; finding none, they quenched their thirst with coconut milk. A cross was set up, and an old woman taken on board and entertained. A chief, too, was seized by force; Quiros had him unbound, and sent him on shore dressed in breeches, a yellow silk shirt, and a hat, with a tin medal and a case of knives. In return the natives gave some fish and water to the soldiers, and the chief sent Quiros his ornamental head-dress of feathers and golden hair. Still in great want of water the ships sailed on, past further islands.[2]

The pilots differed on their position, and the chief pilot became a centre of disaffection. He wasted water and provisions; rumours of mutiny implicated him. Quiros addressed his crew: he himself was determined, he said, to find the new continent and they should do their duty while life remained in them; but the discouraging talk went on—now that the course had been altered they would never find land, and in the end all would perish. The chief pilot asked leave to go on board the *San Pedrico*; leave granted, he would not go. Quiros decided to search for the island of San Bernardo, discovered on his former voyage, and changed course once more north-west to latitude 10° 40′. On 19 February he steered west and two days later sighted what he thought was this island. It was not; it was Caroline, an atoll of abundant fish and coconuts, but no water;

---

[1] The other islands sighted by Quiros up to this time were La Encarnacion (Ducie), San Juan Batista (Henderson), St Elmo (Marutea), Las Cuatro Coronadas (the Actaeon group), San Miguel (Vairaatea)—all between 26 January and 8 February.

[2] La Sagitaria (Raroia, 14 February); La Fugitiva (Takume, 15 February).

some called it the Island of Fish. Quiros was worried; he was
very ill, the mutinous spirit did not abate, the weather was
doubtful, and where so much was at stake he hesitated to run
too great a risk. There was water and a known port at Santa
Cruz—if the fleet were refreshed there, a new start could be
made. To find Santa Cruz therefore now became his purpose,
and he continued his western course. He had to think what to
do about mutiny; his own crew wanted to go direct to Manila,
and one night he was roused by sounds of quarrel to find the
chief pilot with a naked sword in his hand, defiant after wounding a man. Nevertheless, in spite of his dismay, to stern action
he could not bring himself.

At night on 1 March land was sighted, and a fire. Next day
the canoes appeared, their crews singing to the rhythm of their
paddles. They would not come on board, and fastening a cord
to the bowsprit of the launch and dragging for her anchor, tried
to draw her on shore; driven off, they would not go until,
grasping bare swords with their hands, they were astonished to
be hurt and to see blood, whereupon they paddled away at
great speed and in uproar. The wind changing then put the
ships in danger; Quiros therefore stood off and on during the
night and at dawn next morning sent Torres ashore to seize four
natives as hostages for wood and water. The islanders opposed
the first attempt to land, but a second succeeded, with the loss of
the precious contents of a boat which capsized—water-jars,
tools and arquebuses. The people attacked, they were put to
flight, and a village was occupied. Here a boy approached the
Spaniards, 'so beautiful and with such golden hair that to see
him was the same as to see a painted angel'; and presented with
the usual breeches and silk shirt, he climbed a tree and threw
down coconuts. Other natives drew near and the plan seemed
on the point of succeeding, when an undisciplined soldier tried
to enter a native house. The owner, a man of spirit, knocked
him down with a club, before being himself run through by a
Spaniard; other natives were killed and the rest fled. Little
matter, said a soldier, that the dead had been sent to the devil

today, as they would have to go tomorrow—and this, mourned Quiros, 'when they had the Faith of Christ at the doors of their souls'. Torres was forced to see what he could of the island and return without hostages. He found large double canoes sixty feet long and six wide, beautiful mats and woven work, chisels and fish-hooks of shell, dried oysters and a few pearls. The surf was furious, and only with difficulty and danger did he get his men back to the ships, and to a Quiros who was very much annoyed. This island was called Peregrina or Gente Hermosa—the Island of Beautiful People; it was probably Rakahanga in the northern Cooks. The loss of the water-jars from the overturned boat was serious; and with ever-diminishing store the ships stood away west.

They met with fine weather, sometimes misty and with changes of wind; experiencing, too, a total eclipse of the sun. Many days thus passed, while they neither reached Santa Cruz nor brought relief to thirst, and accusation on accusation was made against Quiros—he had taken them all to die solely for his own profit and advantage; the supposed land was a dream; he had deceived the Pope and the king with his stories; he deserved exemplary punishment. Quiros could only reply that all this was not new to him: what his men wanted was 'good health, plenty to eat and drink, little work, many complaints, much grumbling together'; for if they had little love for the voyage, they had much fear of the weather. When a pilots' conference was held to discuss their distance from Callao and from Santa Cruz the behaviour of the chief pilot was so disquieting that he was given into Torres's charge as a prisoner; yet in spite of Torres's importunities, Quiros would carry punishment no further. He did, however, have a block placed at the yard-arm as a threat, and from that time forward lived with the precautions necessary among men he had come to regard as villains. He refused permission to play for money, even if the winnings were devoted to the souls in purgatory; there were better pursuits than gambling, he said—reading and writing, the practice of drill, the study of the spheres and navigation. Nevertheless, whether time was passed well or ill, anxiety grew as the western passage lengthened. All were on a starvation diet, when by good fortune a timely shower of rain quenched their thirst. Soon afterwards signs of land were seen, turtles, coconuts, tree-trunks floating past the ships, and land-birds in the air. At night they navigated very cautiously, with the launch ahead, and on 7 April land was sighted to the north-west, high and black. Next day smoke was seen, and the day after that, while Torres made a reconnaissance, the ships found a port and anchored 'with incredible joy'.

Torres was well pleased with the appearance of the land. On a small reef he had found a village, from which the women and children were hurried in panic to the island. About 150 men took arms against the invaders, but when a musket was fired to astonish them all dived into the water except their chief, who came forward shouting; and the natives laying down their arms, by signs induced the Spaniards to follow suit. The chief held out his hand in friendship, and told his name, Tumai; he was a handsome man of about fifty, with hair and beard turning grey. At Torres's request, he allowed the Spaniards to land in the village, besought him not to set houses on fire, and promised all the help the islanders could give. These signs of friendship Torres reciprocated, dressing Tumai in shot silk. The ships were anchored much nearer the village, and the friars landed and said Mass. The natives imitated the Christians, kneeling down and beating their breasts. The inevitable perdition of so many souls saddened Quiros.

Next day Tumai was received on board the *San Pedro*. He had not seen Spanish ships before, but he had heard of them and their arquebuses. The island, Taumako, was, in fact, not far from Santa Cruz; five days' sail to the west, said Tumai, was the volcano, and Santa Cruz lay in sight of it. Seventy other islands lay in various directions beyond the horizon, and to the south was a very large land called Manicolo.[1] He showed their

---

[1] Malekula in the New Hebrides?—the usual identification. This has been disputed, and Vanikoro, one of the Santa Cruz group, suggested; but no one could call Vanikoro large.

directions, and gave their names, drawing circles to explain their size; while for the large land he opened his arms out wide. To show their distances from Taumako 'he pointed to the sun, then rested his head on his hand, shut his eyes, and with his fingers counted the number of nights one had to sleep on the voyage. . . . He gave it to be understood that in one island they ate human flesh, by biting his arm', but Tumai did not like such people. He departed with various gifts, and Quiros going on shore next day found others to confirm all his reports of land.

The ships stayed for a week at Taumako, or, as Quiros called it, Nuestra Señora del Socorro—Our Lady of Succour.[1] The relations between the Spanish and the natives were excellent—there was no thieving, trust and good fellowship abounded, and names were freely exchanged. Tumai supplied all the wood and water that was needed, and in return the natives were given bells and other trifles. The land was pleasant, the islanders no less so, with their fruit-trees and coconuts and plantains, their clean and airy houses, and their fine outrigger sailing canoes, the prows ornamented with mother-of-pearl. These natives were seafarers, fond of fighting, great archers and hurlers of darts. It is sad to relate that the Spaniards repaid their hospitality by kidnapping four of them; of whom three afterwards leapt overboard to swim to land. While the ships were still at Taumako the difficult Don Diego de Prado moved into the *San Pedrico*. His own story is that he knew for certain that Quiros's crew was going to mutiny; he 'knew who were the mutineers and how they wanted him for head, but he did not want to mix in such conflicts and lose the honour which he had gained in the service of his Majesty', and Quiros refused to listen to warnings. This singular manner of maintaining his honour seems to have caused Don Diego great satisfaction.

Taumako was left at sunset on 18 April. Quiros decided to abandon the search for Santa Cruz and to steer south-east on his original quest of the southern continent, as he now had plenty of wood and water, and a favourable wind. He coasted another

[1] It is one of the Duff group.

pleasant island, Tikopia, where the people thronged the beach urging the Spaniards to come on shore, and gave a mantle of fine palm leaves to Torres, reconnoitring in the dinghy; and then on 22 April thick weather and a strong wind caused the ships to be hove-to for two days. When it cleared Quiros ordered sail to be made. On what course? he was asked, and replied to his pilots to 'Put the ships' heads where they like, for God will guide them as may be right'; and as the course was then south-west, he said it might continue so. The idealist seems at this stage to have overcome the navigator in Quiros. The more sober Torres wished to continue the main search, on which Quiros had already decided; it was finally agreed to seek the islands heard of at Taumako. Islands indeed seemed to stand up on every side. In three days the Spaniards sighted eight, fertile and beautiful to the eye. At one of them, Virgen Maria (the modern Gaua of the Banks group), they took two prisoners, but returned them next day dressed in silk, with plumed hats, tinsel ornaments, knives and a mirror, receiving in exchange two pigs, fruit, and water in large joints of cane. On 29 April what seemed to be extensive land was seen to the south and south-west; in those directions every point to which the eye turned was land, and this day was 'the most joyful and most celebrated day of the whole voyage'. Far away to the south-east rose a massive and lofty line of mountains, their tops lost in the clouds,[1] and as the ships drew nearer, other ranges were seen, apparently part of the same chain. On 1 May they entered a great bay. Next day Torres was sent in a boat to reconnoitre, while two enquiring canoes were put to flight by a gun fired to surprise them. Torres brought back news of a good port, with a river, ballast and fuel, and on 3 May the three vessels anchored there in great joy, 'giving many thanks to God'. So came Quiros and his company to the islands which a later age knows as the New Hebrides. All had been accomplished according to their desires, said a later historian; the weary men held in their

---

[1] Three overlapping islands of the New Hebrides—Pentecost, Aurora or Maewo, and Leper or Oba (Aoba)—were here mistaken for the same land.

hands the most abundant and powerful land ever discovered by Spaniards.

'The idealist seems at this stage to have overcome the navigator in Quiros', it has been written above. It was a change of a sort to make common men hate him and lesser men despise him. His devotion to his southern continent, converted and saved, remained steadfast and unalterable. On none of his men could he impress his own set faith. They were for the most part ordinary sailors and soldiers of that age, who would endure much, but not with patience, in whose minds the precious metals rather than charity shone as the sovereign good. They could not understand the workings of Quiros's mind. He, for his part, could not convince them of his right to command, hardly indeed of his sanity. His actions in the four following weeks have a sort of magnificent futility; in the end he fell a victim to the treachery of wind and sea. His reputation as pilot is secure; but he had none of the abilities of a leader, authority or decision or ruthlessness; he exercised no sway over the minds of men. So the entering of this great bay was Quiros's last triumph. He begins to insist to an undue degree on ceremonies and pageantry.

The first week after anchoring was spent in exploration of the bay, of the interior, so far as it could be penetrated, and the character and intentions of the natives. The land was much admired, for there was a beautiful plain, on which cities might be built, and gentle hills; into the bay flowed a fine river up which frigates might sail—it was called the Jordan—together with several other streams of good water; and the climate was pleasant. Here grew coconuts and plantains, nuts, oranges and yams; fat pigs flourished, fowls, ducks, doves and partridges, 'also many small birds, with sweet songs . . . which, in the mornings, gave us pleasure to hear such gentle and musical voices'. There was excellent ballast, there were fine woods with trees suitable for the yards of ships big or small. Only man was vile. Every attempt to form permanently friendly relations with the people of the country failed. Once or twice the Spaniards came into contact with them, and succeeded in exchanging a silken dress for fruit; but when great numbers of them covered the beach, staring at the boat, arquebuses were fired, and they fled. After this no canoes came alongside the ships and Quiros decided to land an impressive force to take possession of the country. It was met by a great number of natives, a chief from among whom drew a line in the sand, offering to lay down their arms if the Spaniards did likewise and refrained from crossing the line. Torres, in command, refused, and 'as their audacity and insolence was too great' (reports de Leza) the soldiers fired, and a native fell dead. His body was hung by the foot from a tree. The people attacked in earnest; and not till their chief and many others were killed did they flee in despair to the woods. In the next three days the Spaniards marched a short distance into the interior, where the villages were abandoned, and no natives were seen. Their stores of food were taken to the ships. Such was the end of the peace Quiros so earnestly desired.

And now began a curious chain of events. Owing to the risk of attack from the natives, and for the advantage of 'the royal authority, the better establishment of the work, the union of all their wills, and for other hidden reasons', Quiros created a 'ministry of war and marine'. Torres was made camp master, Bernal Cermeño, the captain of the launch, 'almirante', and de Leza chief pilot. A more important ceremony was to follow. On the day preceding Pentecost, Quiros assembled all the ships' companies and created the Order of Knights of the Holy Ghost, in which every man was included. He had long, he said, had in mind the thought of doing so, as well for the good work it promised for God and the king, as for the strengthening of their resolves, and of firmness and hope, which were the qualities needed to achieve great and famous deeds; and he gave each man a blue cross to wear on his breast, that being the sign of the Order. The knights were to be guided by lofty and Christian ends; for if their membership had not cost them much pain and labour, yet what remained in their power to pay was as great as the enterprise on which they were embarked. Quiros confidently expected that the Order would be confirmed by both the Pope and the king. In spite of some sceptical spirits, there was general satisfaction; and the following Saturday all confessed, that they might earn the Holy Jubilee conceded to the expedition by the Pope.

On the eve of Pentecost all three vessels displayed lights and set off rockets; the guns were fired, and their echoes were answered by the shouts of the natives. Drums and bells were sounded, and there was music and dancing on board. Before dawn next day, 14 May, Torres landed with an armed party and set up a 'booth' of branches, surrounded by stakes, for use alternatively as a church or a fort. Then Quiros and all his men went on shore. The three companies were drawn up on the beach with their crosses on their breasts; the Royal Ensign bore the standard, and other flags fluttered in the breeze, to the salute of arquebuses and muskets. Quiros knelt, saying, 'To God alone be the honour and the glory'; then, bending down to the ground, he kissed it, and said, 'O Land, sought for so long, intended to be found by many, and so desired by me!' A cross of native orange-wood was erected in the church, and before it were read proclamations in the names of the Trinity, the Catholic Church, St Francis, John of God, the Order of the Holy Ghost, and Philip III, taking possession of 'this bay, named the Bay of St Philip and St James, and of its port named Vera Cruz, and of the site on which is to be founded the city of New Jerusalem, in latitude 15° 20', and of all the lands which I sighted and am going to sight, and of all this region of the south as far as the Pole, which from this time shall be called Austrialia[1] del Espiritu Santo, with all its dependencies and belongings.' The Franciscans celebrated mass; the whole company took the sacrament very fervently; the banners were blessed, the ships fired off all their guns, and the soldiers their weapons, with

[1] Austrialia and not Australia. The name was in honour of Philip III, who belonged to the house of Austria, and was its archduke.

rockets and fire-wheels. In the middle of this noise, says Quiros, everyone shouted with almost infinite joy, 'Long live the Faith of Christ!' So ended the celebration of the festival. Juan Ochoa de Bilboa, the former chief pilot, taking advantage of it, prayed for pardon; but Quiros, careless of personal offence, would not pardon disloyalty to the royal service. Two slaves were freed at his request: sentries were posted, and all went to dine near a clear running stream, under the shade of great trees.

After the siesta, Quiros, swept off his feet by the thought of his New Jerusalem, before a turf had been cut to give it foundation, proceeded to appoint a municipality and other officers necessary to the capital of a province, in accordance with royal ordinances. Magistrates, a secretary, a chief constable, an accountant, a treasurer, were chosen, and took the oath of loyalty; having done which all proceeded in order again to church. Quiros then went on board his ship and ordered the block to be taken down; 'for the Captain could not believe that persons with such an honourable destiny would do things the punishment of which would be the rope'. Following this Torres led an armed party a league inland, put the natives to flight, and returned with a number of pigs, hens and chickens.

The next week was spent in further reconnoitring expeditions, along the coast of the bay, up the River Jordan, and a certain distance inland. One day Quiros himself went ashore and sowed a quantity of maize and melon and vegetable seeds, to consolidate Spanish possession of the land. Fishing and foraging parties frequently clashed with the native people, without damage to themselves, though they were as frequently in danger and lost no chance of boasting their prowess. What the natives suffered Quiros could only sorrowfully suspect. Three small boys were one day captured; the soldiers would have preferred pigs, but Quiros maintained that he would rather have one of those children than the whole world beside; concluding one of his too frequent speeches by blaming his own sins for the soldiers' wrong-headedness. The feast of Corpus Christi was celebrated with great rejoicings—the church was newly adorned, triumphal arches erected, a garden made with branches and herbs; while the day was clear and serene and the birds sang continually. After mass a procession was formed, and the ships' boys dressed in coloured silk, bells on their feet and garlands round their heads, danced to the sound of tambourines and flutes and guitar. There were salutes from the guns and the drums and at all that pageantry many were touched to tears. 'Having given the souls such sweet and delicious fruit', there was a great banquet, and more dances and music; and now Quiros's secretary, Belmonte Bermudez, a poet of some distinction, was moved to adapt an older verse to the occasion. The poet Alonso de Ercilla had written of the southern continent, unknown, its soil imprinted by no Christian feet, waiting until God should reveal it. Now the continent was Spain's, and Belmonte Bermudez wrote:

> Behold how we have found these lands,
>   Now clearly seen by mortal ken,
> Those are regions now made known,
>   Pressed by feet of Christian men.
> Unknown no longer is their fate,
>   Now full knowledge points them there,
> No longer hid in fleecy clouds,
>   God his secrets now lays bare.

Quiros marched inland a league to see once again the native houses and cultivations, and the seeds he had sown already sprouting; and then he reached a sudden decision. When he came on board he said that as the natives were hostile, and the Spaniards had on their side no chance of success, they would leave the port next day to visit the lands to windward. It was just over three weeks since they had anchored.

So, on the pinnacle of glory, Quiros turned his back; and there began that melancholy retreat the truth of which is so hard to disentangle. For if his decisions henceforth are difficult to understand, they are no less so from the conflict of testimony which surrounds them. A certain amount is plain. Torres asked that another day should be spent in port for fishing. This was agreed to; unluckily a number of poisonous fish, *pargos*, were caught, and all who ate of them, including Quiros, whose health had been so insecure during the whole voyage, fell sick with nausea, vomiting and fever. Nevertheless the following day, 28 May, the ships sailed. The sick became much worse, and the pilots were ordered to keep within the mouth of the bay; next day they returned to port, where in a week all had recovered. Armed natives came to the beach, blowing on shell trumpets and shooting arrows, and the three kidnapped boys were taken on shore and shown to them, that their safety might be known. But they were not given back to their parents, who offered pigs in exchange; and the natives would not take the goats proffered by the Spaniards in their turn. An ambush was suspected, and for the last time these people were fired on and scattered. One of the boys cried pitifully to be put on shore: 'Silence, child!' said Quiros, 'you know not what you ask. Greater good awaits you than the sight of heathen parents and friends and their communion!' Nor would he allow his men to prospect for gold and silver, a work to be done by those who came after and in an hour chosen by God. He decided to leave the bay again, 'to proceed to get a near view of that great and high chain of mountains, desiring by the sight of them to reanimate all his companions; because, if he should die, they would remain with the ardour to continue the work until it was finished'.

The ships sailed again on 8 June. There was a light wind from the east, the direction of the prevailing winds up to that time. Outside the port it veered to south-east and blew strongly, increasing as time went by. All that day no headway was made; for the ships were Peruvian-built and bad under little sail. There was discussion among the pilots. Quiros came to another sudden decision, incomprehensible by the side of his previous reasons for leaving the port. He resolved to return and there winter, 'building a strong house, sowing the land, getting a better knowledge of the season, and building a brigantine to send, with the launch, to discover what was so much desired, it being clear to all that this was very necessary'. The ships beat on different tacks at the mouth of the bay throughout the night and next day. In the afternoon the *San Pedrico* and the launch were near the port, much ahead of the *San Pedro*, which carried little sail. Night fell very dark; the *San Pedrico* and the launch anchored and lighted their lanterns to give the flagship leading marks. Then, when she was less than an arquebus shot from the port, but in water too deep to anchor, a strong squall blew off the land, the pilot was confused by the many lights, some of them native; the ship was near a rock, and it was decided to stand for the middle of the bay. Every time she tacked she went away to leeward with an increasing wind; next morning she was right outside the bay, making leeway rapidly. Quiros, to remedy this, ordered the pilot to make sail; he answered that the sea was so high, and so much against them, that the bows driving into the water would open the ship's timbers; but he would do his best. For three days they strove to re-enter the bay, in vain; and by 12 June Quiros found himself at sea, cut off from his consorts, out of sight of land.

Is this quite the whole story? It is possible, but rather doubtful. Quiros, it is clear, was very sick; was he at this critical moment mastered by the wind and weather only? The subsequent chapter of his own narrative is a medley of blame of his subordinates, of sovereigns who did not give clear orders, of the initial delay in leaving Callao; of explanations which do not explain; of 'sorrowful discourses'. He obviously distrusted his men; he seems to have had little confidence in his pilot. There was certainly reprehensible neglect on the part of Leza and Bernal. Some of the men who sailed later to Manila told Prado, says that officer, that they had mutinied. There was no mutiny. There were pilots who knew what they wanted to do, pitted against a Quiros torn one way and the other. Quiros temporized by deciding to make for the old rendezvous at Santa Cruz, hoping that the other vessels would read his mind and follow him there—irrespective of the fact that Santa Cruz had been abandoned as a rendezvous when he left Taumako. Torres could not read his mind, and Torres concluded simply that there had been desertion. 'From within this bay', he says, 'and from the most sheltered part of it, the *Capitana* departed at one hour past midnight, without any notice given to us, and without making any signal. . . . And although the next morning we went out to seek for them, and made all proper efforts, it was not possible for us to find them, for they did not sail on the proper course, or with good intention.'

Quiros thought he would wait three months at Santa Cruz for the other ships and collect supplies. The ship was in the right latitude on 18 June; the island was not in sight, it might be either west or east, and the weather was threatening. To sail too far westward might mean falling on the south side of New Guinea, in the worst time of the year for a passage thence to the Philippines. Quiros could not tell what had happened to the other vessels: he was convinced that he had made discoveries of inestimable value which it would take several voyages to complete; and he consoled himself in his present failure with meditations on the inscrutable will of God. The other ships, if they were safe, would continue the great work: if they were not, news ought to be carried to Spain of what had already been done. A council was called, which decided to steer towards Acapulco. Quiros still temporized; if further islands were discovered they would build a launch and come to a new resolution; in any case they would sail to 13° N, the latitude of Guam, in the Ladrones, which was on the route from Acapulco to the Philippines. There, taking into consideration all circumstances, a final decision would be arrived at.

The water supply was replenished by rain. On 23 July the pilots fixed the latitude as 3° 20′ N, 900 leagues distant from the coast of Mexico, and 780 leagues east of Manila (a serious miscalculation); contrary winds forbade a course to Manila, and therefore they advised turning to Acapulco. Quiros sadly agreed, bewailing in his misery his 'many great sins', which had made him unworthy to see the end of an enterprise so sacred that only the righteous were qualified for its service. Even then a four months' voyage lay ahead, not lacking in incident, either happy or untoward. As rain supplied the ship with water, so a great shoal of albacore and bonito provided food. It was necessary to go as far north as 38°. There was 'a great trembling of the sea and of the ship' and an eclipse of the moon. Islands off the North American coast were first seen on 23 September. In the mouth of the Gulf of California, on 12 October, a great storm put the lives of all in jeopardy; and Quiros in great haste and anxiety had the two native boys with him baptized and christened Pedro and Pablo. So devout were they that it seemed their conversion and prayers alone must be enough to save the ship; and indeed late in the afternoon, after a last crisis, the wind shifted and sail was safely made. On 21 October anchor was dropped before the desolate beach of Navidad. On all that long passage only one man had died, the aged father commissary of the friars. Refreshment came from settlements inland and from Indian villages; and after four weeks of disputes and complaints the voyage was resumed. It ended at Acapulco on 23 November 1606.

Quiros was immediately misrepresented by his enemies, but the viceroy of Mexico received him kindly. Nevertheless he grew steadily poorer, and none relieved his necessity. The cross of orange-wood, the object of so much Pentecostal veneration, which he had intended to lay in the hands of the Pope himself, with Pedro and Pablo as first-fruits of salvation, he was persuaded to present to the Convent of Barefoot Franciscans at Acapulco; and Pedro and Pablo died. At last a sea-captain gave the penniless man passage to Cadiz. Here he sold his bed, at San Lucar pawned some other belonging, and so reached Seville, much as he had reached Lima nearly three years before. All he had left he sold, and with help from friends arrived at Madrid on 9 October 1607, where he gave away his last small coins to a beggar. He was at the opening of his final campaign.

For in the mind of Quiros the Austral Lands—their settlement, the conversion of their inhabitants—had come to annihilate all other desires. Other things existed only as obstacles: he suffered them with the patience of a martyr, he transcended them with a martyr's faith. For eleven days after his arrival in Madrid he could get no access to authority. At last he saw the president of the Council of the Indies and was suffered to kiss the king's hand; and then began the flood of memorials, printed when he had the money, when not, copied by hand—submitted to the king, distributed to the king's ministers, to the Council of the Indies, to the Council of State. He wrote fifty in as many months. He drew more than two hundred maps. Sometimes they were well received; but no more then than at other times did his business prosper. The Council of State referred him to the Council of the Indies; the Council of the Indies was stiff-necked. He was told to return to Peru, where the viceroy would order what should be done. There was no assurance that anything would be done, and he refused to go. Instead he renewed his memorials. And now, he thought, there must be more hope of success, for where he had been a solitary suppliant, news had come from Torres. The *San Pedrico* and the launch had not been lost; Torres, at Manila, in June 1607 had written him an account of further discoveries. He had written also to the king: what he had said was hardly likely to increase royal confidence in Quiros.

Torres, it seems, after the extraordinary disappearance of his commander, had searched some distance along the coast for wreckage; he found none, nor when he returned to the bay was the flagship there. He stayed in the bay fifteen days, then sealed orders from the viceroy of Peru were produced in front of a council of officers: every effort was to be made to sail to 20° S latitude in search of land; if there were none the voyage was to be continued to Manila, and to Spain by way of the Moluccas and the Cape. These orders, says Torres, it was determined to fulfil, 'although contrary to the inclination of many, I may say of the greater part; but my temper was different from that of Captain Pedro Fernandez de Quiros.' It is evident that we have here to deal with a man of composed daring.[1] An attempt to sail round the island was prevented by the weather and strong currents, and the vessels were turned south-west. 'We had at this time nothing but bread and water', says Torres again: 'it was the height of winter, with sea, wind, and ill-will against us.' In spite of all this, he went down as far as latitude 21°, and he would have gone farther had the weather allowed, his ship being good. It was right to act in this manner, he thought, for these were not voyages performed every day. There was no sign of land, and he stood north-west according to plan, to make New Guinea, and sail round its north-east coast to the Philippines. Then came the critical hour. Did Torres realize the significance of his next decision? He was on the brink of solving a problem which had puzzled generations of cartographers, which fifty years after him still baffled the Dutch; he states his action with the bald simplicity of the commonplace. 'I could not weather the east point, so I coasted along to the westward on the south side.' That is, New Guinea had a south side—was, in fact, an island; it was not the vast northern projection of a continent of the south. This, then, was the solution of one of the major geographical problems of the seventeenth century; and the solution, so brilliantly made, was filed and thereafter ignored.

Of Torres's track through the strait now named after him, a strait fortified with perils, little enough is known. As the ships groped their way great smoke signals rose all along the coast from watching natives. It was a land of great bays and rivers, of many plains, fringed with islands and shoals, thickly inhabited by natives naked except for a bit of bark cloth, fighting with darts and shields and stone clubs made gaudy with feathers. This land and these people the Spaniards claimed for Philip III, capturing many specimens of different tribes for his benefit, and killing others. They had sighted New Guinea about the middle of July; through more than two months they coasted it; once, on 23 September, a great storm nearly sank the ships at their moor-

1 Prado claimed to be the senior officer, but Torres was certainly the effective commander.

ings as they lay in harbour. At last Torres encountered people more civilized, because they blinded their enemies in battle with lime and wore better ornaments; and here also he found iron and bells from China and knew he must be near the Moluccas. All round was 'an infinity of islands'. He came to the western end of New Guinea and there found Mahometans, who wore clothes and used artillery, with which 'they go conquering the people who are called Papuas, and preach to them the sect of Mahomed'. From these conquerors the Spaniards were able to buy a few fowls and goats and some fruit, and biscuit called sago, which was said to keep more than twenty years; not much could be bought because the other ship carried all the articles of barter, as well as all tools and medicines. From them also Torres learnt of events at the Moluccas and of soft gold and pearls and spices in the land of the Papuas. Five days from the island of Bachan[1] a boat appeared, with a person who could speak Portuguese, and knew the men of Spain as valiant cavaliers with swords of gold, whose ardour was astounding. Torres helped the king of Bachan to subdue a revolted chieftain; in return that monarch swore never to go to war with Christians, and ever to be a faithful vassal of the king of Spain. So at last he came to the island of Banda, 'mother of the nutmeg', and to Ternate, where his countrymen were overjoyed to see him, hard pressed as they were to crush rebellion in the island. The launch was left with twenty men, and on 22 May 1607 the *San Pedrico* anchored at Manila. Torres, like Quiros, had lost but one man of all his company. Once in port, it was impossible to leave—he could get no provisions, and even his ship was required of him for other important matters. So Torres passes from sight; of his life no more is known.

The news of Torres's safety and of his voyage was fresh fuel to the fire in Quiros's heart. His memorials grew in scope. Twenty thousand leagues he had gone by land and sea, spending all his estate, suffering so many and such terrible things that even

[1] The island now called Batjan, off the southern end of Halmahera or Gilolo, and on the eastern side of the Molucca Sea.

to himself they seemed incredible; and now the greatness of
that south land was well established—a quarter of the world, its
length equalled that of all Europe and Asia Minor as far as the
Caspian Sea and Persia, with all the islands of the Mediterranean
and the encompassing ocean, including England and Ireland. Its
people assumed ideal proportions and ideal virtues, save only
their ignorance of the Christian faith, and its products grew in
universality and value. Who would not colonize a land of such
excellent black soil, where grew such mace and pepper and
ginger; where there were aloes, sugar and indigo and all things
necessary for silk; ebony and ship-building woods; goats and
bees and even 'indications of cows'; marble (so was coral trans-
muted); and above all, silver, with which the natives pointed
their arrows, and pearls and gold? (The youthful Pedro, before
he died, had learnt enough Spanish to gratify his captor's taste
for marvels.) That land was so central that it was the key to all
the Spanish provinces. But far greater than these things was the
missionary duty of Spain. Was this fair field to be left to the
sowers of false doctrine, the enemies of the Catholic Church?
'My Lord!' cried Quiros to his king, 'this is a great work! For the
Devil wages such mortal war, and it is not well that he should be
able to do so much, Your Majesty being the defender of the right.'

As ever, the enthusiast met with less than enthusiasm. The
Council of State, in September 1608, reflected upon the letter
from Torres. It agreed for once with the Council of the Indies;
fresh discoveries would withdraw population from Spain,
already short of men; they would merely open a way to the
king's enemies; the treasury was exhausted and it was hard
enough to retain what lands were already known. Moreover,
could Spain with a good conscience make conquest of in-
offensive heathen? This Quiros wanted to be a second
Columbus; his design could not be encouraged. Yet lest he
should be driven to despair and have recourse to the enemies of
Spain (his memorials were already coming into the hands of
foreigners), he might be retained as a cosmographer, for his
professional experience should be made use of. Quiros remained

unsatisfied; this man could be neither bribed nor silenced. He managed to get another audience of the king; he was granted a sum of money and ordered to prepare an estimate of his requirements; he was referred to the Council of the Indies. His old enemy Don Fernando de Castro had submitted a memorial against him, arguing that his land was only part of New Guinea. After many months, at the end of 1609, a royal order was at length issued to the viceroy of Peru. Quiros was to go to that country, where he was to be provided with ships and all things necessary for a settlement. He was still not satisfied; royal orders were badly obeyed in distant provinces; he wished his authority to be greater, even if his expenses were to be no more than a cabin-boy's. He became once more the shuttlecock of the Councils. At last, in October 1614, a new viceroy being on the point of departure, both Councils ordered Quiros to accompany him. Life and patience were worn out, said he wearily; he would trust to the magnanimity of this nobleman. He did not know that the viceroy's only orders were to entertain and temporize with him at Lima. They sailed; and at Panama, on the voyage out, Quiros died, unwitting of that last betrayal. It was well that he died.

With Quiros died the heroic age of Spain. Before he left the country letters had been received by the king's secretaries from Don Diego de Prado, from Goa—letters which pursued Quiros with violence and venom. He was a lunatic, a Portuguese, but yesterday clerk of a merchant ship, a liar and a fraud, disloyal, the cause of the Adelantado Mendaña being lost with his fleet; by his fault alone the Spaniards had failed to discover what they sought. However grotesque these accusations, the Council of State must have noted from them one thing: Quiros could not impose himself. It was fairly plain, to professional administrators, that as a leader he had shortcomings. Where personality was so important, so much a part of success or failure, where judgment was as necessary as faith, they could not credit Quiros's schemes with all the virtue that seemed so evident to him. Indeed, they were right. Quiros the sailor had more Pacific experience than had anyone else. Quiros the pilot, the man who had saved the starving rebellious remainder of Mendaña's expedition, was a man of skill and value. Quiros the visionary cosmographer was a man self-deceived. His conceptions were sublime, but they were not geography. That, perhaps, was no reason why they should not contribute to geography; but the Spain of Philip III was not the Spain of Ferdinand and Isabella. The Council of State knew the truth— in spite of all the conquests of Cortes and Pizarro, the stream of silver from the West, the treasury was indeed exhausted. The task of empire for Spain was no longer expansion but assimilation, and there was much she would never assimilate. Statesmen must admit the existence of souls which Spain could never save from perishing; and statesmen reconciled themselves with equanimity to the inevitable.

One voice there was, however, raised after the death of Quiros in defiance of that inevitable. It was the voice of Dr Juan Luis Arias de Loyola, a secular priest and cosmographer of Madrid, in a memorial to Philip III of excessive length, learning and inaccuracy. Dr Arias wrote at the instance of Franciscans in Spain; for the Order desired to undertake the evangelization of the continent. It was a vital matter: 'the English and Dutch heretics, who are instigated by the Devil as much as in his power, roam about avariciously to reconnoitre, discover, and settle the principal ports, which, on this great land, face the South Sea, and to establish there the most poisonous venom of their apostasy'—a thing for lamentation, and deeply offensive to God and His Church. It could be proved (reasoning from the celestial influences of the fixed stars) that a fertile and habitable land remained to be discovered, as great as all the lands of the northern hemisphere, stored with abundance of animals and fruits and precious stones. Remarkable discoveries had been made by Mendaña, Quiros and Torres; there was also the pilot Juan Fernandez, who, sailing from the coast of Chile in latitude 40°, had discovered 'a very fertile and agreeable con-

tinent' inhabited by peaceable, gentle and hospitable people.[1]
Spain had had its days of glory; now, mourned Arias, it had
sunk to such a point that the most inconsiderable nations of
Europe, formerly held beneath its feet, looked upon it as of
small account. But now also was the time to restore the glory
and avert God's indignation, by liberating from the abominable
servitude of Lucifer so many million souls in the southern
hemisphere; that, and that only, would impose a true and
immortal and apostolic lustre on the crown of Spain, divine
sanction on its continued empire.

Arias wrote in vain, as Quiros petitioned in vain. The crown
of Spain persisted in scepticism and in wisdom. It had seen too
much, and suffered too much, to have ambition left. Looking
back on a hundred years, it might well feel that the record of
Spanish endeavour had been a glorious though not an untarnished one, from the day when Magellan, first of men, in a
Spanish keel furrowed that vast and peaceful sea. Pacific it could
be held no longer—of that there was bitter proof; but Spaniards
had ridden out its most calamitous storms. They had given to
Spain or to geography in truth no great continent; but they had
narrowed the bounds in which a continent might be sought.
They had added to knowledge whole clusters of islands; they
had reported strange peoples and unchristian modes of life. Did
Torres, unwitting as he threaded the treacheries of his strait, set
eyes on the northern shores of that last great continent of all? It
seems unlikely, yet no man can be certain. The strait bears his
name, as the east point of the fateful bay of St Philip and
St James bears the name of the impeded and mournful
enthusiast who discovered it; but all those islands are a symbol
of the courage and enthusiasm of Spain and Portugal. Not, it is
true, of their unvarying genius for leadership, not of their
mastery over the discordant desires of men; but where there
was so much of virtue, so much of accomplishment, will history
refuse its measured admiration?

[1]What Juan Fernandez actually discovered in 1563–4 was the island known
by his name.

# CHAPTER VI

# THE ENTRY OF THE DUTCH

THE mind of Quiros, at the beginning of the seventeenth century, moved in a different and an older world from that of his disillusioned masters. The modern age was being born—an age, in discovery, of solidity, without the wild recklessness, the cultivation of forlorn hopes, which had made Spain great. And yet the new age had its birth in an act of defiance as wild and daring and successful as any of the great strokes of Spanish policy abroad. This was the declaration of the independence of the Netherlands in 1581, a year after Philip II, the monarch to whom they were subject, had attained also the throne and the empire of Portugal. There might seem few terrestrial glories denied to that sombre and laborious king; yet within less than a decade the Armada was shattered, and his enemies were breaking in the doors of commerce in the East. The seventeenth century was to be the age of discovery, not of the Spanish or the Portuguese, but of the Dutch.

The independence of the Dutch was not easily secured—it was the fruit of a long and desperate struggle urged not only before the walls of Leyden and with the imminent waters of the dykes, but in diplomacy, in the intellect, in world-wide trade, in battles in European seas and among the archipelagos of Malaya. Their success, it may be said, gave the world political and religious freedom; gave it also a new realization of the potentialities of trade and shipping. For by trade and shipping did the Dutch Netherlands, from their natural and sea-bound insignificance, become great. Before the war their people had interests at sea, in their vast herring fishery, in their oriental trade with Lisbon. One of Philip's answers to rebellion was to forbid that trade. No matter, answered the Dutch; they would themselves dig to the very root of commerce: trade was forbidden with Portugal—then outflank Portugal. Nay, overwhelm Portugal, in her scattered and magnificent empire of the East, and carry to rajah and sultan knowledge of a power greater than that of Spaniard or of Portuguese. The Hispano-Portuguese empire was tremendous in extent, but in its extremities weak; that weakness its enemies were not slow to perceive—and in an age when commerce meant monopoly the perception spelt destruction to empire.

A notable traveller of the last two decades of the sixteenth century was John Huyghen van Linschoten. Born in Haarlem, Linschoten decided against a severely domestic life, and went first to Seville to trade, then in 1583 to Goa, where, in the capital of Portuguese power in the East, he spent five years of observation and note-taking. He reached home in 1591, and in 1595-6 he published accounts of his travels and all he had seen and heard. His writings were influential beyond the bounds of Holland—they were translated into English in 1598; and the English, too, became convinced that the future of the East was theirs. To the East there were, it was now thought, three possible routes, for the English had sought a north-west passage in vain—a north-east passage, that through the Strait of Magellan, and that round the Cape of Good Hope. The English had found tragedy also in the north-east, but, backed by the opinion of Linschoten, the Dutch made three voyages in this direction between 1594 and 1596. They failed. Magellan's route was then followed; Dutch ships reached the Philippines, where the crew of one were garotted as pirates. On this passage the captain, called Gerrards or Gerritsz, driven far south, sighted the great land, with its lofty snow-covered mountains, extending, it seemed, to the Isles of Solomon—so deceptive was vision, so willing was belief. He may, just possibly, have seen the South Shetland islands. After 1595, however, the majority of Dutch expeditions decided on definite defiance, and took the sacrosanct Portuguese route round the cape. Once in the East they bought and sold vigorously and with tolerance towards the natives; they wished to convert not the heathen but his trade; they had no prejudices, except against Portuguese and Spaniards; no fears, except of being worsted in a bargain. They were therefore in some ways popular, and their power grew. 'In the Javas they get such big profits that it will be hard to drive them from the East, where they have done such great injuries in spiritual and temporal matters', wrote de Morga, an excellent governor of the Philippines.

Dutch voyages, up till 1602, were financed by separate syndicates. In that year the whole national effort was thrown into the trade; a United East India Company was formed of almost governmental standing; and to this company were delegated the full powers of war and commerce, with a monopoly of trade or communication with the East, known or unknown, either by way of the Cape of Good Hope or through the Strait of Magellan. The company used its powers with pertinacity and determination. The Portuguese were driven out of Java and their other strongholds—a task the less difficult in that they were a trading empire and had roots neither of settlement nor of affection in the lands they ruled; de Morga's lamentations were fruitless; and Spain was in 1609 compelled to a truce, one of the conditions of which was that there should be no interference with Dutch trade in the East. With that decision empire spread rapidly; ten years later the great governor-general, Coen, founded Jacatra, or Batavia,[1] in Java, a cosmopolitan and unhealthy town which commanded the Straits of Sunda and hence the whole eastern archipelago. The other entrance was captured with Malacca in 1641. Wherever the Dutch went they conquered, from Madagascar and the Red Sea to New Guinea. They took St Helena as a watering place on the long eastward journey; they settled the Cape as a natural halfway house; they occupied Mauritius as a depot for the slave

[1] Strictly speaking, a Dutch factory was first established at Jacatra in 1610 by the governor-general Pieter Both. Coen founded the present city in its stead in 1619: Batavia—now Jakarta—lies on both sides of the river Jacatra.

trade of Madagascar; they drove the Portuguese from the coast of Ceylon and took their place; they set up flourishing factories in India and Cambodia and Formosa; they carried on commercial battle with their rivals in Japan; and they planned even to enforce a monopoly of trade on China. To found their empire on an unassailable basis they drove from the East Indies not only the Portuguese but the English. The English were supported by no national feeling. Their East India Company was not popular; and in a sporadic warfare they were beaten from those eastern seas. Their persecution was crowned by the 'massacre of Amboyna'—the torture and execution of English traders of that island on a trumped-up charge of conspiracy. This barbarous triumph was the index of Dutch supremacy in the East Indies—a supremacy which lasted for more than two centuries—and the English retired to the hazards of an unknown future on the coasts of India.

The interest of this story is not specifically geographical. But the geographer is concerned to note that the chances of history had brought the Dutch into the position most favourable for further exploration in the Pacific, and that their interests as traders and their abilities as seamen combined to make certain that any exploration they did would be valuable. The possession of the East Indies, as once the possession of the Americas, was now the key to the ocean. Dutch ships were much superior to those of the preceding century, more seaworthy, better rigged, easier to work; Dutch captains rarely displayed genius, but expertness and doggedness were their common possession. In the mystery of the chart-maker there had been much technical advance. And in the Dutch character there was a sober sense of proportion, which, while it may have precluded dazzling triumphs, yet saved individuals from Quiros's loyalty to the impossible. All things, it might seem, if the Dutch willed it, joined to make their East India Company a great and successful agent of discovery.

Yet the company was a trading company, and trading companies are apt to regard their first business as trade. Trade of the sort the company followed in the seventeenth century, however, was apt also to lead to discovery. This discovery was not at first the fruit of a definite policy, and in the Pacific proper the company through all its history could point to but one voyage of ample scope and achievement made under its orders —that of Tasman. Exploration for forty years was with the Dutch almost a by-product: it was incidental to the conduct of voyages of narrower purpose. Out of these voyages, at first like a dim surf-beaten phantom, later with firm and charted distinctness, emerged New Holland—the west and north coasts of Australia and part of the south; not *Terra Australis incognita*, for of the peopled civilization of that vividly pictured continent there was no sign, but in amplitude and potentiality a continent indeed. Those shores may be deemed to be hardly of the Pacific, and certainly in the west it is the waters of the Indian Ocean that wash them; nevertheless to comprehend the greater voyages of Tasman and of Cook it is necessary to see Australia assume her form, as it were, on every side.

The voyages which revealed those three barren sides of the new continent were expert rather than great. Dutch skippers were plain men, ambitious for the most part only to bring their ships to port, and they displayed little enthusiasm at the sight of so inhospitable a land. None the less, though knowledge of Australia was almost a casual accretion, the country was first sighted by an exploring expedition. Not only the conquering Moors whom Torres met, but the Dutch also had heard of the gold and spices of the 'Papuas'; it seemed worth while to investigate New Guinea on the south, and in November 1605 a pinnace called the *Duyfken* was sent from Bantam, where the company had a factory, to see what the unknown coast afforded in the way of gold. The *Duyfken*, says the Dutch record, coasted New Guinea on the south and west for about 880 miles, from 5° latitude to 13¾°; that is, the little ship sailed as far as the passage of Torres's discovery, and then, apparently unaware that it was a strait, crossed to the west coast of the northern extremity of Australia, the Cape York peninsula, and followed this some distance south. It was a coast desert for the most part, but in places inhabited by 'wild, cruel, black savages', by whom some of the *Duyfken*'s crew were murdered; it seems therefore that the Dutch landed on that unattractive shore. They could get no water nor provisions, nor learn anything more intimate of the country; so, calling the farthest point of land they reached Cape Keer-Weer, or Turn Again, they sailed back to Bantam, with a report that could hardly be made cause of jubilation. They reached port in June 1606, two months before Torres sailed through his strait.

Ten years later another Dutch ship came on the west coast of Australia. This discovery arose from a change in the route followed by the merchant fleets of the East India Company on their voyage out from Holland. The route adopted by the Portuguese had been hitherto followed by the Dutch; from the Cape of Good Hope they had sailed north along the coast of Africa or Madagascar, and then with the south-west monsoon east to India and so to their destination in the Indies. A shorter way was discovered in 1611. In that year Commander Brouwer, picking up westerly winds (which were not, like the monsoon, seasonal), took his ship eastwards from the Cape 4000 miles, and not till then turned north; as a result he reached Batavia in half the usual time. The advantages of this plan were proved by further experiment in 1614, in which year three ships sailed from Holland, two taking the old route, one the new; the former two arrived in the East Indies in sixteen and eighteen months, the third in six. From that time the company ordered all its vessels to follow Brouwer's course. Thus sailing, Dirck Hartog of Amsterdam in his ship the *Eendracht*, in October 1616, came upon 'various islands, which were, however, found uninhabited'. He took shelter in 'Dirck Hartog's Road' behind an island known still as Dirck Hartog's Island; and on a post on that island nailed a flattened pewter dish engraved with the record of his three days' visit. Eighty years later, Willem de Vlamingh found the post upright, though rotten, with the dish still attached. He flattened out a new dish, copied on to it the inscription, and added a second recording his own visit; this he nailed up in place of the old one, which he took to Batavia. From Batavia the governor-general and council of the company sent it home to their superiors in Amsterdam, who, they thought, would 'no doubt stand amazed that the same has for so long a series of years been preserved, in spite of its being exposed to the influence of sky, rain, and sun'; and in the Rijksmuseum of Amsterdam Dirck Hartog's dish rests to this day. Vlamingh's dish was in its turn found by a French expedition in 1801, half covered with sand, lying near its post. It was nailed up again, but a later French expedition brought it to Paris, where it was lost until 1940; and it, too, is now in a museum, at Perth in Western Australia.

No journal or account of this *Eendracht*'s voyage has survived; there is only the pewter dish to tell us what coast Dirck Hartog had come upon, while a map drawn in 1627 by the company's cartographer, Hessel Gerritsz, gives a very definite piece of coastline. From this it seems that the 'Land of Eendracht' stretched from the modern North-West Cape of Western Australia down to about 28° S. But almost every succeeding year added something to the Dutch knowledge of Australia, and piece by piece there was built up a more coherent idea of the coast. Before even the news of Dirck Hartog's discovery had reached Holland another ship, the *Zeewulf*, in 1618, made it slightly north of Eendrachtsland—a low-lying shore of great length, wrote the supercargo, though whether it was continuous land or only a series of islands they could not tell. 'Only the Lord knows the real state of affairs. At all events it would seem never to have been made or discovered by anyone before us, as we never heard of such discovery, and the chart shows nothing but open ocean at this place.' The captain suggested that ships sailing with the western monsoon might make this land so as to get a fixed course for Java; and after that year, 1618, Dutch skippers on their outward passage kept a look-out for it, though it was rarely sighted by two of them in the same place.

In 1619, on 19 July, Commander Frederick de Houtman with two ships bound for Batavia 'suddenly came upon the Southland of Beach in 32° 20'', a considerable distance south of the point first seen by the *Eendracht*, just south indeed of the modern Perth. Houtman, as his journal implies, was of the opinion that this must be the coastline of the 'Beach' or 'Locach' of Marco Polo, with its fabulous riches; accordingly he determined to do his best to get some knowledge of it. It seemed to him a very good country, but continual surf and heavy seas kept him from landing; until at last, after nine days, persuaded that the risk to heavy ships and costly cargoes was too great, he was forced to continue his journey in the hope that it might be more fully explored later on. Land was out of sight by the evening of 28 July, and thinking himself in the open sea, he shaped a course north-by-east. But during the next night, three hours before daybreak, he again unexpectedly came on land— 'a low-lying coast, a level broken country with reefs all round it'. These were dangerous shoals, Houtman justly thought, and the Dutch called them by a fitting name, Houtman's Abrolhos —*abrolhos* being a Portuguese word meaning 'open your eyes'.[1] They made the best of their way out of danger, but three days later came on another long stretch of land in 27° 40'—evidently this time the Eendrachtsland of Dirck Hartog; and it seemed certain that all the land thus seen was one uninterrupted mainland coast. That part of it in 27° 40' was red mud; might it not therefore prove to be gold-bearing? At any rate, a Dutch map of 1639 boldly identifies the land, not very well defined, with the *Beach provincia aurifera*—the golden province of Beach—of the sixteenth-century continent of Mercator and Ortelius. It was not, in fact, a very good guess, as became apparent later. The earlier map of Gerritsz is more faithful to ascertained fact, and it proves that the Dutch had made soundings on their journey up the coast. This newly seen coast was named after Jacob Dedel, the supercargo of one of Houtman's ships. Then

[1] Hence 'Look out! Take care!' The word is properly three, *abre os olhos.* It was used more than once by other people as the equivalent of shoals.

three years later land was seen south again of this tract, how we do not know; but on Gerritsz's map a coastline is marked which changes direction at 34° to south-east and runs thereafter to 35°; it is inscribed 'land made by the ship *Leeuwin* in March 1622'. It was low-lying, covered on the south-east with dunes.

A great deal of this coast had now been seen at one point or another. Houtman agreed with the captain of the *Zeewulf*, that it was a good point for outward-bound ships to make; it might even become a refreshing place between the Cape and Batavia. Houtman and his supercargo had agreed also on the necessity of further exploration of the coast they had seen, and they had seen only a part of it. What, then, intervened between the northern point of Eendrachtsland and New Guinea? These were interesting questions, practical and theoretical: there was a point more vital still—the danger of shipwreck on a shore most imperfectly known. Houtman's Abrolhos were to take their toll; before that happened, but not till after several Dutch ships had been in grave danger, disaster came. On 5 July 1622 a ship's boat arrived at Batavia with ten men; three days later it was followed by another with thirty-six. These forty-six men had come in their small boats over the Indian Ocean; they were all that was left of the crew of an English ship, the *Trial*, which at night-time, in fine weather, without having seen land, had run on 'certain rocks situated in latitude 20° 10', in the longitude of the western extremity of Java'. A heavy swell had carried the ship on to the rocks, and filled it with water; there was great disorder, and when the forty-six survivors got away they left ninety-seven men behind them, whose fate was known to God alone. The Englishmen, wrote Governor-General Coen, said that they had met with this accident through following the course of the Dutch ships; and they intended to dissuade their fellow countrymen from imitating them. This eastward course of 4000 miles from the Cape, he continued, made it necessary that great caution should be used, and the best measures be taken to avoid such accidents.

These fatal rocks, on which the *Trial* had made her desperate end, were, according to the survivors, near a number of broken islands lying very far apart, and Gerritsz marked them on his map in the spot indicated. But neither rocks nor islands were ever found in that longitude; and the conclusion is that the ship was wrecked on the reefs about Barrow Island, or Trimouille Island, one of the Monte Bello group, about ten degrees east of her fancied position. What was certain was that this wreck and loss of life on the ordinary route to the East argued the urgent necessity of a full exploration of the new and unknown coasts. The Directors of the company in Holland had already earnestly enjoined the sending of yachts to make discovery of the South-land; Coen, too, was convinced of the desirability of finding whether any of these southern regions were inhabited, and whether trade could be established with them. Accordingly in September 1622 he issued instructions to two yachts to discover and explore, 'and to ascertain as much of the situation and nature of these regions as God Almighty shall vouchsafe to allow them'. These instructions, if they could have been carried out, would have left little of the coastline of Australia to be discovered in later days, and they are an index of Coen's thoroughness and his conception of the scope of a voyage of discovery. They envisaged the complete circumnavigation of the continent and the careful examination of its peoples and products, down to the kidnapping of natives who might be 'turned to useful purpose' when occasion should serve. They were never carried out, for the two yachts did not even leave port. More urgent matters called, and at the beginning of 1623 Coen himself returned to the Netherlands. But all plans of exploration were not abandoned; in January of the same year Governor van Speult of Amboyna, the hero of the 'massacre' of the succeeding month, sent out two other yachts, the *Arnhem* and *Pera*, under the command of Jan Carstenz. Van Speult aimed somewhat lower than Coen; his plan was to enlarge on the discoveries made by the *Duyfken* in 1605 and 1606. These, it will be remembered, were of the south coast of

New Guinea and the west coast of the Cape York peninsula; but, apart from the route to be followed, the instructions given to Carstenz were in general similar to Coen's exhaustive model. In pursuit of these instructions the *Arnhem* and *Pera* made some interesting though commercially most unprofitable discoveries.

They sailed from Amboyna on 21 January 1623, and on the way to the New Guinea coast received the submission to Dutch authority of three East Indian islands. New Guinea was sighted in latitude 4° 45′ and from here Carstenz followed the whole south coast as far as Torres Strait, finding it to be unbroken. It seemed a pleasant land; there was a snow-covered mountain range inland, and the Dutch, like Torres, noticed the many valleys and fresh-water rivers. But of what fruits, metals or animals it contained they could give no report; nor of the customs of the natives, beyond the fact that they were savages and cannibals, and refusing to hold parley with the Dutch had even fallen on them and slain the skipper and nine men of the *Arnhem*, who had been careless of their safety. Coal-black, stark naked, their noses pierced by bones, they were in appearance more like monsters than human beings. Perils human were followed by perils of the sea; for in 9° 6′ the ships came into a mesh of sand-banks, reefs and shallows—which Torres again had had difficulty in negotiating. The boats, sent out to sound, reported shoals everywhere: so, though a chart that was being used left a conjectural opening to the east, Carstenz deemed it clearly impossible to follow the coastline any farther in that direction. His ships seemed caught in a trap; the best he could do was to get out of it 'with extreme difficulty and great peril' by retracing his course, and when he did so he praised God for his deliverance. This difficult tangle of shallows and reefs appeared to the Dutch as not a passage but a bay, and they accordingly resolved to call it 'Drooge Bocht', or Shallow Bight. The land to the south must accordingly be New Guinea still; the coast along which they had sailed they called the 'West End of New Guinea'.

Carstenz sailed south. The land he followed now was undeviatingly, depressingly flat and low-lying, dry and barren, growing only brushwood and stunted wild trees; and undoubtedly, as he followed the track of the *Duyfken*, the prospect was discouraging. 'We have not seen one fruit-bearing tree', he reported, 'nor anything men can make use of. There are no mountains nor even hills, so that it may safely be concluded that the land contains no metals, nor yields precious woods. In our judgment this is the most arid and barren region that could be found anywhere on the earth. The inhabitants, too, are the most wretched and the poorest creatures that I have ever seen.' But he took his ships past the *Duyfken*'s Cape Keerweer, till he came to a salt-river inlet in 17° 8′ which was called the Staten River, and then he, too, decided to turn again. The prevailing winds were from the north, and Carstenz was afraid of falling on a lee shore in some vast bay. It was 24 April: a wooden tablet was nailed to a tree recording the date and the visit, and the *Pera* sailed back the way it had come to Amboyna, where it arrived on 8 June. The *Pera*, not also the *Arnhem*: for on 25 April that vessel, already a source of annoyance, deserted the commander—'on purpose, and with malice prepense'.

Carstenz's observations on this part of 'New Guinea', or the Cape York peninsula, rendered his journal a joyless one for his commercial masters. He had landed and made short expeditions in from the coast, which had merely confirmed his bad opinion of the country. It had hardly any fresh water and what there was had to be dug for; the rivers were salt; there were no harbours. The natives seemed to be less cunning, bold and ill-natured than those of New Guinea proper, but he suspected them of cannibalism. They were, he thought, utter barbarians, black, ignorant of precious metals and spices—'poor and abject wretches, caring mainly for bits of iron and strings of beads'. They dragged their wives and children over the rivers on sticks and boughs of trees; their weapons were spears, tipped with human bones or fish bones, which they hurled with throwing-sticks. From beings of such a level it was hardly to be expected that much information could be gleaned; nor could the Dutch learn anything more about their numbers or study individuals at leisure. For when they tried to capture specimens, these people were strangely reluctant to be rescued from their barren home. They were shown their coveted bits of iron and strings of beads and so tempted to await the approach of the sailors; but when a man who was weaponless was seized, noosed about the neck and dragged to the pinnace his fellows rushed furiously to the rescue with their spears, and one was killed. It seemed ingratitude to Carstenz, who regarded his countrymen as kind and gentle beyond the ordinary; yet everywhere they were received as enemies and in one place were attacked by no fewer than two hundred. Misguided savages, to defend their freedom thus!

What meantime had happened to the *Arnhem*? Carstenz thought she would have gone to the island of Arua, or Aroe, 'to have a good time of it', but at Aroe he got no news. The mutinous vessel, he found later, had preceded the *Pera* at Banda by three weeks. There exists no journal of her voyage, and the governor of Banda wrote that she had done nothing worth mentioning. He was wrong, however, as later maps and records prove. On the days following the separation of the two ships off the 'New Guinea' coast there were easterly winds; the *Arnhem* had been blown right across the gulf, the 'vast bay' which Carstenz suspected, and had discovered the coast on the other side. To this land her crew gave the names of their ship and of van Speult, the governor who had sent them out. The name Speultsland is no more; Arnhem's Land still persists. To these 'vast lands' the Dutch commander Pool was directed to sail in 1636; the fruits of the voyage were 'great lands . . . named van Diemens and Marias land'—in reality the Cobourg peninsula, the northern entrance to Van Diemen Gulf, and Melville Island, westward of the *Arnhem*'s discoveries. At this point knowledge of north-eastern Australia rested for eight more years. But of discoveries of other parts of the coast two more remain to be recorded.

The story of neither of these discoveries is known in full

detail. The evidence comes from charts and brief mention in
the *Daily Register* of Batavia. The first was made by the ship
*Gulden Zeepaert*, skipper François Thijssen, which sailed from
the Netherlands on 22 May 1626, and arrived at Batavia on
10 April 1627. The *Gulden Zeepaert* for some reason had not
made the usual course to the coast of the South-land; she had
on the contrary in January 1627 followed round the south-
western extremity of that coast, south of the part discovered by
the *Leeuwin*, and so in curiosity right along the uniformly bare
and arid shore of the Great Australian Bight, as far as the two
little groups of islands which the Dutch called by their present
names, the islands of St Francis and St Peter. On board the ship
was the Honourable Pieter Nuyts, an 'Extraordinary Councillor of India', and that vast land was named after him Pieter
Nuyts Land. The *Gulden Zeepaert* brought to Batavia an excellent chart of the coastline, a chart that was used a century and
three-quarters later by French and British explorers; but no
ship before 1802 went farther east than that Dutch voyager.
She brought few other details of the new discovery, and could
have brought none that was attractive; for not even the most
hopeful rhapsodist could invest with excitement that long
monotonous wall of cliffs defending an interior which might
well seem the last completion of sterility. The islands of St
Francis and St Peter were not more to be praised. A coast as
barren and uninviting was that encountered in 1628, the succeeding year, by the ship *Vyanen*. This was on the north-west
coast of the South-land, in about 21°, where the *Vyanen* was
driven ashore. A great quantity of pepper and some copper was
thrown overboard, and through God's mercy, said the thankful
Dutch, she got off again without further damage. They sailed
200 miles along the coast, which they did not like; inland there
were green fertile fields, and inhabitants who were barbarous
and exceedingly black. A chart of 1628 calls this land 'G. F. de
Witsland', apparently after one of the ship's company.

So much for the discovery at this time of the Australian

coastline. Bit by bit the Dutch had obtained some knowledge of nearly half of it; bit by bit in this incidental, sometimes accidental way, with the help of two or three small exploring expeditions, the solid, unexcited merchant captains had enabled their chart-makers and geographers to build up the outline of an authentic South-land: great in extent, it seemed certain, though so far giving little indication of the riches and the civilization, the towered cities, the elephants and glittering kings of the Great South Land of Marco Polo and those imaginative cosmographers who built on his foundation. Beach, that auriferous province, was one thing. The South-land of Dirck Hartog and his fellow skippers was less enchanting. Its kings, if it had any, were coal-black and did not glitter. When they were attacked, they defended themselves. The immediate interest of the South-land to the Dutch, in fact, was mainly the interest of the dangerous. Eendrachtsland, as its earlier discoverers had recommended, was a good mark to pick up on the outward journey to the East Indies—as long as the navigators could manage to avoid the desperately perilous, almost invisible Houtman's Abrolhos. The coast was not laid down properly on the charts; furthermore, different charts placed the Abrolhos in different places. There was the difficulty of longitude; there was the difficulty of making a regular landfall in latitude 26°. The Abrolhos lay in about $28\frac{1}{2}°$; and so, as Coen observed, Dutch ships were in 'daily peril'. Once he himself narrowly escaped destruction. He had been sent to Java for a second term as governor-general; and suddenly, one afternoon, in the fatal latitude, the breakers were descried less than half a mile away. According to different maps, the ship was fifty, a hundred, or even three hundred miles from land. 'If we had come upon this place in the night-time,' he said, 'we should have been in a thousand perils with our ship and crew.' What might happen when a ship did come upon this place in the night-time received a lurid illustration in the wreck and mutiny of the *Batavia*.

Commander François Pelsaert, of this ship, sick in bed, was

awakened on the night of 4 June 1629 by a violent shock. He ran up on deck, found it a bright moonlit night, and fair weather. In every direction as far as the eye could reach the sea was covered with a white froth; the ship, with all her sails set, was grinding on a reef and apparently surrounded with rocks and shoals. The master, upbraided, admitted having perceived the froth at a distance, but a shipmate had assured him it was caused merely by the rays of the moon. What was to be done and where they were, he said, God only knew. The cannon were thrown overboard to lighten the ship, but she remained fast. An anchor was dropped; but a storm of wind and rain sprang up and she struck continually. The mainmast was then cut away, but could not be got clear of the rigging and only increased the danger. The sole land visible was an island about three leagues away; and nearer, two other islands so small as to be not much more than rocks. In the morning the master was sent to examine these barren islets and reported that at least they were not covered at high water; and as the ship was encumbered with crying women and children, sick people and many 'out of their wits with fear', it was decided to take the risk of landing them. One hundred and eighty persons were placed on the larger islet, forty on the smaller; and the vessel beginning to break up, every effort was made to land stores and water, of which there was none on shore. These efforts were impeded by the brutality and indiscipline of the crew, who seized the opportunity to get drunk and could make no more than three trips in the day. Towards evening the sea ran so high that Pelsaert could not return on board for more water, and was forced to abandon seventy men on the vessel at the very point of perishing.

The position on the islets was serious; on the smaller one there were but eighty pints of water for forty people, on the larger still less. It was accordingly resolved that Pelsaert should take the pinnace and search for water on further islets which day had discovered near by. The little that was found was brackish; it remained to go and look elsewhere. A deck was added to the boat and Pelsaert put to sea. He sighted the coast of the continent, low, bare and rocky, but as he approached a little creek the weather became threatening, and next day he came near destruction. The rain, he thought, would at least be some relief to those left on the islets. When the weather cleared he steered north along the coast, on which sea and rocks together made it impossible to land. On 14 June, however, smoke was seen, and six of his men determined to swim ashore. They did so, much bruised and battered, and spent the whole day in an unsuccessful search for water, while four black and naked savages, who approached on hands and knees, fled in panic when they were seen. Next day, the sea being calmer, the whole boat's company were able to land, almost exhausted with thirst, and vainly dug wells in the sand. At length rain-water was discovered in clefts of the rocks, and their agony was relieved. Landing again the following day, they found no more, however, and were able to observe nothing but ant-hills so large that they were taken for the habitations of the 'Indians', a few of these 'Indians' themselves, who fled like the four already encountered, and a plague of flies. The wind then changed to the north-east, so that they could no longer follow the coast, and being in latitude 22° 17′, Pelsaert decided to sail to Batavia and secure assistance. He made the Java coast on 27 June, and five days later met with a Dutch vessel which took him to the capital. Here he was given a frigate with which to go to the rescue of the castaways, and approaching the wreck on 17 September, saw to his joy that from the islets smoke still rose.

Pelsaert immediately jumped into a skiff, with bread and wine, and rowed ashore. At the same time a boat hastily approached with four men, one of whom, Weybehays, ran and implored him to return to the frigate as speedily as possible, for his life was in danger; and the hurried words recounted a horrible story of murder and betrayal. Among the seventy men who had been abandoned in the *Batavia* was one Jerome Cornelis, the supercargo, formerly an apothecary at Haarlem. The life of an apothecary, or even that of an ordinary sailor, evidently lacked incident to Cornelis' mind: already, off the African coast, he had plotted with the pilot and others to seize the ship and take to piracy. This plan was abandoned, but his mind remained at work. He was able to exist on the wreck for ten days after the vessel struck, drifted for two days more on the mainmast, and finally floated on a yard to the larger islet. In Pelsaert's absence he, as supercargo, became commander, and the conspiracy was resumed. Its object was now to get possession of the remains of the wreck, and when Pelsaert returned to seize his ship and cruise piratically in the Indian Ocean. Success in this scheme, however, meant the elimination of all honest men, and Cornelis and his fellow conspirators, before beginning their deeds of blood, agreed upon a written compact of fidelity to one another. They then assailed those whom they distrusted on the larger islet and killed thirty or forty. Meanwhile Weybehays had been sent to a third island to look for water; after a search of twenty days he found some, but his signals were fortunately not seen by Cornelis's party. The survivors of the massacre were able to fasten together pieces of wood, on which they floated to Weybehays's island; and he, having forty-five men with him in all, thereupon determined to resist vigorously any assault made. Cornelis indeed intended no half-measures, nor did he intend more to risk being forestalled with Pelsaert and the rescue ship. He had no difficulty in killing all the men on the small islet, leaving alive only seven children and some women, who were appropriated to the use of himself and his men as part of the booty. The mutineers then broke open the chests of merchandise saved from the wreck, and dressed in rich and noble stuffs; while Cornelis, lavish in his regard for the dignity of command, had himself elected captain-general in a formal document signed by all his companions, and appointed a bodyguard whom he clothed in scarlet, with gold and silver embroidery. There remained to be consummated only the murder of Weybehays and his party. But, like many another talented leader, Cornelis found there was a limit to success. Two attempts were repulsed. He then tried guile. A treaty of peace was proposed and agreed to: Weybehays and his men were to stay unmolested and to receive material for clothes, giving up in return a small boat in which a sailor had escaped from Cornelis's island. Once again the desperado overreached himself; during the negotiations he wrote to some French soldiers among Weybehays's men, offering them £6000 apiece to assist him in his design. The soldiers remained incorruptible, the letters were shown to Weybehays; when Cornelis came next day with the stuffs he was attacked, some of his men were killed, he was made prisoner, and a last assault on his behalf was routed. It was at this moment that Pelsaert arrived with the frigate.

Scarcely had he heard Weybehays's report and regained his vessel than the two shallops came alongside, full of armed men clothed, as Weybehays had said, in gold and silver embroidery. Pelsaert demanded the reason for their armament; they replied that they would tell him when they came on board. Thereupon he ordered them to throw their weapons into the sea or he would sink them where they lay. The plot had failed, the weapons were abandoned, and as the mutineers stepped on deck they were placed in irons. In the evening Weybehays brought Cornelis on board. Next day those still left on the islet surrendered unconditionally; and Pelsaert was able to salvage what he could of the spoil. All the looted jewels were recovered except a gold chain, and though the *Batavia* was in fragments, five chests of silver also, while the position of another was marked with an anchor and a piece of artillery. Then, after ten days, an icy wind from the south making further salvage impossible, Pelsaert held a council to decide whether to take the prisoners to Batavia for regular trial or to execute justice where they were, on the scene of their exploits. They were many in number, and the frigate was loaded with a valuable freight; it was decided to avoid all risk, and Cornelis and his men were forthwith condemned and hanged. With that signal act of justice Pelsaert put the Abrolhos behind him, a melancholy memorial of a savagery perhaps beyond the ingenuity of the black and naked wretches of the mainland, whose behaviour was so often a scandal to the company's Dutchmen; whether his narrative is relieved by the mention of a 'species of cat . . . very strange creatures', discovered on the islands, which walked on their hind legs alone, may be a matter of varying estimate. Wholesale murder now being added to the history of Australia, so to its natural history was added the wallaby. Farther up the coast, on the passage to Batavia, two criminals were marooned, in the pious hope, says Pelsaert, that some day they might be rescued alive with trustworthy information about 'these parts'. So also might the company be served.

It remains to consider, very much apart from the discovery of Australia, and standing by itself amid Dutch exploration of the seventeenth century, a voyage made in defiance of the company's authority—the first conspicuous Dutch voyage indeed in the Pacific proper. This was the voyage of Schouten and Le Maire. Isaac Le Maire was an Amsterdam merchant of European reputation; he was an enemy of the East India Company, and his 'Remonstrance' to the States-General in 1609 against its increasing powers was defeated only after much agitation and intrigue. Nevertheless in the following year a company formed by him was given permission to trade in Tartary, China, Japan, 'Terra Australis' and the islands of the South Sea—permission which might well make the greater company indignant. But the company was still protected by that clause in its charter which gave it the exclusive use of the passages by the Cape and the Strait of Magellan; and Le Maire, much as he wished to extend his trade, could derive little enough comfort from that. He took council with Willem Corneliszoon Schouten, a famous navigator who had already sailed three times to the East Indies and whose eagerness to visit strange lands was unabated: and a plan was evolved. Magellan had doubted whether the land to the south of his strait was a continent, and Drake had been driven by storm beyond the southernmost point of America; accordingly Dutch and English cartographers often represented here not a great expanse of land, but a sort of archipelago. Le Maire and Schouten believed therefore that south of the strait a passage might be found, by means of which they might discover the rich continent of Quiros's memorials, while if that failed them it would be simple to sail to the East Indies and there carry on a profitable trade. Each agreed to raise half the necessary funds from his friends and admirers; Schouten, Le Maire with his son Jacob and three burghers of the town of Hoorn were appointed directors, and in a short time the money was collected. Two vessels were equipped, the ship *Eendracht*, 220 tons, with a crew of sixty-five, and the yacht *Hoorn*, 110 tons, and twenty-two men. In the *Eendracht* sailed Schouten as skipper and Jacob Le Maire as supercargo and commander of the voyage. The skipper of the *Hoorn* was Jan Schouten, a brother of Willem. The officers and crew were engaged to go wherever the skipper and the supercargo should please, for the destination of the voyage was kept a secret. 'Wherefore,' it is said, 'very diverse opinions obtained among the crews concerning this voyage and these ships, which were finally called the Goldseekers, but the aforesaid directors called their assembly the Australian Company.' The vessels were inspected in state by the sheriff and aldermen of Hoorn, and at the end of May 1615 they sailed.

On 4 July rationing began, as was customary on long voyages—each man got a tankard of beer a day, four pounds of bread and half a pound of butter a week, and five cheeses for the whole voyage. It is not surprising that by the middle of August the men were fast contracting scurvy, and as it was now too late for a quick passage across the equator, it was resolved to put in at Sierra Leone to provision. Here they watered, and from the blacks of the African coast got 25,000 lemons—'all for a few beads and some poor Nuremberg knives'. Sailing again, they encountered on 5 October the first of their marvels: such a din arose at noon that day that the skipper thought a man must be overboard, and then to his astonishment he saw that

the sea was red with blood. When later the ship was beached
for cleaning it was found that a great horned sea-monster had
struck the bow with most wonderful force; sticking in it below
the waterline was a horn of exceedingly hard bone, like the end
of an elephant's tusk. Towards the end of that month the crew
were told the object of the expedition, at which there was great
joy; for each one hoped to profit himself somewhat. At last,
after a long passage of the Atlantic, otherwise without incident,
they came on 7 December to Port Desire in Patagonia, in
latitude 47° 40', and next day anchored. A strong wind, in
spite of double anchors, drifted both vessels to the shore, where
they settled on rocks in such a position that at low tide the men
could walk underneath them. They were convinced that the
ships were lost and the voyage over before ever the Pacific had
been sighted; until the tide rose and, the weather keeping calm,
all was secure. This good hap, however, was followed by ill;
for when the vessels, beached in a more orthodox fashion, were
being cleaned, the *Hoorn* was accidentally set on fire, and burnt to
the water's edge. What remained of her was broken up, and
the guns, anchors and other valuable fittings were stowed in the
*Eendracht*.

While at Port Desire there were observations to make other
than nautical ones. Ostriches were seen, and animals shy like
deer, only with very long necks—the llamas of the South
American pampas; heaps of stones on a mountain provoked
curiosity, and when one was overturned it was found to conceal
the bones of a human being ten or eleven feet high; so here was
a giants' cemetery. But these were incidents, however engross-
ing, not the end of the voyage; and on 13 January 1616 it was
resumed by the now solitary *Eendracht*. Early on the morning
of the 24th land was sighted to starboard, about a mile away,
a country of high mountains white with snow, running east by
south. This the Dutch coasted, coming to the end of it about
noon that day; but to the east they saw more land, very high
and dangerous. A channel intervened about eight miles wide;
it seemed a good one, and there was a strong current to the

south. As they made for it they saw numberless penguins and 'whales by thousands'. Next morning they were close to the more easterly land, which extended east-south-east as far as they could see. Possibly this might be the southern continent; it was, at any rate, named Staten Landt, while the land on the other side of the channel was called after the Dutch prince Mauritius de Nassauw. There seemed to be good anchorage and fine sandy beaches on both sides, and though no trees could be seen, penguins, seals, birds and water were abundant; later on, even, albatrosses came and sat on board the ship, so unaccustomed to the sight of men that they allowed themselves to be seized by the sailors and killed. In the evening the wind veered to the south-west, the sea was deep blue and there was a heavy roll from that direction; and they ran southward, 'certain that we had open and deep water on the weather-side, not doubting that it was the great South Sea, whereat we were very glad, holding that a way had been discovered by us which had until then been unknown to man, as we afterwards found to be the truth'. This was the passage now known as the Strait of Le Maire. Two islands with a few rocks around them were named the Islands of Barnevelt, and on the evening of 29 January the extremity of the land south of the Strait of Magellan was seen. Unromantically, but lastingly, it was called Cape Hoorn. There was still blue water and a heavy swell from the west— there was, indeed, an open way to the South Sea.

The weather turned stormy, and for a month the adventurers suffered much cold and hardship, steering always a northerly course. The beginning of March brought them to the island of Juan Fernandez, though they could not approach near enough to the roadstead to anchor. They caught plenty of fish, however, and got some water, and after two days' delay sailed on lest they should waste a favourable wind, 'to the very great pain and sorrow of the sick, who thereby saw all their hopes of life lost, but God gives relief'. He did not give relief to Jan Schouten, who died on 9 March. A month later, 10 April, the *Eendracht* arrived at the first of a close series of islands: she was now among the Tuamotus. This first one was Honden, or Dog Island—Pukapuka, perhaps the speck, San Pablo, sighted by Magellan a century before. Then on the 14th came Eylandt Sonder Grondt—Bottomless Island, the atolls of Takaroa and Takapoto. Here there was no anchorage, even close to the shore, but tattooed natives paddled out to the ship from Takapoto, at first timid, though bolder at the sight of iron—one pulled the nails from port-holes in the *Eendracht*'s gallery, others tried to drag free the bolts which kept the ship's timbers together. Here, too, began the melancholy story of shooting and killing; a boat was sent to the shore, and natives who came from the woods and tried to disarm the crew were shot dead or mortally wounded. These had slings, and spears pointed with the swords of sword-fish. The course was then changed to a westerly one, and at the next island, Waterlandt (Manihi, or perhaps Ahe), on the 16th, water was obtained in spite of a great surf; a sack of herbs was also gathered, with crabs and shellfish and 'snails of very good flavour'—the boiled herbs being found an excellent remedy for scurvy. This island was uninhabited. Another uninhabited atoll, on the 18th, Vliegen Eylandt (Fly Island or Rangiroa), was so plagued with flies that the ship, although it fled, could not get rid of them for three or four days. This was the last seen of the Tuamotus. Later on a sail was sighted coming from the south, a double canoe; being unacquainted with the rules of international warfare, it would not stop at a shot fired across its bows, and the shallop was sent in pursuit. Some of the unfortunate savages were killed, while two men were taken on board, falling down before the Dutch and kissing their feet and hands. These people surprised their captors by drinking salt water; they were 'red folk who smeared themselves with oil, and all the women had short hair like the men in Holland, whilst the men's hair was long and painted very black'. The captives were put back in the evening with beads and knives, in return for which they gave mats and coconuts.

The ships still sailed the same course. On 10 May two more

islands were seen, close together, where it was possible to anchor. One was very high, the other longer and comparatively flat. Natives came alongside with bananas and coconuts, 'obas roots' or yams, small pigs, and dippers of fresh water; they had double canoes, like the one already met with, very swift, and steered from the stern with two oars. They were surprised at the size of the ship, and knocked against the bottom with a stone to see how strong she was. But there was more firing when the shallop, looking for a better anchorage, was surrounded by canoes; and a state visit from the chief, accompanied by the present of a pig, ended in an attack on the ship, repulsed with musket-balls and old nails fired from the guns. The high island, called Cocos by the Dutch, was Tafahi; the other, called Verraders or Traitors' Island, was Niuatoputapu. They were the most northern outliers of the Tongan group. On 13 May Schouten and Le Maire left them, next day found another small volcanic island—Goede Hope, or Niuafo'ou; then altered course further to the north. At last, on 19 May, they came to a more agreeable place, two high islands where they anchored in a bay opposite a village by a fresh-water river; and here, after a little skirmishing, friendly relations were established.

In the village the visitors saw a number of circular huts about twenty-five feet round and ten or twelve feet high, tapering to a point at the top and covered with leaves. The men were strong, and all the people were well made, brownish yellow in colour, and intelligent. The native king was friendly, hostages were exchanged, and nothing was stolen except a sword, which was returned. To gratify savage curiosity the guns were fired, at which there was general flight to the woods. But social relations went forward, the supercargoes were presented with crowns of feathers, the Dutch blew their trumpets to amuse the king, and in the evening the sailors and the savages would dance together; 'we got to be as free and easy there as if we had been at home', said the Dutchmen. There are accounts of native customs and accomplishments: of how Le Maire and three others, becoming weary on an exploring expedition, were led to a coconut grove, where 'the under-king tied a bandage round his feet or legs and climbed with great dexterity and swiftness up a straight tall tree, and in a moment brought down ten coker-nuts, which he opened very easily in a moment by a peculiar knack with a small piece of wood'; and of how in the evening maidens danced gracefully before the king, to music made by thumping on a piece of hollow wood. There is the story, too, of how the king of the neighbouring island visited his royal brother, and of the strange ceremonies which accompanied this occasion, the visitor 'falling with his face to the earth and praying incessantly, with much shouting and raving, and with very great zeal'. The Dutch sounded their trumpets and drums for the additional benefit of these happy monarchs, 'who were seated together and took exceeding pleasure therein'. After that there was the rite of *kava*-drinking. A number of natives came to the kings with a quantity of some green herb; then they chewed it into fragments, which were placed in a large wooden trough, covered with water, and stirred and kneaded together. This mixture was served to the kings and their nobles; it was indeed offered also to the Dutchmen, but for them the sight was sufficient. The kings inspected the ship; they each presented the Dutch with a roast pig and some live ones; and in return they received three small copper pails, four knives, twelve old nails and some beads—with which precisely enumerated barter they were well satisfied.

In spite of such mutual compliments, the natives heard with enthusiasm the announcement of their visitors' departure. The South Sea islander could never have had an altogether comfortable feeling in the presence of these extraordinary appearances from an unknown world, with their great ships and potent weapons, their white skins and strange angers. The bay where the ship anchored was called Eendracht's Bay, the islands the Hoorn Islands—they were Futuna and Alofi;[1] and on 1 June the Dutch put once more to sea, with the loss of two anchors in weighing. It seemed to Le Maire that these islands, and the

[1] The collective name is now Horne.

others they had so recently visited, must be the Solomons or at least near the Solomons, near even the continent defined with such loving, if imaginative, detail by Quiros; for much that had been described by the Spaniards, he thought, was matched by the observed character and habits of the amiable savages. The Dutch were, in fact, among the islands between the groups now known as Fiji and Samoa, rather to the north-east of the former. Le Maire was anxious to sail to the west to make sure of the continent; Schouten was unwilling to do so. For the southern coast of New Guinea was unknown and feared—Torres's report was buried among Spanish official papers, not to be revealed for the benefit of foreigners and enemies—a passage to Java by way of this southern coast was at best problematical, and failure to find one might be fatal. The seamanlike course now was to sail north-west, and thus round the north of New Guinea to the Moluccas and safety. Schouten's view, the view of the practical sailor, experienced in East Indian navigation, prevailed; the *Eendracht* ran for a while west-south-west, and then turned northwards, making good progress. Islands were passed and added to the chart—Marcken,[1] Green Islands and others;[2] till on 25 June the coast of what was thought to be New Guinea was sighted (it was, in reality, New Ireland). The people were very primitive, black and quite naked, with rings hanging from their nostrils, and came out in canoes to pelt the sailors from slings. Next day there was further fighting, in which the Dutch showed little moderation. Three prisoners, however, were bandaged, one of whom was ransomed for ten pigs; another died, and the third was set on shore with little hope of life. The battered canoes went to the galley fire.

Water was obtained here, and friendlier natives were afterwards encountered, with handsomer canoes and the beginnings of clothing. There was still fighting, however, as the *Eendracht* drifted along the coast in the first days of July, sometimes

[1] The Tauu islands, about 130 miles west-north-west of Ontong Java.
[2] Green islands, five in number, about 130 miles from the Tauu islands. The others were the Feni islands, called by the Dutch S. Jans (St John's).

varied by bad weather. Many islands were passed, and more than one volcano. Schouten and Le Maire knew they were off the coast of what was generally imagined to be New Guinea; beyond that they were ignorant of their position. They were running short of supplies; all pottage—peas, beans and barley— was gone, and all their meat, bacon and fish; rations were confined to bread, oil, Spanish wine, and one glassful of brandy a day. They sailed on through July, always in sight of land. One day they anchored and tried to land to collect coconuts, but were driven off with darts by ambushed blacks; on the succeeding days relations improved, and the natives brought off nuts and bananas to exchange for old nails, rusty knives and beads; and fish were caught. Herbs were noticed which it was thought must have come from a Spanish source, and the people did not seem curious about the ships; others met later had pieces of Chinese porcelain—obviously this region was within the bounds of civilized trade. A large island was christened permanently Willem Schouten Island; beyond that the sight of land was qualified by bad weather, terrific thunder and lightning, and an earthquake. So July passed, and August; at last the adventurers came to a people who spoke Malay, which one of the Dutch knew well; some also spoke a few words of Spanish and wore bright-coloured clothes and silk breeches. There was news of Dutch ships in the neighbourhood; and on the evening of 17 September the *Eendracht* anchored at Ternate. Schouten had brought her into the heart of the Moluccas, sixteen and a half months after her departure from Hoorn. She was well received by the Dutch; fifteen of her crew who wished to enter the service of the East India Company were here discharged, and after a week's stay the voyage was resumed to Jacatra, where on 28 October 1616 it came to an end.

This voyage, resulting as it did in the discovery of little of importance in the Pacific, none the less deserves our highest respect. It was conducted with more than ordinary ability, and, though it failed in its primary object from the very nature of the quest, the absence of crisis throughout its course indicates the advance over a hundred years of the technique of navigation and the design of ocean-going ships. Out of eighty-seven men only three had died—one off the coast of Portugal, early in the voyage, then Jan Schouten, and a sailor at Jacatra, the first of all the crew of the *Eendracht*. Scurvy for once had been defeated: Dutch vessels were far less crowded than the older Spanish ships, and this reacted favourably on the general health. Nor was it a small feat to have discovered the Strait of Le Maire, and to have sailed a vessel for the first time round the Horn; or to have made known a greater portion of the northern coastline of New Guinea. The islands encountered in the Pacific with their laconic Dutch names, so violently contrasted to the sonorous sanctity of the Spanish, are of less importance; yet the Horne group was added to the map of the southern hemisphere, though its exact position was not easily established by Le Maire's successors. And the voyage, it has been noted, has a further historical importance—it was an effort, unlike the other Dutch exploration of the seventeenth century, definitely addressed to the discovery of the unknown southern continent—*Terra Australis incognita*.

The continent remained a hidden one; it may be wished that Schouten and Le Maire could have returned to their native land at least with the honourable credit of able circumnavigators. That was denied them. Three days after their arrival at Jacatra, Coen, then 'president' at Bantam of the East India Company, also arrived. On 1 November they were arraigned before him: on a charge of infringing the company's monopoly their ship and all their goods were confiscated. Strictly speaking, they were not guilty of that infringement—they had come to the East Indies neither by way of the Cape of Good Hope nor of the Strait of Magellan. Coen refused to believe their story of a newly discovered passage; Le Maire, Schouten and ten of their men were sent home in the fleet of Joris van Speilbergen, an admiral who was on the last stage of a voyage round the world (he had entered the Pacific in Magellan's track); and the rest of the crew remained in the East Indies in the service of the company. Schouten reached the Netherlands; not so Le Maire. To the great grief of his shipmates he died on the passage, it is said of a broken heart, at the age of thirty-one. But that did not close the story. Old Isaac Le Maire was content with the confiscation no more than with the earlier transactions of the company. Once again he had recourse to petitions and to litigation, and after two years he found his cause justified; the company was ordered to return the confiscated vessel and its cargo, and to pay all costs with interest from the date of seizure. The report of the new strait at last carried conviction; and not for a quarter of a century was the theory of the continent of Staten Land seriously threatened. 'The Gold-seekers', it was held, had deserved well of their countrymen.

# CHAPTER VII

# TASMAN

THE wreck of the *Batavia* in 1629, it may be said, marked the end of a short period of considerable achievement, achievement only in a minor degree the result of careful planning or a settled policy. Except for the mutiny, it has not the dramatic interest of the great Spanish voyages, and there is little interest of personality; nor in great degree can we attribute those characteristics to the voyages which followed. Tasman and his fellows were markedly able, technically expert, skilled navigators and admirable seamen, but they were more workaday than heroic, more competent than brilliant. They determined the direction of all future discovery in the Pacific, and that was an accomplishment not to be despised. Yet, though they did the work, and accomplished much, they were not, with one exception—that of Visscher—the architects of their own eminence: this distinction belongs to the great governor-general, Anthony van Diemen, whose plans and resolution unify the most ambitious of Dutch voyages in that century. And he in essentials followed the vast scheme of his predecessor, Coen.

In detail van Diemen's early life is obscure. He went to the East Indies apparently to escape his creditors; there his abilities elevated him rapidly from a clerkship to the position of a Councillor of the Indies, and so, through more extraordinary dignities, in January 1636 to the seat of governor-general at Batavia. Three months later he despatched the first of his exploring expeditions, that of Gerrit Thomasz Pool, already briefly mentioned. There was general willingness among officials in Batavia to investigate the South-land; van Diemen lost little time in providing the ships. What was the problem

with which he was faced? It was briefly, in modern terms, the
nature of Australian geography between the Cape York
peninsula and Arnhem's Land, and of the north coast of the
continent from Arnhem's Land westward to North West Cape;
in addition, of the east coast, and of the south coast eastward
from the islands of St Francis and St Peter. What the Dutch
already knew of the South-land has become clear. Beyond the
limits of their discovery anything might emerge. There might
be islands, archipelagos, ocean passages or vast seas. Was the
Gulf of Carpentaria, for example (named after the governor-
general Carpentier), indeed a gulf? Might a ship not sail southwards to Pieter Nuyts Land, with New Guinea on the left hand
and the east coast of Eendrachtsland on the right? These were
questions which Pool was set to answer. He was to sail from
Banda to Arnhem's Land; thence to cross the gulf to 'New
Guinea' (or Cape York), and to follow the coast south to the
farthest known limit and beyond. Possibly this coast joined that
of Eendrachtsland, and he was to try to follow it as far as
Houtman's Abrolhos, and farther still if his provisions held out,
the condition of his men allowed it, and his yachts remained
seaworthy. On the way back to Batavia he was to touch at the
Trial Rocks and gain what information he could about their
situation. If he found channels, he was to explore them, for they
might lead into the South Sea. If the gulf itself proved to be
such a channel, he was to sail down the east side and up the west,
and so as before to Eendrachtsland and Batavia. The men whom
Pelsaert had marooned, if they showed themselves, were to be
offered a passage; and if possible some place was to be found on
the coast where fresh food and water might be obtained by the
company's ships on the outward voyage from Holland. In these
instructions van Diemen included a salutary passage: the
natives, he said, were to be treated 'with great kindness, wary
caution, and skilful judgment. Whoever endeavours to discover
unknown lands and tribes, had need to be patient and long-
suffering, noways quick to fly out, but always keen to ingratiate
himself.'

The voyage was well planned, but Pool was not fated to carry it out. Before it had well begun he, like the captain of the *Arnhem*, and at the same place, was murdered by the savages of New Guinea; and his ships returned, as we have seen, having discovered only parts of Van Diemen's Land, a continuation to the west of the coast of Arnhem's Land. There was no civilization—the shore was wild and barren, and though many fires and smoke-clouds had been seen, not a native was visible, not a house, not a boat, not a fruit-tree. Van Diemen, however, was not discouraged: his plans even developed. The next expedition he despatched was not a repetition of Pool's, but one in the North Pacific. There was a report, or legend, of islands somewhere east of Japan in about latitude $37\frac{1}{2}°$—Rica de Oro and Rica de Plata[1]—where gold and silver were so common that the natives made their kettles out of them. Spanish ships had been driven there in a storm, but the Spanish, it was deemed, being by God held unworthy, had never rediscovered this desirable shore. But if the Dutch could do so, the profits might enable the company to surmount the financial difficulties under which it was labouring; and the Directors in Holland were enthusiastic. Van Diemen also was sanguine; and in June 1639 two ships sailed on the discovery commanded by an excellent captain, Matthijs Quast. The skipper of the second ship was Abel Janszoon Tasman, a man in his middle thirties. If the chief purpose of the voyage failed, they were to explore the coasts of Korea and Tartaria; for the prospects of the Japanese trade were dubious, and in case of its loss adequate compensation was desirable. Again, if this was prevented by contrary winds, the Ladrones were to be investigated, in hope of discovering the rendezvous of the Spanish treasure-ships from Manila to Acapulco —a booty which might usefully supplement the profits of trade. None of these purposes was fulfilled. Quast reached a point six hundred miles or more east of Japan, but saw no islands; scurvy and other illness prevented the completion of alternative tasks, and after wandering about the North Pacific for twenty

[1] 'Rich in Gold' and 'Rich in Silver'.

weeks in bad weather the ships returned with forty-one men dead out of a company of ninety. Beyond aiding the correction of charts, the voyage was fruitless; nevertheless Tasman's observations and Quast's journal together determined the out-lines of Dutch exploration in that region. Tasman himself was eager to take part in such exploration. Though Quast and he had seen no land, they had, they affirmed, seen unmistakable signs of it; and the directors resolved to send him out again. He did not go; his destiny lay in a different part of the ocean. It is on the great voyage of 1642 that his fame is based.

In this voyage three minds found full scope. Behind the work of Tasman the executor lay the strong ambition of van Diemen and the careful thought of one of the ablest of Dutch pilots, Frans Jacobszoon Visscher. Tasman himself was no theorist; he was born in 1603 in a Groningen village, of a family not otherwise distinguished; he lived poorly, but learnt to write, and in 1633 for the first time shipped to Batavia before the mast. He must have been more than ordinarily able, for in the following year he was skipper of a yacht on general East Indian service—that is, trading, suppressing smugglers and native rebellions, taking part in the constant search for safer routes in those perilous seas. In 1636 he returned to the Nether-lands; but after two years sailed again with his wife, being now bound to the company's service for ten years. His first important mission was the voyage with Quast; to it succeeded more general service from peaceful trade to kidnapping. His success in these employments, together with his capacity as a sailor, so impressed his masters that of all the Dutch captains it was he who was chosen for the prospective discovery and exploration of the 'rich Southern and Eastern lands'; to which discovery he found himself 'strongly inclined'. Of Visscher less is known. He had certainly had great experience as a pilot and as a surveyor and hydrographer on the Japanese coast—indeed, of such experts he was esteemed first in those seas; and he had written memoirs on other aspects of navigation. Certainly his contribu-tion to the voyage was vitally important.

Visscher in January 1642 produced a *Memoir concerning the Discovery of the South-land*, which formed at once the basis of the instructions actually given to Tasman and a statement of the main problems of the Pacific as they posed themselves to a very able and practical Dutchman. It would be necessary, he wrote, to use the long days of the summer season for making discoveries, and it would be necessary also to call at Mauritius for water and firewood; therefore the expedition should sail about the middle of August or at latest the beginning of September. Sailing south it should be in the latitude of 52° or 54° by the beginning of November, and so have between three and four months to carry out its work with minute care. If in that latitude it had met with no land, it should sail east till land was sighted or till the longitude of the east side of New Guinea was reached; if there was then still no land, it should sail north by west to New Guinea and so to the starting-point. Alternatively, it might run on as far east as the longitude of the Solomons and then steer north so as to discover them and return round New Guinea. This seemed to Visscher the best plan to follow, 'since we do not in the least doubt that divers strange things will be revealed to us in the Solomon Islands'. But there were larger schemes possible. The ships might start their voyage from the Netherlands, sailing to the Cape and thence south to 54°; or they might make their first objective the Strait of Le Maire, explore Staten Land thoroughly, and then sail east—so as to explore not merely the South Pacific but also the South Atlantic —and north as before. In this way 'one would become acquainted with all the utterly unknown provinces of Beach'. Then what of the only remaining unexplored region of the south? Visscher's fertility was unexhausted. If the Dutch could secure a suitable station for refreshment on the coast of Chile, he suggested, ships might run with the trade wind to the Solomons, somewhere between 12° and 15° latitude; refreshing again here, they would have to sail south so as to fall in with westerly winds—perhaps to 50° or until land was encountered. With these winds a ship could sail east again to the Strait of Le Maire or the Strait of

Magellan; this would make it possible to discover 'the Southern portion of the world all round the globe, and to find out what it consists of, whether land, sea, or icebergs, all that God has ordained there'. One problem would then remain, and one that seems small in relation to these giant schemes—that of the region between New Guinea and Eendrachtsland. This could be solved by recourse to van Diemen's instructions to Pool, and a voyage down the coast of 'New Guinea' to latitude 22°.

If all the work so planned by Visscher had been completed, there would have been little for later ages to do but verify the results. Certainly it seems to prefigure the greatest achievements of the succeeding century. Certainly it would have exhausted the energies of a commercial company. But some great voyage might be carried out, and in 1642 the circumstances were favourable. Both the government at Batavia and the Worshipful Masters in Holland were inclined towards the scheme; peace with Portugal freed the necessary ships, though even then there was delay before vessels returned from Persia and India. There was, however, no want of officers and men or supplies. By August 1642 two ships were appointed to this service, the *Heemskerck*, a small war yacht, the flagship, and the *Zeehaen*, a flute—a long narrow ship, a quick sailer, of small draught and plenty of shiproom. They were to carry sixty and fifty men respectively, were victualled for twelve months, with rice for eighteen, and were provided with 'divers commodities and minerals'—an extraordinary selection indeed of everything in which the company traded, for which it was hoped to find a profitable market. In command was Tasman, with Visscher sailing also in the *Heemskerck* as 'pilot major' and chief adviser; with the additional advice, as was the Dutch custom, of a council of the ships' officers.

Tasman's instructions were issued on 13 August. The 'remaining unknown part of the terrestrial globe', which he was to find, was supposed to exist somewhere in the same latitude as the gold- and silver-bearing provinces of Chile and Peru. He was to sail first to Mauritius, as Visscher's *Memoir* had suggested, and thence southward till he came to the unknown South-land; if he had not met with it within 52 or 54 degrees of latitude, he was to sail eastward as far as the longitude of the eastern extremity of New Guinea or of the 'Salomon Islands', coasting along any land he might meet. But if after mature deliberation he deemed it more expedient, he might sail east from his southernmost point only to the longitude of the islands of St Francis and St Peter, then due north to touch at them, and so eastward again to find how far the land extended, whether it joined New Guinea with an unbroken coastline or whether channels and passages intervened. If there was a passage north he might sail through it and then turn west to explore the South-land coast as far as the northernmost point of Eendrachts-land. This passage might exist, but the governor-general and his council doubted it; they therefore thought the first plan would be the more fruitful. On Tasman's eastern course, there-fore, he might even go eight hundred miles beyond the longitude of the Solomons, to investigate the possibility of a shorter route to Chile—a route which might be of great advantage to the company; for a trade with the Chileans would enable it to snatch rich booty from 'the Castilian', who would never dream of Dutch ships coming that way. If this quest was successful a trial cargo would be sent.

From Tasman's most eastern point he was, if possible, to sail with the south-east trade wind for the Solomons and explore them; for this purpose he was given a Spanish description of the islands and a vocabulary of words used by the natives of those seas. Then he was to make for the eastern end of New Guinea, and follow Le Maire's track along its north coast, trying to find some passage through it leading south to Cape Keerweer; and if he reached this to sail west with the south-east trade wind to the northern end of Eendrachtsland, ascertaining on the way whether any passages led to the South Sea. Eendrachtsland he should reach between May and July 1643, whence he was to return without further delay to Java.

Such was the course to be followed, such the discoveries

envisaged. As they went the explorers were to gather all manner of information. Good behaviour, combined with caution, was to be maintained towards the peoples discovered, and though any native who wished voluntarily to visit civilization might be brought back, none was to be carried off by force. It was held unlikely that Tasman would meet with civilized men: if he did so he was to enlarge on the advantages of trade— especially, said these most realistic instructions, 'trying to find out what commodities their country yields, likewise enquiring after gold and silver whether the latter are by them held in high esteem; making them believe that you are by no means eager for precious metals, so as to leave them ignorant of the value of the same; and if they shall offer you gold or silver in exchange for your articles, you will pretend to hold the same in slight regard, showing them copper, pewter, or lead and giving them an impression as if the minerals last mentioned were by us set greater value on'. From an expedition so greatly planned, and from enquiries thus discreetly pursued, it might be confidently expected, in the words of governor-general and council, that the expense and trouble that must be bestowed on the eventual discovery of so large a portion of the world would be rewarded with certain fruits of material profit and immortal fame.

There is a fuller account of this voyage of Tasman's than of any other of the time. It is contained in a copy of his own 'daily register', illustrated with drawings both careful and interesting; a register which begins with the pious invocation of the Divine blessing. It was on 14 August that the ships sailed, and by 5 September, after a passage unusually short and without accident, they were anchored at Mauritius. This good start, however, was of little use, because it was necessary to spend more than a month at the island carrying out repairs. The upper work of the *Zeehaen* was half rotten, and a great part had to be renewed; to the Dutch commander at Mauritius the equipment of the ships for such a voyage seemed hopelessly unsatisfactory —he was compelled to provide them with firewood, canvas, cordage and various other necessaries—but by 8 October they were able to set out on their real task. On the 27th seaweed was seen, and the ships' council, being convened, decided to put a man at the mast-head, and to offer a reward of three pieces of eight and a can of arrack for the first sight of land, shoals or sunken rocks. Next day they met with more seaweed and fragments of trees, but the weather was so dark and foggy, in spite of its being early summer, that it was 'hardly possible to survey known shores, let alone to discover unknown land'. At night muskets and guns were fired to keep the ships in touch. The plan was to sail south as far as latitude 52° or 54°; by 6 November they were already in 49° 4', in a storm from the west, with hail and snow and a high sea, and the men began to suffer badly from the severe cold. Tasman could do nothing but run before the wind under reduced sail. Next day Visscher submitted some formal notes of advice; it was impossible to sail south as far as had been intended, and he thought it best to return to latitude 44°, sailing east along that parallel to longitude 150°, then north to 40°, and then east again to longitude 220°;[1] after which they might sail north, so as to get the trade wind from the east of the Solomons and New Guinea. As there was more hail and snow, Tasman decided with the council of officers of the *Heemskerck* to accept this advice, anyhow so far as it would bring him to longitude 150°. This decision was communicated to the *Zeehaen* by enclosing the necessary papers in a wooden canister-shot case, well waxed and wrapped up in tarred canvas, and sent adrift from the stern of the ship. The *Zeehaen* hoisted a flag to show its agreement. The sea was still running high from the south-west, an argument at least that no continent lay in that direction. On 17 November it was calculated that the longitude of the islands of St Francis and St Peter had been passed, but there was apparently no thought of following the coast of the South-land farther east from Pieter Nuyts Land. A week later, in good weather, land was sighted, very high, bearing east by

[1] This is the contemporary Dutch reckoning of the longitude: 220° is 160° west of Greenwich.

north, about forty miles away. This was Anthony van Diemen's Land, so christened by Tasman after his 'illustrious master'. There was a calm on 25 November, and a council was held with the *Zeehaen*'s officers. On succeeding days the weather was so variable that the ships could do no more than beat off and on, making south as they did so. So far off-shore that they could barely see the land, they rounded its southernmost point and sailed north up its east coast, at first into the great bay now called Storm Bay,[1] whence they were driven by a gale round Cape Pillar; and at last, on the evening of 1 December, found good anchorage off a small island—Green Island.

Tasman wished both to examine the country and to obtain refreshment; next day, therefore, Visscher was sent off with the pinnace and ten men to a bay on the north-west—the modern Blackman's Bay. He brought back various vegetables, and reported a land high but level, covered with excellent timber and vegetation, 'not cultivated, but growing by the will of God'; and a water-course in a barren valley, so shallow, however, that the water had to be dipped out with a bowl. Certain human sounds had been heard, and something like a small gong, but no one had been seen—though the Dutch had noticed two great trees, with notches up the trunks five feet apart; from which it seemed that a race of giants must climb after birds' nests in this way, or else the natives had some device to aid them. They saw footprints something like a tiger's, mussels but no fish, many gulls, ducks and geese, and trees with a hole burnt into their trunks at the foot to form a fireplace. 'So there can be no doubt there must be men here of extraordinary stature', said Tasman, who did not land himself, by a process of reasoning that remains obscure. On the following day a landing was made on the other side of the bay, where the only water found was brackish. In the afternoon, when it was intended to

---

[1] Tasman first tried to find anchorage in a smaller bay on the west side of the present Storm Bay, but he was driven from it by a strong gale. This smaller bay he called Storm Bay; Furneaux, identifying Tasman's discoveries wrongly in 1773, called it Adventure Bay, and the greater opening received Tasman's name.

land again and to raise a post as a sign of possession, surf put the boats into some danger; so the carpenter was ordered to swim ashore, and planted the post with a flag on it, 'as a memorial to those who shall come after us, and for the natives of this country who did not show themselves'—though it was suspected that some of them were at no great distance and closely watching the proceedings. Next day, 4 December, Tasman left this bay to look for a better watering place farther up the coast.

This northern course was sailed for a day only; for the coast fell off to the north-west, and the wind being almost dead ahead prevented progress in that direction. The ships' council was therefore convened, and it was decided to resume the eastward course as far as the longitude of the 'Salamonis islands'. For five days they had variable weather, calm or squally, with generally favourable winds, and good weather for the two days following; then on 13 December, towards noon, they saw high land, bearing south-east and about sixty miles away. Tasman turned straight for this land, resolving to take advantage of the weather and touch on it as quickly as possible, for there was a great sea running and a heavy swell. Here it was indeed that the Pacific rollers beat on the western shores of the southern island of New Zealand—shores as inhospitable as most to ships and seamen— which rise through forest-clad heights to the snowy summits of the Southern Alps. Thick clouds hid those summits from Tasman's vision, although next day he was near enough to the shore to see the surf breaking; there seemed no possibility of an immediate landing, and he shaped his course, still in good weather, northwards up the coast. The country looked very desolate, without sight or sign of human beings. Then, on the morning of 17 December, having worked round a point where the land fell off abruptly (the point later named by Cook and still known as Cape Farewell), he saw smoke rising in several places. The coast here was low-lying and covered with dunes, and on the 18th Tasman decided if possible to find a good harbour and get ashore.

In the afternoon of that day the pinnace and the cockboat

went out to reconnoitre, and at sunset the ships anchored. An hour later lights were seen on shore and two canoes approached. The people in them called out with rough, hollow voices, and blew what sounded like a Moorish trumpet; the Dutch shouted their answers, and musical sailors were ordered to play tunes on European instruments. This double concert continued till the dark fell, when the natives paddled off, the Dutch keeping a good watch, with weapons ready. Next morning a canoe came within a stone's throw of the ships, and their people called out again, unfortunately in words unknown to the vocabularies of New Guinea and the Solomons. The men in the canoe, those seventeenth-century Maoris, were of ordinary height, strong-boned, their colour between brown and yellow; their black hair was tied in a tuft at the top of their heads, surmounted by a large thick white feather. They were naked from shoulder to waist, round which they wore woven mats and some material which looked like cotton. Their canoe was a double one, fairly fast, with long, narrow, pointed paddles. Despite all gestures of invitation and the display of white linen and knives, they would not set foot on shipboard; but their intentions appeared friendly, and when the officers of the *Zeehaen* came to a council on board the *Heemskerck* it was resolved to anchor as close inshore as possible. Seven more canoes paddled out towards the ships, and two drawing closer, the skipper of the *Zeehaen* sent his quarter-master and six men in the cockboat to warn his second mate against allowing too many natives on board. Then came tragedy. The cockboat had delivered the message, and was returning: when it was half-way the natives in a large canoe began to paddle furiously, and rammed it; the quartermaster was thrust overboard with a long blunt pike, and the others attacked with short clubs so fiercely that three were killed and another mortally wounded. The quartermaster and two sailors swam to the *Heemskerck* and were picked up; the natives took one dead body into their canoe, threw another into the sea, and set the cockboat adrift. The Dutch fired, hitting nothing, as the canoes made for the shore out of reach of shot; the cockboat was picked up with its dead man and its dying one; and since friendly relations seemed impossible, Tasman gave up the hope of obtaining water or refreshments there and weighed anchor.

The historian must regret this unfortunate encounter; for he would like to know more about those seventeenth-century Maori people. In the following century the tribe concerned was harried by its enemies out of existence, and it left no tradition of consequence or detail. Tasman records no act of provocation. We can only guess that in that corner of Polynesia strangers were enemies; and summer was the season of war parties. The Dutch were singularly unsuccessful even in exacting vengeance. When under sail they counted twenty-two canoes near the shore, of which eleven, crowded with people, were making for the ships; and although Tasman reserved his fire till the foremost were within range of his guns, the few shots he did fire harmed none, while the *Zeehaen* hit only one man. They had perforce to content themselves with the sound of canister-shot striking on the bows of the canoes, which fled, paddling with great speed and hoisting sails. The record is at least a variation on the tale of indiscriminate slaughter which stains so much of Pacific exploration. Tasman convened his council, and it was resolved to coast along to the east in search of some place of refreshment. He branded the place of his anchorage Murderers' Bay; but what was the land itself to be called? 'In honour of Their High Mightinesses the States-General', wrote Tasman, 'we gave to this land the name of *Staten Landt*, since we deemed it quite possible that this land is part of the great Staten Landt, though this is not certain. This land seems to be a very fine country, and we trust that this is the mainland coast of the unknown South-land.' The course they had sailed from Van Diemen's Land was named Abel Tasman's Passage, 'because he has been the first to navigate it.'

Next day, 20 December, land lay on all sides. Tasman had fully expected a passage here into the South Sea, and so to Chile; now, to his grievous disappointment, it seemed to prove quite otherwise, and he concluded provisionally—though still in some doubt—that he was in a great bay. The wind was westerly and he attempted to tack out, but the sea ran so strongly into the bay that he could make little headway. Then for four days there was stormy weather from the north-west, and most of this time the ships rode on their anchors. On the 24th another council was held—Tasman had renewed hopes of a passage eastwards; the tide was running from the south-east, and he was of opinion that as soon as wind and weather permitted the point should be investigated; fresh water also might be obtained. The Dutch were, in fact, held among the treacherous winds and tides of Cook Strait. When the weather cleared the wind was in the east, and it was decided to abandon the search. Yet, though the chart in one copy of Tasman's journal here shows a bay, 'Zeehaen Bight', that in a second leaves an opening; only actual discovery could elucidate the problem. The voyage continued in another direction. On Christmas Day, lying at anchor, it was possible to refit the tops and yards, and next day to sail to the west, with the intention of making round the land northwards. But all that night and the following day they were forced to lie-to. It was not till the 28th that real progress could be made; and at noon on that day the Dutch saw the peak of Mount Karioi, which they at first took for an island. Fog had hidden the beautiful cone of Egmont. Sailing steadily northwards, and charting the general outline of the coast, they found themselves on 4 January 1643 near a cape with an island to the north-west. The land at this cape—Cape Maria van Diemen, so named after the governor-general's wife—fell away to the east, and there was a heavy sea running from that direction. Could there be a passage to the South Sea here? A council resolved to touch at the island in search of the vegetables and water so much needed—it was called Three Kings island, because they anchored on Twelfth Night Eve. The following day Visscher and the supercargo of the *Zeehaen* took the boats to look for water. They entered a small bay, cautious of sudden assault, and saw plenty of good fresh water falling down from a steep mountain; here the surf threatened too dangerous a landing. Once again the Dutch passion for giants was gratified —they saw also, on the highest hills, thirty or thirty-five men of great stature, armed with sticks or clubs, who took enormous strides, calling out loudly with rough voices. There was a little cultivated land near the fresh water; on the beach were only two canoes, one of which was broken—obviously not a promising place. Another attempt to water was made on 6 January, but this time a strong current against the wind, as well as the surf, prevented success. There was seen only another tall man: and so a council resolved to run east again to longitude 220°, north to latitude 17°, and then west to Le Maire's Cocos and Hoorn Islands, to refresh there.

The wind, however, forced them north-east, and on the afternoon of 19 January they saw land again, in latitude 22° 35′. On the chart of the South Sea which Tasman had were marked here, by chance we must think, four islands, to which he believed he had come. To the first, which he could not approach because of the wind, he gave the name of Hooge Pylstaert or 'High Tropic-bird' island, after the narrow-tailed tropic-birds which flew about it; next day he was near the two which he called Amsterdam and Middelburg. This group was Tonga, or the Friendly Islands, as Cook afterwards named them; Pylstaert was the small though high Ata; Amsterdam was the low flat Tongatapu; Middelburg was Eua. They were islands friendly to Tasman also; it was at Tongatapu that he was at last able to refresh, and that abundantly. At first three men came off in a narrow canoe; one of whom dived for a piece of linen that was thrown them, and 'put it several times atop of his head, in sign of gratitude'. They were presented also with nails, a Chinese looking-glass and some beads, and gave the Dutch a mother-of-pearl fish-hook. Later on other canoes came with coconuts to exchange for old nails; and though a pistol and a pair of slippers were stolen, they were taken back with no sign of dissatisfaction. These cordial relations were improved when the chief sent off a large hog, yams and coconuts, while provisions of the same kind were obtained constantly by barter.

To gratify the chief, though much to his terror, a gun was fired; and when other people came off to the ships their leader was dressed in a shirt and a pair of drawers, in which he thought himself a very gallant object. They were greatly astonished at the playing of trumpet and violin and flute; Tasman adds, as a thing remarkable, that they had no knowledge of tobacco. No one wore arms, so that 'it was all peace and amity here'. On 23 January the Dutch were entertained ceremonially by the 'king', and besides hogs and fowls and fruit, were able to get some good water. It was not enough; so when the *Heemskerck*'s anchor dragged and she drifted to leeward, it was resolved to go on and touch at any other islands met with. On the 25th anchor was cast at Nomuka, called by Tasman Rotterdam, a little to the north, where, though the natives were exceedingly thievish and stole whatever they could lay hands on, the Dutch remained till 1 February. Water, as well as fruit, was plentiful, and the casks could be filled at leisure. By this time discipline was bad, and a council at the end of January imposed penalties on sailors who neglected their watch or committed other misdemeanours. There was not quite the natural virtue on board that there was on shore—the natives, says Tasman (whose observations are sometimes more interesting than accurate) had neither king nor government, yet they were aware of evil; for when complaint was made of the theft of a pike all took part in the punishment of the evildoer, who was battered with a coconut till it broke. Furthermore, they never killed flies, and there was much indignation at the breaking of this rule by the harassed chief mate.

By 1 February nearly all the water-casks were full, and as the ships were on a lee shore it was decided to sail. Tasman was here fairly certain of being far enough east not to miss Le Maire's islands, and sailed a course roughtly north or northwest. On the 6th, in latitude $17\frac{1}{2}°$, the ships found themselves entangled in a multitude of islands—eighteen or twenty were counted that day. They were among these islands, in the Fiji group, with their shoals and breakers for three days, and Tasman was both puzzled and anxious—the weather was bad, and so dark that the Dutch could hardly see a distance of two or three ship's lengths. At one moment they escaped disaster simply by charging full tilt over a reef—which luckily had enough water on it.[1] Although Tasman thought he must be in Le Maire's track, the chart recorded no such islands. Islands there were marked in this latitude, but eight hundred miles farther west. It was possible that the calculations of the longitude were thus much in error, for the voyage had been long and stormy, and there had been a good deal of guesswork; Tasman therefore called the council of officers, from whom he got signed opinions of the best course to pursue. He was faced, indeed, with the problem that had confronted Le Maire and Schouten in the same vicinity in 1616—was it more advisable to sail west and risk running on a lee shore, the south-eastern side of New Guinea or some land south of New Guinea, perhaps unknown islands or shoals, or to play for safety and sail north? Tasman himself, certain only of the uncertainty of their position, and 'seeing that the weather we now have is such that one might easily miss a known coast, let alone an unknown one', it being the bad season when the south-east trade wind and the north monsoon met, was in favour of running due north as far as latitude 4° S and then due west to familiar New Guinea. Visscher and the other officers agreed; and it was finally resolved to sail north to 4° or 5°.

Throughout February the weather did not improve; on the 26th Tasman noted that for three weeks past they had not had a dry day, while on some days the ships made but little progress. So February passed into March, when for twelve days they were not able even to observe the latitude. But on the 14th of that month the wind turned to the south, and there was almost a calm; the ships dried and thenceforth the weather was generally good. Branches of trees floated by, and a week later,

---

[1] This was the Nanuku reef. The islands were the Ringgold islands, eastern outliers of Vanua Levu, the large northern 'half' of Fiji, and Vanua Levu itself.

on 22 March, land was seen straight ahead. It proved to be about thirty islets, surrounded by reefs; and it enabled Tasman to fix his position. These islets were Ontong Java, so named by Tasman himself[1]—Tasman indeed, like Le Maire, had taken a wide sweep right round the north of the Solomons and all the islands of Spanish discovery. He did not land at Ontong Java, sailing on to anchor two days later at Le Maire's island of Marcken. Here natives brought out coconuts, though they seemed to despise the nails offered in exchange. They were rough and savage beings, armed with bows and arrows, less polite and more naked than the friendly inhabitants of Amsterdam and Rotterdam, and with blacker skins than any of the peoples previously seen. On the 28th Le Maire's Green Islands were sighted; from which, while the ships drifted in a calm next day, natives still more savage came off, with bows and arrows and spears, stark naked, quite black, their hair curly and their faces daubed with lime. They brought one old coconut to exchange for the beads and nails of commerce, and Tasman passed by without landing. On 1 April he was off Cape Santa Maria, still thought to be a projection of the New Guinea coast—in fact, the north-east point of New Ireland—and was within calculable distance of his destination.

Tasman's instructions, it will be remembered, had directed him on coming to the north coast of New Guinea to search for a passage through that land to Cape Keerweer, whence he might explore the unknown coast between the cape and the extremity of Eendrachtsland. He found no passage, though in one place, the Bay of Good Hope, he sought in some expectation. Thus, using Schouten's chart and Le Maire's vocabulary, he passed along the whole north coast of New Guinea, trading on the way for hogs and fowls and fruit. In the last days of May he reached its western end, too late in the season to go then to

[1] Onthong Java in Tasman's journal. 'Onthong'/'Ontong' is, one presumes, the Malay *untung*, luck, fortune, destiny, fate; so that the name may be equivalent to 'Java luck', Tasman thereby congratulating himself on the improved circumstances.

Cape Keerweer and begin a new chapter of exploration; and making direct for Java through the Moluccas, on 14 June he brought his ships to Batavia, after a voyage of ten months. The last entry in his journal, like the first, is one of piety: 'Item, the 15th do. In the morning at daybreak, I went to Batavia in the pinnace. God be praised and thanked for this happy voyage. Amen.'

To the modern mind, contemplating the ocean Tasman sailed, and picturing the ships in which he sailed, he may seem not to have done badly; and the planning brain of Visscher approved his course. The company, however, manifested no excitement. The governor-general and council awarded the officers two months' pay, and the crews one, so it is to be presumed that these elevated persons attached some credit to the seamen. But they were men of business—were elevated indeed precisely because of their devotion to business—however tolerant of exploration, or even interested in it as a subsidiary pursuit; nor does van Diemen himself seem to have judged the matter with a disinterested intelligence. Certainly, they agreed, Tasman had made a 'remarkable voyage', but he 'had been to some extent remiss in investigating the situation, conformation and nature of the lands and peoples discovered, and left the main part of this task to be executed by some more inquisitive successor'. No treasures nor store of profitable commodities had been laid bare; whether the regions discovered might become of importance to the company's trade was uncertain; and though a passage into the South Sea, and so to Chile, seemed promising at Cape Maria van Diemen, it was unproven. Nor had Tasman given any information as to what lay between his Staten Land and Le Maire's, beyond the guess that they were the same. Nevertheless an attempt might be made to sail by this route to Chile and there form a trade connection—and also perhaps plunder the Spaniards on the coast of the South Sea. A voyage was actually planned for October 1643, though owing to renewed war with the Portuguese it was first postponed and then abandoned. It was resolved to appoint Tasman and Visscher to the command once more. With the passage of months their achievement had bulked larger in the minds of the council, which was now, it seems, convinced that a way into the South Sea did exist.

In the meantime there was another voyage which they could undertake, unimpeded by war—they might attempt to solve those problems of the South-land which still remained; and on this voyage they were sent in February 1644, with the two yachts *Limmen* and *Zeemeuw*, and the galiot *Bracq*. First, there was the question, not yet finally decided by the Dutch, of the possible strait between New Guinea and the South-land, where previous explorers had reported only a treacherous bay. Tasman, anchoring south of this bay, was to send the galiot into it for two or three days, to try whether it did not after all lead to a passage into the South Sea—and so to South America, its trade and its booty. This question settled, he was to sail down the west coast of 'New Guinea' (namely the Cape York peninsula) to the farthest known point, 17°, and then to follow the coast in whatever direction it trended, to see if it was divided from the known South-land—that is, he was to answer another question which had been troubling the Dutch for years. If there was a division, 'a fact which might easily be ascertained from the heavy and slow swell of the seas', he was to run down it south to Van Diemen's Land, and to ascertain whether this was an island, or united either to 'New Guinea' or Pieter Nuyts Land. Then he was to visit St Francis and St Peter, sail back up the channel north, and along the still unknown part of the northern coast to De Witsland and the Willems River, where Eendrachtsland ended; after which, say these instructions confidently, 'the whole of the known South-land would have been circumnavigated, and found to be the largest island in the world'. If, on the other hand, as seemed probable, there was no passage south from the Gulf of Carpentaria, he was to sail along westward, closely examining the coast, and then if possible south as far as Houtman's Abrolhos. Here he was to try to fish up the sunken chest of dollars from the *Batavia*, to look for the two men marooned by Pelsaert, and in about 26° or 28° latitude seek out a convenient place for refreshing ships bound to the East Indies. If it were not possible to sail south, Tasman was to run east again to explore Arnhem's Land and Van Diemen's Land—that in the north—to see if they were, in fact, the same, and then to discover what other islands were situated between Timor and the South-land.

There was thus, as with Tasman's first voyage, no lack of work projected for an enterprising captain to do. A detailed account of what he and Visscher actually did has not survived. A chart embodying the track, and a letter from the governor-general and council to Amsterdam, supply an outline of the voyage. The ships had sailed in February according to plan. There was no strait south of New Guinea. Neither was there any channel leading south between 'New Guinea' and Een-drachtsland: there was 'a large spacious Bay or Gulf', from which gulf Tasman had sailed westward in shallow water along the coast to Willems River, whence, finding it too late to continue south, he had in August returned to Batavia. His masters were no more satisfied with this second voyage than they had been with the first. Its results were highly important certainly; but Tasman had found nothing that could be turned to profit; he had come across only 'naked beach-roving wretches, destitute even of rice . . . miserably poor, and in many places of a very bad disposition'. What the country produced no one knew, since the explorers had done nothing but sail along the coast; but 'he who wants to find out what the land yields, must walk over it in every direction; the voyagers pretend this to have been out of their power, which may to some extent be true'. Nevertheless Tasman had, in his two voyages, sailed right round the South-land, which it was thought must contain 8000 miles of coast; and in a country of this vastness it could hardly be supposed that no profit of any kind should be obtainable. The governor-general and council intended to have everything more closely investigated, and by 'more

vigilant and courageous persons than had hitherto been employed on this service: for the exploration of unknown regions
can by no means be entrusted to the first comer'.

Tasman, then, had scarcely given satisfaction: he had not
walked over the South-land in every direction, nor extracted
the profits of a rich trade from the destitute and naked aborigines. He had, in fact, committed the cardinal sin of doing what
was possible and no more. Yet, faced with these shortcomings,
van Diemen and his council revived their visions. They could,
it seems, blow hot as well as cold. The visions grew in magni-
tude even; at the end of 1644 they held within their ambit the
further discovery of Tartary, the northern parts of America,
'the South-lands recently discovered in the East', and the
Solomon Islands. Mines were necessary to the company's pros-
perity—gold and silver mines would therefore be found; there
was always the prospect, pleasing to Dutchman and God alike,
of looting the Spaniard; and all these things would be for 'the
solace of the shareholders'. These far-reaching schemes, these
siren notes, stirred no response in the breasts of managers in
Amsterdam. They had had their moments of enthusiasm for
discovery, but their hands felt no itch to grasp the world. They
had ignored the news of the voyage of 1642. They were
business-men; and their view of what was for the solace of the
shareholders exhibited some difference from van Diemen's.
Further discoveries would cost money, and so far there had
been no return on expenditure; there were nations in Europe
more populous than they, who might seize the fruits of Dutch
exploration—if those fruits were more exciting than the
parched solitudes of the South-land already investigated, or
the savages, coconuts and plantains of Tasman's Staten Land
and the islands; and the company already had knowledge of
more countries than it could trade with. Nor did they anticipate
success from a search for mines. 'These plans of Your Worships
somewhat aim beyond our mark', they wrote to Batavia. 'The
gold and silver mines that will best serve the Company's turn,
have already been found, which we deem to be our trade over

the whole of India, and especially in Taijouan[1] and Japan, if only God be graciously pleased to continue the same to us.'

Van Diemen, the prime mover and restless brain behind these projects, in whom was all the rare brilliance of the Dutch ideal, died in April 1645, before he knew of this decision. The second voyage to Tasman's Staten Land had never sailed, and the Dutch came to that mountainous shore not again. Its identity, also, had become even more doubtful; for in 1643 Hendrik Brouwer, on a voyage round the south of Tierra del Fuego, had found that Le Maire's Staten Land was but an island nine or ten leagues long, obviously not the great southern continent, either of Marco Polo or of Quiros; pearls and elephants there were none. Whatever Tasman's land was, therefore, it was not Staten Land; and some time within the decade it had received the name—perhaps as a counter to New Holland—of Nova Zeelandia or Nieuw Zeeland, a name that was to be more permanent. Tasman himself did not sail on another long voyage. His life became again the miscellaneous one of a skipper of the East India Company on general service—his salary was raised, he plotted against Spanish ships at the Ladrones, and planned improved courses for Dutch ships on the outward passage to the Indies and to Manila; he became a member of the court of justice at Batavia; forestalled the English in the buying of pepper in Sumatra; harassed the Spaniards in the Philippines, the Moluccas and Malaya. He fell into disgrace for a piece of drunken brutality against two of his own sailors, and was deprived of his office, pay and membership of the Batavia church vestry. But he was a useful man, if intemperate, and was given further work under the company —indeed, within two years he regarded himself as so far reestablished in public estimation as to ask for higher rank and an increased salary. Restored in 1651 to a status of honour and respectability, his last years are not fully chronicled; he evidently left the company's service and experimented in private trade with a ship of his own, became one of the largest land-

[1] Taiwan or Formosa.

holders in Batavia, and died there in 1659, leaving a sum of money to the poor of Luytegast, the village of his birth.

He left behind him also a reputation for seamanship to which history, in spite of the reluctance of his masters' praise, has done full justice. Tasman was not a genius, nor even a man of extraordinary mind; none the less as a sailor and a discoverer he had more than ordinary capacity, and his service to the company was one of more than ordinary versatility. He attacked no new problems of geography, nor solved in a masterly fashion many of the old ones; but he did, it may be argued, what few other men of his time could have done. Urged not so much by his own original impulse as by the driving force of van Diemen, his great voyage taking the course it did largely because of the systematic planning of Visscher, yet he was 'earnestly inclined' to the work, and his was the executive hand. His was the ultimate responsibility, and that being so, he was, says Burney, the historian of Pacific exploration, both a great and a fortunate discoverer. He found no southern continent, but even his negative results were valuable to geography; his exploration of an unknown sea in a latitude higher than had before been attained restricted the limits of the supposed continent more than the work of any other navigator between Magellan and Cook. And his results furnished the basis for the effort of all later discoverers within his sphere—of Dampier on the north coasts of Australia and New Guinea, of Cook in the whole western Pacific. His discoveries, except New Zealand, were portrayed in the map of the two hemispheres inlaid on the floor of the new Town Hall at Amsterdam in 1655, they were incorporated as common geographical knowledge in maps drawn thereafter, and before the end of the century an abstract of his journal of 1642-3 had been published to the world. If the intermittent light which shines on his character is but a dubious one, it may at least be held that in his treatment of native peoples he displayed a moderation rare in any age. His name is commemorated in the Tasman Sea, that *Abel Tasmans passagie* over which he sailed to New Zealand, and in that Van Diemen's Land of his discovery which midway through the nineteenth century became Tasmania.

Anthony van Diemen died; Tasman sailed no more; the vision of a Dutch Pacific faded. The hard outline of a monopoly trade was the familiar and comforting form which filled the eyes of the Directors of the East India Company; that was something concrete, it had tangible results, nutritious to the soul of commerce. 'It were to be wished', they wrote in 1645, in answer to news of some promising lands, 'that the said land continued still unknown and never explored, so as not to tell foreigners the way to the Company's overthrow.' Nor is it for a later age to scorn them; like Quiros's masters in their day, they knew the limits of their assimilation. It may be accounted to the Dutch for geographical virtue that they did not, even in the sacred cause of monopoly, conceal their discoveries from the world. But the company in that century pursued no further geographical enquiry. Their ships continued to be wrecked at intervals on the coast of Eendrachtsland, and vessels were sometimes sent from Batavia to the rescue, and to chart a fresh portion of that deadly shore. Of the crew of the *Vergulde Draeck*, for example, which in 1656 struck a reef between latitudes 30° and 31°, only seven reached Batavia in the small boat which brought the news; 118 perished in the waters, and of those others who reached the shore not one was ever found, nor anything of the ship and its cargo except wreckage. In 1696 Willem de Vlamingh searched in vain for traces of another lost vessel, though he examined more closely than any of his predecessors the whole coast from the Swan River (rowing up to the site of the present Perth and disturbing the black swans of the neighbourhood) to the North-West Cape. He it was who found Dirck Hartog's pewter dish, nailed to its rotten post, where it had stood on that remote island for eighty years while the world went its course, and left his own inscription for the French a hundred years later. In the bay behind the island the

Dutch caught great sharks and enormous turtles, beyond which limited booty the whole of the long coast provided no hint of a refreshing place for ships or a country grateful to men—only a shore desolate, barren, and forbidding. For water, north of the Swan River, they dug in the sand and found an evil brackish fluid, injurious to whomsoever drank it.

Nine years later, in 1705, it was again proposed to explore more closely the coast of the northern Van Diemen's Land—which some believed to consist entirely of islands—and the whole of the Gulf of Carpentaria. It was still hoped, in spite of Tasman's work, that a passage might lead thence to the South Sea. The ship sent evidently did not examine the Gulf of Carpentaria. She sailed forty miles into Van Diemen's Gulf, and her company concluded that that inlet ran right through the country to its south side. The South-land, they thought, not at all improbably consisted in a great measure of islands; for islands there were in plenty on the south side, and the character of the people, rude, barbarous and malicious, was much more that of islanders than of the inhabitants of a continent—a psychological generalization that was perhaps too hasty.

With that generalization, the effort of the Dutch East India Company ceases. It was an effort of no inconsiderable result, and its chief voyages were cardinal to the elucidation of the hemisphere. On their first voyage to the East, in 1595, the Dutch circumnavigated Java. They knew, without detail and without confidence, the Moluccas, and whatever other island had blown its spices and its gold into the eager mind of Linschoten, among the Portuguese at Goa. By the end of the following century they knew, with something like geographical precision, most of the East Indies, a good half of the coast of New Guinea, and nearly three sides of the enormous island that had become known as New Holland. They had struck into the Pacific through a new strait at its south-east corner; on the west they had begun the advance towards the Antarctic, and had charted part of the coastline of two new countries. The South-land of their knowledge was not the Beach of the romancers; and over a great part of the hemisphere which that astonishing continent might occupy they found nothing but the long roll of the southern ocean. Nor, eager as they were for the enlargement of commerce and the depredation of 'the Castilian', were they entirely self-devoted in their voyagings. Monopolists they were. We have seen in them also the ambition to know, the technical obligation to explore 'the best way of using the sea and of finding out the winds that would enable ships to navigate it all the year round'. That sea, those winds the Dutch never mastered entirely, and the fatal islands which Houtman first descried, which so many captains after him failed to descry till too late, remained the symbol and the instrument of their defeat. The Abrolhos were visited in 1840 by Englishmen. They found the last bleached timbers of a ship that still rotted in the sand, and a coin or two from some drowned seaman's pocket. They found, too, other relics of a more various nature; bottles shaped like Dutch cheeses, arranged in orderly rows on the ground; some large brass buckles, once gilt; a number of small clay pipes; and a brass gun with vermilion paint still on the muzzle. To those glass bottles, so neatly arranged, and those clay pipes, the magnificence and the monopoly of the seventeen Masters of the United East India Company had come.

# CHAPTER VIII

# THE GROUNDWORK OF THE EIGHTEENTH CENTURY

THE seventeenth century, in the development of the modern world, has a significance not negligible, nor even single. It was an age of growing freedom of the mind, it was notable for the emergence of the idea of political liberty, it saw the decay of Spain and Portugal and the birth of newer and more strenuous empires; it was also the witness of an influence still more potential—the first great expansion of modern scientific thought. The age of Dutch conquest in the East was the age of the maturity of Bacon and of Kepler; Galileo died the year that Tasman discovered New Zealand, and in that year also was born Newton, who was to illuminate more than any other man the mind of the succeeding century. It was in 1660 that the Royal Society first met in England and discussed the promotion of 'Physico-Mathematicall Experimentall Learning', and mathematics, physics and astronomy were to remake the foundations of the world. Mathematics and astronomy, moreover, form the fundamental structure of the science of navigation; and to that scientific labour of the seventeenth century is due the success of the eighteenth in geographical discovery. But a new navigation, it is obvious, could not spring to life with the earliest thought of Newton, and so the brilliant achievement of Newton's century was not reflected with a similar lustre in the voyages of the Dutch. It was not till the following age that the theoretical became the practical, that intellectual discovery became invention, that first principles were turned to applied science. Yet even before the change in outlook brought by the chronometer, before newer modifications in naval architecture and a new accuracy in geographical statement, one man at least travelled and observed and wrote with the disinterested passion of the scientist. This man was William Dampier.

Dampier was a natural genius: he had the scientific mind and observed with an intentness as painstaking as it was unusual, he recorded his observations with precision and vividness, not because of training or an interest in the academic. No man was less a student of the abstract, none less devoted to hypothesis. Even in exploration his plans seemed to proceed not so much from an exhaustive study of the field of geography as from his own past experience and limitless curiosity. For Dampier was a rover, and his eminence in the story of the Pacific arises not from the weight of his achievement, though that was sufficient, but from his place as a precursor. With the equipment of the seventeenth century, he had the attitude of the eighteenth. His taste was not for marvels, but for the examination and adequate description of natural phenomena, whether plants, beasts, tides, winds or the ways of strange tribes and peoples. For a man of his time, he had remarkably little interest in gold and spices, and not much in his own enrichment. He was untroubled by ambition in any usual sense; his satisfaction, to use his own words, lay in 'the Discovery . . . of the various and wonderful Works of God in different Parts of the World'. He had little talent for command, nor was his experience such as to cultivate it. From his portrait his face gazes still, set round with its Caroline hair, hardly the face of a man of action, brooding, a little heavy, saturnine yet not without humour, certainly full of experience; certainly not the face of a distinguished buccaneer.

For buccaneering, technically considered, was Dampier's profession for a good part of his life. It was in his day a profession comparatively respectable; but the distinction with which he was popularly credited in its practice was not his by right. Like his other activities, it was simply a department of travel—it was a convenient way of seeing the world; and regarding it from this point of view, he took no trouble to rise to eminence. Dampier was born in a Somersetshire village in 1651 and had the schooling proper for a youth destined for trade. When his parents died his guardians were so far agreeable to his own inclinations as to allow him to go to sea. He sailed to Newfoundland, to the Dutch East Indies; he enlisted in the navy during the Dutch wars; he spent six months on a Jamaican plantation and six months in a coastal vessel of that island. It was during the passage to Jamaica in 1674 that he began to keep the journal on which is based his most secure fame; and by the end of his coastal service he was already well versed in the technique of navigation, of pilotage and hydrography. Then he shipped to the Bay of Campeachy, west of Yucatan, and in 1676 became a logwood-cutter. The logwood-cutters were habitually buccaneers, and after a visit to England, Dampier returned to the West Indies and the inefficient career which took him for the first time into the Pacific—for in 1681 he visited Juan Fernandez. He cruised in the Caribbean Sea, he lived in Virginia, he made a piratical voyage to the coast of Africa and sailed round the Horn into the South Sea again. There, on the Mexican coast, he joined the *Cygnet*, a vessel whose captain had been forced into piracy by his crew; and with this unhappy man reached Mindanao in the Philippines.

Here Dampier first seems to have discussed in his journal the prospects of discovery. The islanders of Mindanao were hostile to the Spaniards and thought the buccaneers had been sent by the English East India Company to form a factory. Dampier's mind was fired by the idea—why indeed should they not build a fort and settle down at once? The Dutch were in the East Indies, and therefore trading voyages would have to be made by way of Cape Horn; but on those voyages it would be possible to stretch over to the unknown east coast of Nova Hollandia and make some profitable discovery, or even touch on the continent of *Terra Australis incognita*. A certain buccaneer, Captain Davis, had told Dampier of a land he had sighted about 500 leagues (so runs the printed record) from Chile in latitude 27°—might not this be that identical coast? But the crew of the

*Cygnet* had little taste for settlement and trade; after a period of heavy roystering they sailed away, leaving their captain behind them. Dampier was on board, and so came to Tonkin and Cochin China, to Formosa and the Bashi Islands;[1] and then it was decided to go to Cape Comorin by way of the Spice Islands and south of Timor. Off Timor the buccaneers quite casually agreed to stand over to the coast of New Holland, 'to see what that country would afford us'. On 4 January 1688 they saw land in 16° 50' and anchored in a bay full of islands— Cygnet Bay and Buccaneer's Archipelago. New Holland afforded them remarkably little, and yet they stayed till the beginning of March. The only water was obtained from wells, there was no food except turtle and manatee, and no trees which bore fruit or berries. As for the natives, they were 'the miserablest people in the world. The Hodmadods of Monomatapa, though a nasty people, yet for wealth are as gentlemen to these . . . setting aside their human shape, they differ but little from brutes.' They were ugly and black, with costume only of 'a piece of the rind of a tree, and a handful of grass or bough'; without houses or tools; alternately gorging on fish and starving from the lack of it. Ragged clothes which the buccaneers dressed them in they threw off again, they could not be prevailed upon to carry casks of water, and they admired nothing new that they saw. Dampier's opinion, in fact, coincided with that of his Dutch predecessors.

Thus the first Englishman visited mainland Australia. Dampier was growing exceedingly weary of his companions, and they can hardly have felt that the spirit of this singular student was altogether in tune with theirs; for they offered to maroon him on the New Holland coast. At long last, at the Nicobar Islands, he got ashore in peace; and with seven companions sailed thence in a small canoe, through a terrific hurricane, to Sumatra, 150 miles across the Indian Ocean. And then he went to Tonkin and Malacca and Madras and to Sumatra

---

[1] Now known as the Batan Islands: on the other side of the Bashi Channel, south of Formosa.

again; bought a half-share in the person of an unfortunate native, elaborately tattooed, to be shown for money in England; and finally began to sigh for his native land. In September 1691 he came again home with only the 'Painted Prince' and his sea-stained journal, and the Prince had to be sold at once for ready money. The journal was little enough, by ordinary standards, for a distinguished buccaneer to accumulate.

Yet this journal was Dampier's fortune, or at least determined his future. He decided to publish it, and in 1697, after some delay, the greater part did appear as a book dedicated to the Earl of Halifax, the President of the Royal Society. The *New Voyage Round the World* had a success immediate, lasting and merited. It was not merely an exciting and extraordinary account of adventure; it was also an exceptionally accurate, detailed and many-sided record of observation that can truly be called scientific, conveyed in a style short, close, workmanlike and vivid—a travel-book not second in interest and variety to the *Voyages* of Hakluyt's collection. It made Dampier known at once to the polite world and to the learned; members of the Royal Society patronized him and he dined with Pepys and Evelyn; he was consulted by the government over the concerns of Darien, and his reputation as a geographer, hydrographer and expert on the winds of the world was that of an accepted authority. Meanwhile a summary of Tasman's journal had been published in London, in 1694, and the English were becoming interested in *Terra Australis incognita*. Halifax introduced Dampier to Orford, the First Lord of the Admiralty, and he was asked to suggest some voyage which might be serviceable to the nation. England, that is, began to take an official interest in exploration. Dampier proposed that he should be sent on a voyage to 'the remoter part of the *East India Islands* and to the neighbouring coast of *Terra Australis*': there were several places that might be visited with advantage, but no larger tract undiscovered than this,[1] 'if that vast space surrounding the South

[1] He evidently here identifies *Terra Australis incognita* with New Holland.

Pole, and extending so far into the warmer climate be a continued land, as a great deal of it is known to be'. This land,
surely, must produce a great variety of valuable commodities.
None of its European neighbours could think themselves
injured by such a scheme, nor was there need to interfere with
them, as there was a clear ocean passage to New Holland either
east or west. For such a voyage, said Dampier, he would want
a practically unlimited commission—he could not expect to
return under three years, and it was impossible to foresee a
thousand accidents which might push him aside from the
original design and perhaps offer the chance of some more
valuable discovery. He would need two vessels well provided
in every way; 'and considering the Temptations our Seamen
have had of late to break loose and turn pirate when they come
into the nither parts of the World I should be glad that some
good encouragement might be proposed to those whoe should
goe in this Voyage upon their return'.

The Admiralty agreed with these suggestions, up to a point.
Dampier was commissioned to go on a voyage to New Holland,
but not with two ships well provided. He was given the
*Roebuck*, 290 tons, a vessel so rotten that the survival of her
company must be considered one of the principal miracles of
the age. She was provisioned for twenty months, and had an
inadequate crew; while her lieutenant, Fisher, despised Dampier
because he was not a regular naval officer and distrusted him
because he had been a buccaneer. The crew, besides being too
few, were dirty, incompetent and without stomach for the
voyage. Finally there were interminable delays in fitting the
ship out. Dampier's first plan had been to enter the Pacific by
way of Cape Horn and begin a coasting voyage round New
Holland on the unknown eastern side, going northwards to
New Guinea. Such an enterprise would have been of cardinal
importance. It entailed sailing in September, so as to pass the
Horn in summer; but although Orford had agreed to the
voyage as early as March 1698, it was not till 14 January 1699
that it could be begun. This later start would mean a Horn

passage in the depth of winter, and that Dampier would not contemplate; the route was changed to the Cape of Good Hope, and with it went most of the utility of his scheme.

To get refreshment and favourable winds he first stood over to the coast of Brazil, though he was scarcely out in the Atlantic before the ignorance and insubordination of his crew began to hinder him. They would not believe that he knew his work—than whom there was no abler navigator living— and as a commander his past was against him: the natural calms and changes of the wind, even, encountered in crossing the line 'made them, who were unacquainted with these Matters, almost heartless as to the Pursuit of the Voyage'. He was apprehensive of a mutiny, and was driven to sleep on the quarter-deck with small arms handy. 'I mention thus much of it in general for my own necessary Vindication', he says, 'in my taking such Measures sometimes for prosecuting the Voyage as the State of my Ships Crew, rather than my own Judgment and Experience, determin'd me to.' At Bahia, exasperated beyond endurance by the unasked but freely tendered advice of Lieutenant Fisher, who seemed the head and fount of mutiny, Dampier committed him to the mercies of a Portuguese prison, and left him—a modified form of marooning which earned grave censure from a subsequent court-martial. The *Roebuck* remained at Bahia a month, while Dampier got the crew into some sort of order, observed the country and collected plants; then, to give his men no further chance, he omitted to call at the Cape of Good Hope and sailed directly to the coast of Australia, sighting land somewhere near the Abrolhos on 31 July 1699. His instruments of navigation were quite inadequate, even for those days, while he was driven to write pages on the variation of the compass. For one thing he could be thankful—the *Roebuck* steered 'incomparably well', and a gale which blew up just after the Cape had been left behind did no damage. On the Australian coast two courses were possible—to sail either south or north. It was midwinter and he had no taste for cold; he doubted the behaviour of his crew in high latitudes after the long run from Brazil; more-over, the parts worth discovering for their gold and spices must lie, he thought, near the equator. It seemed logical therefore to turn his back on Cape Leeuwin and Pieter Nuyts Land and to coast north and east, and so later round by the east and south sides of New Holland in the summer-time.

Seeking a place where he could refresh, Dampier came to Dirck Hartog's Island and the great bay behind it. Four days' dig-ging brought no water, and he had to content himself with only the fragrant wild flowers and the many strange and beautiful shells. He called the bay Shark's Bay, because of the sharks his men caught—which they found very savoury 'boil'd and press'd, and then stew'd with Vinegar and Pepper'; kangaroo rats also were good meat, but the turtles were 'indifferent sweet'. Dampier had had a wide experience of food: he had 'eaten of Snakes, Crocodiles and Allegators, and many Creatures that look frightfully enough, and there are but few I should have been afraid to eat of, if prest by Hunger'; but one thing he found which he could not stomach—the New Holland 'guano', or iguana lizard. In the absence of water, however, there was nothing to do but sail on past North-West Cape, and on 21 August he came to the group of islands now called Dampier's Archipelago, one in particular of which he named Rosemary Island from the wild flowers he found growing on its dry and rocky surface. He was not satisfied indeed with Tasman's chart, which he was using, and had difficulty in believing that the coast was one and continuous, as Tasman had laid it down—though mainland there might be farther back. Was there a great river hereabouts? Tasman had marked several openings on his chart; but, said Dampier, 'by the great Tides I met with a while afterwards, more to the N. East, I had a strong Suspicion that here might be a kind of Archipelago of Islands, and a Passage possibly to the S. of N. Holland and N. Guinea into the great S. Sea Eastward'. Lack of water prevented him from inves-tigating this passage immediately; there was however the probability that coasting round New Guinea and the eastern side of Terra Australis he might save some time by sailing into its eastern end and out again at Rosemary Island. The existence of some passage, though not into the South Sea, was not disproven till Flinders's voyage of 1802; Dampier's guess was, as a matter of fact, a likely one. The search for water continued along the coast without success, except that digging deep down the men found a brackish runlet, fit only for boiling porridge, in Roebuck Bay, in latitude 18° 21'. Beyond this there seemed nothing but sand-hills, a poor scrub, numerous flies and a few dingoes, the native dogs, lean and hungry skeletons, until the day the voyagers had an unhappy encounter with a band of hostile natives. So far from obtaining from these blacks what he wanted, knowledge of the whereabouts of water, Dampier was forced to shoot one of them to save the life of a young sailor. Their appearance lacked charm, while the streaks of white paint which bedaubed their chief, surrounding his eyes, down his nose and on his breast and arms, 'added very much to his natural Deformity; for they all of them have the most un-pleasant Looks and the worst Features of any People that ever I saw, though I have seen great variety of Savages'. Such was Dampier's final verdict on the Australian aboriginal.

The *Roebuck* had now been five weeks on this hopeless coast, and as a last resort Dampier determined to go to the *Cygnet*'s old anchorage to dig for water there. But shoals, tides and wind defeated him, his men were growing scorbutic, and the only pleasure he had got from New Holland was that, he said, which results from the discovery even of the barrenest spot upon the globe.[1] He sailed to Timor, as a stopping-place on the way to New Guinea. Here he got excellent refreshment and entertain-ment from both Dutch and Portuguese and was able to resume his journey in good heart. On 1 January 1700 he sighted New Guinea, a green and pleasant prospect, sailed round the western end and then east, far out of sight of the coast, till he saw it again at what is known now as the island of New Hanover.

[1] Cf. Cook's sentiments on the north-east coast of Australia, pp. 313-14 below.

That is, Dampier, like all his predecessors, thought this was part of New Guinea, and in that faith coasted its eastern side, that of New Ireland and that of another island larger still, until he discovered and sailed through Dampier Strait, a passage which cut off from New Guinea the three islands he named as one, New Britain. The strait between New Britain and New Ireland he took to be a bay, calling it St George's Bay. His 'Nova Britannia' he praised exceedingly, with its flourishing woodlands, green savannahs, and strong well-limbed natives. These natives were shy, but he thought might be easily habituated to trade, and the island, it was probable, was as rich in commodities as any in the world. Incidentally, the discovery that New Guinea was thus divisible seemed an added argument against the doubted unity of New Holland.

Dampier's intention had been to sail down the east and round the south coast of New Holland, or at least to search for the eastern end of the supposed channel from near Rosemary Island; and he now had his men more under control, though they were hoping to turn homeward. Difficulties nevertheless accumulated—further exploration would require much time and caution, and the ship's condition was appalling. So he sailed back along the north coast of New Guinea, past burning islands and a shore now fairly well known, to Timor, and then in a wide loop to the south to Batavia. Although meaning to search for the Trial Rocks, he fell sick and his men could not navigate the ship, and Batavia was his only refuge. Provisions were bought, and the carpenter made an attempt to refit the vessel, but the leaks grew on her and she had to be careened. From 17 October 1700 till 22 February 1701 she laboured on her way home as far as the island of Ascension in mid-Atlantic. There the plank about a great leak was found to be so rotten that it broke away like dirt, and the *Roebuck* 'founder'd thro' perfect Age'. The company got ashore safely, with some rice and water and most of their belongings—though Dampier lost many of his books and papers; and on rice and the island turtles they lived uneasily for five weeks, at the end of which four English ships came into the harbour and took them on the final stage of their journey.

The ship had been lost; it remains a matter for astonishment that the captain and crew had not been lost with her. At any rate, whatever Dampier's virtues as a navigator and explorer might be, he was met on his return to England with a court-martial. For the loss of his ship he was plainly not responsible, but in regard to the truculent Lieutenant Fisher the evidence was not so plain. Fisher, freed from Portuguese prisons, had been back in England since the end of 1699, assiduously working up his case; there was a great deal of swearing and counter-swearing and raking up of nautical scandal; and the outcome was that Dampier was found guilty of 'very hard and cruel usage' towards his unpleasant subordinate. Without some modification, this verdict seems surprising—even more surprising is the penalty: for Dampier was fined all his pay and adjudged not a fit person to be employed as commander of any of the queen's ships.[1] The return to Dampier for his remarkable knowledge and skill, and the comparative success of the voyage —though it fell enormously short of his hopes—may seem inadequate; possibly he got some sour comfort from the reports of the masters of the English ships he had met at Batavia: 'Most of them had been unfortunate in their Officers; especially Captain Robinson, who said that some of them had been conspiring to ruin him and his Voyage.'

In spite of this censure, Dampier retained his reputation, rather undeservedly; for though no man was better fitted to navigate a ship, he was certainly not a great captain. Yet, within a year of the court-martial, when a London syndicate was fitting out a privateering vessel, the *St. George*, to harry the Spaniards on the Pacific coast in a new war, it was Dampier, as an expert and knowledgeable buccaneer, whom they chose for

---

[1] He was probably not a fit person to be so employed; but probably also he was no worse than a great many ornaments of the Royal Navy. The court-martial consisted of four admirals and thirty-three captains; this, it may be hazarded, was hardly giving a simple ex-buccaneer a chance.

the command—in which capacity he received a royal commission. The expedition was a desolating failure; it took a few small prizes and split up into malcontent parties who made off to the East Indies in captured barks. The *St. George*, with a bottom 'eaten like a honeycomb', was as rotten as the *Roebuck*. Finally Dampier left it to drift and founder somewhere in the Pacific and took the remnants of his crew in a small captured Spanish ship in their turn to the East Indies, where, Dampier having mislaid his commission, the vessel was seized by the Dutch. He had not, however, been for the last time to the Pacific; another syndicate, this time of Bristol, was fitting out two privateers under the very able command of Captain Woodes Rogers, a man with none of Dampier's capacity in navigation, but one who could handle successfully even the seamen of that insubordinate, ill-provided age. Dampier went as pilot. The voyage lasted from 1708 to 1711; it was more successful than any since the days of Drake and Cavendish, and paralleled their exploits in its climax, the capture of the Manila silver galleon. Woodes Rogers took his ships finally across the Pacific to Guam and Batavia and home round the Cape of Good Hope—the fourth of Dampier's great voyages and the third circumnavigation in which he was concerned. He sailed no more: his declining years were spent in litigation over his share of the proceeds of this last expedition, the only financially profitable voyage he ever made; and in March 1715 he died in an obscurity which does not match the documented excitement of his life.

The popularity of Dampier's writings did not soon wane; and, curiously enough, he remains to later times the representative seaman of his age. In some ways perhaps he was, for though his varied and extraordinary life was in its fullness that of few among his contemporaries, to his experience most of the departments of his profession made contribution. He was a merchant-sailor, a buccaneer, a privateer, he served in the navy, he explored little-known coasts. But he was much more, and here lies his real and rare distinction. Himself discovering only

a part of the fringe of the ocean, to his countrymen he discovered the whole South Seas. He made them aware of a new
life and a new fashion of looking at life. As a buccaneer and a
captain he fell far short of the first rank; as an observer of the
incidentals of travel, as a reporter of the unfamiliar in men and
natural history, he is a precursor of Banks and Darwin. As a
continual investigator of hydrography and of the variation of
the compass, of winds and the many minutiae of navigation, he
is fundamental to all future discovery, and the appreciation
accorded to him by men so diverse in professional genius as
Cook and Nelson establishes the measure of his ability. To
compare the precise observations of Dampier with the magnificent visions of the Spaniards, the rule of thumb of the Dutch, is
to compare intelligences of a different order. Dampier, whether
pressing through the flooded forests of Darien or digging deep
in the barren sands of the Australian coast for the water that so
many sailors had vainly sought, retained his principal passion.
Experience and observation he never elevated into a system, but
to bring the passion of science into nautical discovery was
significant not alone for the exploration of the Pacific but for
that of the whole unknown world.

Thus, though at the opening of the modern era of scientific
exploration there had been little added to knowledge of the
Pacific since Tasman's second voyage, the ocean was more in
men's minds than it had ever been before, and they were
becoming more adequately equipped to deal with its problems.
Dampier had made it known to the English reading public, a
place of far romance, the abode of surprising and profitable
possibilities. It signifies much that the fever of speculation which
swept the country in 1721 was known as the 'South Sea Bubble',
though the South Sea Company, founded ten years before,
never sent a ship to the Pacific even to trade. The War of the
Spanish Succession already had stimulated the interest of
Englishmen in a region so largely monopolized, where it was
known, by one of their opponents, and it was becoming

evident that that monopoly would be assailed by more than the irritating, if sporadic, operations of the buccaneers. Dutch rights in the East Indies and New Holland, also, could no longer be granted an unlimited and permanent recognition. Nor did the South Seas fail to make their contribution also to the literature of the age. Robinson Crusoe, though he was much indebted to the experiences of Alexander Selkirk and other solitary inhabitants of Juan Fernandez, was cast away upon an island in the mouth of the Orinoco; but when Swift sent Gulliver on his travels it seemed natural that that gifted navigator should make three of his astounding discoveries within the bounds of the Pacific—Lilliput was north-west of Van Diemen's Land, and Gulliver sailed through what is now New South Wales; Brobdingnag lay somewhere to the east of Japan, and was perhaps part of that golden land which Quast and Tasman failed to find; while over the northern ocean the empire of Balnibarbi stretched out towards California.[1]

Yet though interest was thus aroused, the first half of the century witnessed no exploratory voyages of major significance, and only one of interest, and this was Dutch. Anson's voyage round the world in 1741–4, though it created vast excitement, added nothing to discovery. The time was one of history and theorizing, of the collection of thick volumes of *Voyages*, of

---

[1] See also the *Tale of a Tub*, sect. iv, and the appended *Project for the Universal Benefit of Mankind* (1704) for the manner in which the southern continent could be pressed into the service of current controversy:

'The author, having laboured so long, and done so much, to serve and instruct the public, without any advantage to himself, has at last thought of a project, which will tend to the great benefit of all mankind, and produce a handsome revenue to the author. He intends to print by subscription, in 96 large volumes in *folio*, an exact description of *Terra Australis incognita* collected with great care and pains from 999 learned and pious authors, of undoubted veracity. . . . This work will be of great use for all men, and necessary for all families, because it contains exact accounts of all the provinces, colonies, and mansions of that spacious country, where, by a general doom, all transgressors of the law are to be transported. . . . After this business is pretty well established, he has promised to put a friend on another project, almost as good as this, by establishing insurance offices everywhere, for securing people from shipwreck, and several other accidents in their voyage to this country,' etc.

dogmatic discussion elevated frequently enough on the slenderest basis of data. The chief collections were English and French, but the attention and resources of those countries were mono- polized by the national struggle which occupied so much of the century. Even in the sacred name of trade, therefore, little was done, for the great trading organizations were fully engaged elsewhere, and the English South Sea Company realized its ambitions in the Asiento treaty with Spain; while the East Indies trade gave ample scope to all the energies of Holland. It was not till the rivalries of France and Britain were settled, temporarily, in America and India by the Seven Years' War that those nations began to look with new purpose to the Pacific; and until then the vague proprietorship which the Dutch East India Company exercised, with little satisfaction, over the disappointing shores of New Holland was left un- challenged. Nevertheless, in that half-century after Dampier's death the idea of Pacific discovery grew to a fruitful maturity.

Nor, as already remarked, were the Dutch entirely inactive. Jean Pierre Purry, one of the company's servants, in 1717 and 1718 addressed to his masters two memorials urging the colonization of Pieter Nuyts Land. What was known of the country, it was true, was not in its favour, but it was hardly possible that between Dedelsland and New Zealand there were not many lands so good as to make choice an embarrassment. If the coastline was in truth barren and deserted by all but a singularly ignorant and unattractive race of savages, exploration would probably discover an interior as rich as Mexico and Peru, a country of gold and silver, the potential bearer of every harvest that was most desirable. Slaves, or labourers from Java, could colonize it with the greatest advantage, as a place both of refreshment for the company's ships and of supply to its settle- ments in the Indies. Tasman, certainly, had reported the existence of giants in that vicinity, who might possess engines of war better than ordinary bombs and cannon; so a body of picked soldiers should first be sent to reconnoitre. Purry was urgent: a settlement would no doubt involve great expenditure, but a levy on produce would fully compensate for that. Nor should the ignoble caution of commerce impede the Dutch. For the moment was fleeting—to a land of such massed riches the British and the French must inevitably turn their gaze; New Holland would shelter no Hollanders, and by the side of new empire would wither their power in the Indies itself. The dark prophecy fell on unheeding ears. There was no Dutch settlement in Australia, and New Holland became a name for historians to explain. The last great Dutch voyage in the Pacific, that of Jacob Roggeveen, was sponsored not by the East but by the West India Company, and its reception at Batavia underlined the decision to do no more.

The Dutch West India Company had been founded in 1621, and was given by the States-General a monopoly of commerce on both the Atlantic and the Pacific coasts of America. Roggeveen's father, a man of some enterprise, framed a project for the discovery of the southern continent and its adjacent islands, which he presented to the company in 1696. The company promised him every assistance as soon as its affairs would permit; but before that day arrived the projector died, bequeathing his scheme in trust to his son. The young Roggeveen entered the service of the East India Company, became a councillor of the court of justice in Batavia, and retired with a handsome fortune; and then, in 1721, bethinking himself of his promise to his father, renewed the application. His memorial also was well received, and the West India Company fitted out a squadron of three ships, the *Arend*, the *Thienhoven* and the *Africaansche Galey*. With these Roggeveen sailed from the Texel on 21 August 1721. After touching at the Falkland Islands, he passed through the Strait of Le Maire, and that he might be certain to get round Cape Horn sailed south beyond latitude 60° —in these high latitudes, even though it was midsummer, experiencing three weeks of furious west winds, hail, snow and frost. He was apprehensive of being driven on icebergs in the thick fog; and these, so many of which he saw, convinced him that the southern continent extended to the Pole—for such vast masses of ice, it seemed certain, could neither be produced in the sea nor 'formed by the common force of cold'. It seemed no less certain that the cold currents in the ocean must all proceed from the mouths of rivers, which flowed down from a high continent into the sea with such force that they retained their impetus long after they had entered it; and if a further argument were needed, there was the great number of birds. The continent, even though frozen in the winter, might quite well be inhabited by fishermen, like Greenland or the borders of Davis Strait in the north.

From these speculations Roggeveen sailed to Juan Fernandez, which stimulated no less enthusiasm. Here, he thought, was one of the finest countries in the world, with a climate equally pleasant and wholesome, admirably fitted for settlement and capable of sustaining six hundred families at least. As a base for the discovery of the Southern Ocean, and for refitting after the voyage from Europe by way of the Strait of Magellan, no place could be more suitable; and whoever should make such a settlement would become in a few years master of a country as rich as Mexico and Peru, or Brazil. This indeed, pronounced Roggeveen, was 'the best-laid scheme for promoting southern discoveries that ever yet entered the head of man'; and he decided himself to take the initial step of settlement on his return voyage. He was eager to begin discovery, and to find that part of Terra Australis which lay within the latitudes of 30° and 36°; in both the northern and the southern hemispheres, he argued, between those degrees lay the lands most agreeable and advantageous. First, however, he sought the coast in 27° which the buccaneer Captain Davis had told Dampier about. There was no continent, but on Easter Day (5 April) 1722 he came to a small island, which he accordingly named Paasch or Easter Island. It seemed to be very fertile, and from the quantities of smoke which arose, populous, and the ships spent some days in refreshment. The natives though thievish were friendly—so friendly indeed that even the death of a number of them at the hands of a large landing party, gratuitously alarmed, did not long affect their behaviour; still they kept their women in the background. They were a well-proportioned race, much tattooed, and wore ornamental plugs in their ears so large that very often the lobe hung down to the shoulder. 'When these Indians go about any job which might set their earplugs waggling, and bid fair to do them any hurt', noted Roggeveen, 'they take them out and hitch the rim of the lobe up over the top of the ear, which gives them a quaint and laughable appearance.' They wore wraps of some vegetable material neatly sewn together; but their canoes were not equally well made, and were narrow, flimsy and unseaworthy. More remarkable, though Roggeveen did not describe them at length, were the great volcanic tuff figures at the sea-edge, colossally featured, which the islanders appeared to worship, kindling fire and squatting down with bowed heads, raising and lowering the palms of their hands. A remarkable place certainly: where, then, was the continent of Captain Davis? On 12 April, after a week's stay, they sailed on, in hope that the high and wide-stretching land might soon appear; and that perplexing island was left for a half-century more to the silent monarchy of its ancestral memorials, gazing from their platforms by the sea with grim and infinite melancholy on the land before them.

Yet the southern continent did not raise itself above the horizon. Roggeveen stood north-west into the latitude of Schouten and Le Maire's discoveries, and here his hopes rose. He sailed without landfall for upwards of 800 leagues, frequently changing his course, so that it is now in detail impossible to follow; till at length, in the second week in May, between latitudes 15° and 16°, he came into the northern fringe of the Tuamotus, whence he did not emerge till a month later. Pleasant were those islands, but with a deceptive charm; on that which Roggeveen called Schadelijk, or Disastrous (it was Takapoto, the Bottomless Island of Schouten and Le Maire in 1616), the *Africaansche Galey* was lost (her crew was divided among the other ships) and here five sailors deserted; and shortly afterwards only with difficulty were the other two ships extricated from the group of reef-fringed atolls which Roggeveen named the Labyrinth.[1] Then, on 2 June, a landing was made, again with fatal consequences, shared this time by the Dutch themselves. To clear the beach for landing Roggeveen's men opened fire on a crowd of islanders unarmed and peaceable, whom they afterwards pacified with outward success by means of signs and presents. But next day, attracted by the native women, they were led into an ambush, beset with a hail of stones, and forced to retire, leaving ten men dead behind them and carrying many wounded. Nevertheless Roggeveen was able to refresh to great advantage at this island, which he consequently called Verkwikking or Refreshment (it was Makatea), and before he left it he held a council which determined the remainder of the voyage. If he could make no discovery of importance in the latitude where he now was, his instructions were to return home. Already one vessel had been wrecked, and in the subsequent time of peril he had had trouble with his company, whose wages he had been forced to guarantee because of the Dutch custom that when a ship was lost its crew lost also their pay. The fleet had been at sea for ten months, provisions would not last indefinitely; the crews were diminished in number and scurvy-stricken, while the continent of Quiros was nowhere apparent. It was resolved therefore neither to search those seas longer, nor to return to settle Juan Fernandez, but to go straight to the East Indies; for to delay would be to miss the monsoon and remain compulsorily in the Pacific six months longer. So from Verkwikking a north-west course was steered, to round New Britain and thus reach Batavia.

The immediate result was to bring Roggeveen north of the Society Islands, among which he sighted in the distance Borabora and Maupiti; these he took for Le Maire's Cocos and

---

[1] His individual islands were Bedrieglijke, Doubtful or Deceptive (because at first he thought it was Le Maire's Honden)—Tikei; Schadelijk or Disastrous —Takapoto; Dagenraad or Dawn—Manihi, or Ahe; Avonstond or Evening— Apataki; Meeder Zorg or More Trouble—Arutua; Goede Verwaghting or Good Expectation—Rangiroa; Verkwikking or Refreshment—Makatea.

Verraders. In mid-June he came to the lovely islands of the Samoan group, called by him variously Bouman's Islands—after the captain of the *Thienhoven*, the first to sight them—Thienhoven and Groeningen. These were in order the Manua islands, and the larger, high islands of Tutuila and Upolu. The inhabitants were 'a very harmless good sort of people', unusually fair in colour, painted—that is, tattooed—down from the thighs to the legs. They brought out fruit in exchange for beads and looking-glasses. But Roggeveen would not stay, in spite of those of his officers who now thought that the land of Quiros could be easily discovered, and that there the expedition might recuperate for renewed voyaging. So, harried always by disease, it continued its north-west course, between the Gilbert and Ellice islands, by Schouten's route north of the Solomons and New Guinea and through the Moluccas. Roggeveen thought of burning one of the vessels, for scurvy was carrying off three, four or five of his best hands every day. He refrained, nevertheless, and sighted Java towards the end of September 1722. At Batavia the fate of Schouten and Le Maire awaited him; the East India Company seized and sold both ships as interlopers, and sent his company back to the Netherlands virtual prisoners. Roggeveen, true to his word, paid all their wages; and a great lawsuit between the two companies resulted in restitution. Although Roggeveen's voyage had failed to discover the unknown continent, to few did the failure seem conclusive. Certainly the non-existence of the continent had not been proven; of its existence Roggeveen's officers at least were convinced. In the absence of further practical experiment the matter rested for some years in the hands of geographers and the compilers of *Voyages*.

In 1705 a collection had been published by John Harris, the formidably named *Navigantium atque Itinerantium Bibliotheca*. Of this a new edition appeared in 1744–8, edited by John Campbell, a fervid patriot and moralist whose ethic was the exaltation of commerce. To commerce, he declared, his country owed its wealth, to commerce its strength, and not without serious purpose was his book dedicated to the 'Merchants of Great Britain'. And in mid-eighteenth century what more fruitful source of commerce could exist than even the discovered portion of the South Sea? Campbell was convinced that New Guinea, Carpentaria (or the Cape York peninsula), New Holland, Van Diemen's Land and the land discovered by Quiros all formed one continent, from which New Zealand, perhaps part of another continent, seemed separated by a strait. *Terra Australis incognita* therefore must lie between New Zealand and South America, and probably included not merely New Zealand but the various 'promontories' sighted by voyagers from Quiros and Le Maire to Roggeveen. Anson returned in 1744 laden with booty; it was evident that Britain had no need to pause before the ghost of Spanish monopoly, nor to make obeisance to the outmoded might of Holland. Roggeveen had proved the existence of the southern continent; let, then, British merchants proceed to exploit its riches, and adopt Roggeveen's plan of the settlement of Juan Fernandez and the Falkland Islands. Even before the *Terra Australis incognita* should be discovered, New Holland—*Terra Australis Cognita*—lay ripe for settlement. The Dutch had made no use of it; they had published no description of it and their opinion that it was worthless carried no conviction. Reports of its unpleasant heat Campbell frankly disbelieved; the climate on the whole was 'the happiest in the world'. Great heat in any case meant great riches; and Quiros, Dampier, Le Maire and Roggeveen united in praise, the first of the almost incredible riches, the others of the fertility of the continent. The Dutch being in the East Indies had the vantage-point for settlement; but it was open to the English East India Company to send a squadron on the track of Tasman; or the Royal African Company might settle a colony in Madagascar; or the South Sea Company, becoming in truth what its name implied, might colonize Juan Fernandez, whence trade to New Guinea, New Britain, Van Diemen's Land and Terra Australis would be perfectly feasible—nay, the endeavour was a patriotic duty. Such (and one thinks of Jean Pierre Purry) was the exhortation of Campbell.

It was taken up in France. There, geographers were convinced not merely of the patriotism implicit in southern colonization, but also of the fact that to the French nation was due, in the words of one of them, 'the honour of the first discovery of the Austral lands sixteen years before the departure of Magellan'. This conviction was founded on the story of the adventures of the Sieur de Gonneville—a nobleman who, sailing to the east in Vasco da Gama's track, was driven off his course and arrived at a large country which he called Southern India; whence, returning to France, he took a native prince who was to be restored, instructed in all the arts of Europe. But on his passage home de Gonneville was captured by an English privateer and lost all his possessions, even his journal, so that in painting the attractions of Southern India he could unfortunately give no sufficient indication of its position. The prince was not restored to his people; he remained in France, became a Christian, and married into de Gonneville's family. In 1663 his grandson, an 'Indian priest', published a book recounting the story, and proposing that he should be sent as a missionary to the Austral Land. As nobody knew where it was, this presented some difficulty; it was one of those convenient places that the geographers could put where they liked, from Brazil to Madagascar. The story did not cease to interest the French, and the eighteenth century made the most of it. It remained to solidify the claim of ownership. Authoritative opinion seemed to hold that de Gonneville's land lay in the South Atlantic, and was perhaps in the region of the 'Cape of the Austral Lands'— another dubious discovery which may have been Tristan d'Acunha or Gough Island; and the French East India Company was persuaded by Lozier Bouvet to grant him a commission for the discovery of these lands, which, he held, were admirably situated both as a place of refreshment for the company's ships on their long voyage to India and for trade with La Plata or Brazil, while the prospects of the conversion of the heathen were exceedingly happy. He sailed in July 1738, and finding no cape thought the discoverer might have been deceived by a fog-bound iceberg; then on New Year's Day 1739 he found a cape of his own, the Cape of the Circumcision, so called in honour of the appropriate feast. This was in latitude 54°, slightly west of the longitude of the Cape of Good Hope; though in continuous fog, for some weeks Bouvet thought he saw land, and believed he had actually coasted the Austral continent. He was rapt by the story of Quiros, and with Quiros's dazzling vision he identified his continent, admittedly unattractive as in this part it was. He breathed the spices, he handled the pearls and silks of Espiritu Santo, he heralded a trade which would make France unassailably great. It was his ambition to sail again to the Cape of the Circumcision, and thence south of New Holland to Espiritu Santo and home round the Horn. The company lacked his enthusiasm, and Bouvet did not make a voyage which might have disproved his own thesis; for he, too, had been deceived, and his cape and continent were, in fact, but the small island which now bears his name. The land of de Gonneville remained a matter for speculation.

France of the eighteenth century, France of the *philosophes* and the noble savage, was the headquarters of speculation. Reason and benevolence were twin watchwords, and among those things 'useful for the human race, and curious for scholars', on which the mathematician Maupertuis expanded to Frederick the Great,[1] was progress in the knowledge of the unknown south. Both for commerce and for science was the discovery of these regions important. In islands of the South Sea, travellers reported, they had seen savages, hairy men with tails, who were a kind of mean between the monkeys and ourselves. Entrancing thought, to talk to a man with a tail! The enthusiasm of Maupertuis stimulated to expression the most thorough of the French chroniclers of Pacific voyages, Charles de Brosses, president of the Parlement of Dijon. First in memoirs, and then, owing to the interest he had excited, in his

[1] In his *Letter on the Progress of the Sciences*, 1752.

*Histoire des Navigations aux Terres Australes* of 1756, de Brosses enlarged on what was known and what might be discovered about the lands of the south; and he spoke with the authority of an exhaustive student.

He discusses, like so many other writers, the 'utilities of discovery'—in a new spirit. Not commerce, but glory, should be the object and reward of him who through discovery should benefit both his country and the human race. Through geographical enterprises, not in war, had kings and their subjects in the past gained greatest glory, and he would be the most famous of modern sovereigns who gave his name to the Southern World. 'What comparison is to be made', writes de Brosses, 'between the execution of a project such as this, and the conquest, unjust perhaps, of some little ravaged province— of two or three cannon-shattered fortresses, acquired by massacre, ruin, desolation, amid the sorrow of conqueror as of conquered, bought at an expense a hundred times greater than that needed for the whole of the discovery proposed?' By no single person, not even by a commercial company, could the great work be carried out, but only by a nation; for only a nation could possess the spirit and the ability to take views long enough, to build foundations deep enough, to undertake voyages of pure curiosity—voyages that, however great their ultimate benefits to mankind, would pay no immediate dividend. And by what nation could the task be more fittingly undertaken than by the French?—men who, in spite of the deeds of Spaniards and Portuguese, could look back to the brave de Gonneville for their example. Furthermore, if the glory of contributing to knowledge was first and most to be desired, knowledge meant might and wealth, discovery led to commerce, commerce to sea power; and sea power, while Great Britain visibly affected 'the universal monarchy of the Sea', was no mean thing to contemplate.

Useful so great a discovery must be. More than one-third of the globe lay included in the *Terres Australes*, part known, part still to find. Unknown but existent—the argument from the balance of the earth in itself was adequate proof—a continent, its centre at the Pole, projected far northwards in the capes and promontories that so many voyagers had seen. Within the bounds of these southern lands what interest and profit! What peoples, customs and religions! What inconceivable variety of natural phenomena; what trade in gold and jewels, in medicines and spices, dye-woods and silks and skins, the liberal return for brandy, cheap looking-glasses and iron; what profit to the Australian in the acquisition of a pair of French scissors—nay more, of French culture, of which they were a symbol and an earnest! Barbarous as might be the natives encountered by Dampier and the Dutch, might there not exist in the interior of their country civilizations from which even France could learn?

What, then, of the divisions of discovery? The President de Brosses was systematic. He placed the southern world in three parts—Magellanica, or the south Atlantic; Polynesia, or the south Pacific; and Australasia, or the southern Indian Ocean. In Magellanica let Bouvet's discovery be followed up; here, too, the Falklands might be settled and in time of war the mastery of the two oceans be secured, a valuable trade be maintained with Patagonia, Tierra del Fuego and China, and the precise dimensions of the Patagonian giants be ascertained. From Magellanica one passed to Polynesia, where in the south the continent must lie, unexplored by navigators who had all sailed a too northerly course. Since Mendaña and Quiros no one had visited the Solomons or Espiritu Santo; yet how many other islands had been discovered, charming and fertile, the abode of a felicity unknown elsewhere in the world! To found a French colony useful both to science and to navigation would be easy. For the scientist there were problems of geology and the study of man, primitive certainly but simple, dignified and intelligent; for the navigator the investigation of New Zealand and the southern continent. Juan Fernandez would be much better settled and fortified by the French than as a perpetual refuge for English pirates. But of all places for settlement,

Australasia, a region probably of great islands separated by undiscovered straits, remained the most suitable—a region where France, through colonization, might emulate the glories of Spain, Portugal and Holland, and completing a great and noble task assume even in this distant sphere the rank she held in the European Republic!

The question remained, where to settle the colony that was to earn such immortal praise. There were sufficient objections to all the divisions of Australasia except New Britain, and of this fortunate island Dampier and Roggeveen united in praise. It was fertile, as a commercial centre no place could be more conveniently situated, as a base for exploration none be more admirable. Once the colony had been founded the transportation of orphans, beggars and criminals, both men and women, would be useful to itself and to its mother country alike; for in that pure air vice would wither away and a society of virtue grow to happy maturity. Not the Spanish, but the Dutch colony was the model to emulate and refine upon, a colony rooted in the ever-fruitful soil of commerce, not the gold-mine; sustained by a strong marine and itself cherishing afar the power of the state. For not in conquest is true glory, reiterates de Brosses, but in colonization. Empire is not to be confined to the bounds of Europe; the colonist remains a Frenchman, the author and agent of mutual advantage. 'He who is master of the sea is master of the land.' Colonization is not the destruction of the state but its fulfilment.

Not in conquest, not in wasted cities, is true glory: the comment of the age was the Seven Years' War. To fight for trade in settled lands, rather than found it in new, was the preoccupation of France and her rival, and humanitarianism and philosophy had little voice in the process. Nor was the mastery of the sea to repose with the French. Ten years later than de Brosses's *Histoire* appeared the first of the three volumes of John Callander's *Terra Australis Cognita*. The British had deprived France of her colonial empire; now, with as little scruple and considerably less trouble, a Scotsman appropriated de

Brosses's work and de Brosses's programme. For Callander is little more than a free rendering of his predecessor, with the natural modifications of a conqueror securely in the vanguard of European expansion, and the arrogance of the usurper of ideas. Vain, he wrote, were exhortations addressed to a nation so denuded of naval strength as the French. Far other was the position of his own happy island: 'United among ourselves, respected by foreigners, with our marine force entire, and (humanly speaking) invincible, aided by a set of Naval officers superior in every respect to those of the nations around us, with a sovereign on the throne who is filled with the most ardent and laudable desire of seeing his native country great and flourishing'—ineffably blessed as Britain was, Terra Australis presented a field worthy of the most attentive consideration. Dampier had discovered New Britain; let Dampier's country-men settle it. So much for *Terra Australis Cognita*; what of the unknown? 'It is very certain', said Callander, 'that the discovery of *Terra Australis Incognita* is considered, by many wise and knowing people, as a kind of philosopher's stone, perpetual motion, or, in plain *English*, as a chimera, fit only to take up the empty brains of wild projectors. Yet there seems to be no sufficient reason, why such as are competent judges of the matter in dispute, should decide, peremptorily, that there is no such country: or, if there be, that it is not worth the finding. These sort of hasty conclusions are extremely fatal to science in general and to the art of navigation in particular.' It was to the consideration of this problem that Alexander Dalrymple, a man of more original talent, now addressed himself.

Callander, unscrupulous, may have been a patriot; Dalrymple was a student and geographer of positive accomplishment, a correspondent of de Brosses and the great French cartographers. He had been a servant of the East India Company, and later became its hydrographer, and the first hydrographer to the Admiralty. Columbus and Magellan were the heroes of his youth, and the emulation of their deeds was his ambition. In Madras he saw a Spanish manuscript account of the voyage of

Torres. Returning to England in 1765, he became a propagandist of trade in the East Indies and discovery in the South Seas. He secured a copy of the memorial of Arias, printed in 1640. He was certain there must be a strait south of New Guinea. A strait of some sort was even marked in the atlas of Jean Rotz, a six-teenth-century Frenchman, which he subsequently found in the British Museum. He was not content with what seemed to him to have been so clearly ascertained. He was a man of imagination easily fired, and his imagination caught light from that of Quiros. Henceforth he was in England the chief upholder of the claims to exploration of Quiros's continent. That explora-tion, he hoped, he himself would lead.

Dalrymple in 1770 published a *Collection of Voyages in the South Seas*, but his more significant is his smaller work, *An Account of the Discoveries made in the South Pacifick Ocean, Previous to 1764*, which was printed in 1767, though not published till 1769. In this volume (which contained a map marked with Torres's approximate course) Dalrymple described what was known of the islands of the Pacific, examined the conduct and courses of previous explorers, and analysed the future possibil-ities of discovery 'as well from the analogy of nature, as from the deduction of past discoveries'. He discussed the continent with confidence. He assumed that the proportion of land to water must be the same in both hemispheres; but while from the equator to latitude 50° N the proportion was nearly equal, in the south the land hitherto known was not one-eighth of the space supposed to be water—there must therefore be valuable and extensive countries still to discover. Another argument he drew from the winds: tropical regions in wide oceans had con-stant easterly winds, but where land was extensive they were less steady and were interrupted during some months of the year from the west; now, in the Pacific the voyagers reported all sorts of winds, and the existence of a great chain of land followed. Not only must the continent exist as a deduction from elemen-tary principles, but it had been seen by a long list of explorers and seamen in different latitudes from 64° to 40° S—and the unfortunate Roggeveen received the blame justly due to one who had turned his back on infallible indications of its presence. The space unknown in the Pacific Ocean from the equator to 50° S must be nearly all land. Whether New Zealand was part of this great mass, or merely islands, remained doubtful; most probably it was the former. Thus Dalrymple concluded that the coast of Terra Australis ran northward a little west of the usual route to Juan Fernandez, turned west about latitude 28°, joined the land of which Quiros saw the signs in 26° and 17° and thereafter probably extended south to New Zealand— 'so that it appears this Continent in the latitude of 40° extends about 100° of longitude, which in this latitude is 4596', a greater extent than the whole civilized part of Asia, from Turkey eastward to the extremity of China'. A continent so often seen no person at this time could *discover*, remarked the enthusiast; but the immense interior still remained unexplored, and there was no intercourse with its inhabitants. Rejecting with scorn the proposition, attributed to Roggeveen, that the southern continent was the abode of the lost ten tribes, he added (in 1770) that if the American colonies with a population of two millions were the source of little but trouble to their mother country, if trade were declining and profits waned, here was a greater continent of perhaps fifty million inhabitants: 'the scraps from this table would be sufficient to maintain the power, dominion, and sovereignty of Britain by employing all its manufacturers and ships'.

So, appealing at once to history, geography, hydrography and cupidity, Dalrymple erected the most compelling and definite continental hypothesis which theorists had yet evolved. It came before his fellow geographers while exploration in the Pacific was already threatening its stability, and the next ten years were to witness its utter and complete demolition.

# CHAPTER IX

# THE CIRCUMNAVIGATORS: BYRON TO BOUGAINVILLE

THUS did scholars make their compilations and patriots exhort their fellow countrymen, and with an equal fervour, with 'rapture', they were read. 'Circumnavigations of the globe', it was said within a few years, 'have been of late the universal topic of all companies.'[1] This was interest stimulated predominantly not by books, but by the voyages to which the governments of England and France gave their support now that they were released from the more absorbing business of war. Important as some of these voyages were to geography, it is clear that from another aspect they were simply a continuation of the struggle that had just formally ceased. The first was that of Commodore the Hon. John Byron, than whose proposed activities nothing, it was held, could redound more to the honour of Great Britain as a maritime power, to the dignity of its crown, and to the advancement of its trade and navigation. And though Commodore Byron had been wrecked on the Chilean coast during Anson's expedition, his qualifications as a discoverer indeed do not seem to have gone much farther.

Nor was the exploration of the Pacific the essential object of Byron's voyage. The real essential was the gaining of a base in

---

[1] J. R. Forster, preface to the *Voyage round the World* of Bougainville (1772), p.v. The 'rapture' is indicated by the biographer of Cook: 'The writer of this narrative fully remembers how much his imagination was captivated, in the more early part of his life, with the hypothesis of a southern continent. He has often dwelt upon it with rapture, and been highly delighted with the authors who contended for its existence, and displayed the mighty consequences which would result from its being discovered.'—Dr Andrew Kippis, *Life and Voyages of Captain James Cook* (1788), p. 184.

the South Atlantic—the Falkland Islands most desirably, perhaps (though unlikely) something else—which would make for control of access to the Pacific. The idea of de Brosses was also an English idea: Anson had preached it, not without effect, and had even planned a voyage in 1749 both to survey the Falklands and to carry out exploration in the South Seas. Spanish opposition negatived the plan. After that there was a return in part, after nearly two centuries, to the ambition of the Elizabethans. Parliament in 1745 had already passed an act offering a reward of £20,000 to the British subject who in a British ship should first discover and sail through a strait between Hudson's Bay and the South Sea.[1] Byron was therefore to leave either the Cape of Good Hope or Rio de Janeiro to search the South Atlantic for land between latitudes 33° and 53°, and to identify 'Pepys Island', supposed to lie somewhere in the neighbourhood of the Falklands; to survey the Falklands; and after wintering at Pepys Island or some suitable spot on the South American coast, to go to New Albion, to Drake's harbour, and from there search the coast as far north as practicable. If a likely passage to Hudson's Bay presented itself, he was to sail home through it; if there was none he was to cross the Pacific to China or the Dutch East Indies, and return by way of the Cape. The actual voyage was far other in its course.

Byron was given two vessels, the frigate *Dolphin*, coppersheathed, with 190 officers and men, and the sloop *Tamar*, Captain Patrick Mouat, with a company of 115. These vessels were well prepared for the voyage and the *Dolphin* carried a 'machine' for purifying water—a not unnecessary appliance, for barely a month after they sailed their water had become foul and 'stunk intolerably'. They left the Downs on 21 June 1764, and in late November came to Port Desire, on the Patagonian coast. Here they took in water and ballast, fresh meat and fish; and proceeded to make an unsuccessful search for Pepys Island. Then, not trusting to the existence of sufficient wood and water at the Falklands, Byron decided to sail into the Strait of Magellan,

[1] The reward at this time, however, did not apply to the Royal Navy.

spending a week at Port Famine, the scene of the ill-fated Spanish colony of 1581. In spite of the name, wood, water and fish were plentiful, and fragrant wild flowers, and the port was used by whatever ships were in the strait. Sailing east again in January 1765, he examined the Falklands, came to the conclusion that they were identical with Pepys Island (as indeed they were) and took possession of them. On the whole the group seemed barren and desolate; and Byron, after sailing seventy leagues along the coast and finding himself on a lee shore, stood to the north, and then once more over to the strait. At Port Desire he was met by a store-ship from England, which was sent back from Port Famine, with a letter informing the Admiralty that the *Dolphin* and *Tamar* were 'too much disabled for the California voyage', and that he had seen some remarkably large men on shore.[1] He had also seen, in the strait, to his surprise, a French vessel; and would have been even more surprised to learn that she was his competitor on the coast of the Falklands. The *Dolphin* and *Tamar* made a difficult and dangerous passage of the strait, and it was not till 9 April that they emerged, seven weeks and two days after entering it; yet, thought Byron, at the proper season a large squadron might make the passage in three weeks, while the quantities of fish, wild celery, scurvy-grass, berries and vegetables to be found were sovereign specifics against scurvy and other diseases. He had already decided to sail a course of his own, and to look for the Solomon Islands.

Once in the Pacific, Byron struck north for refreshment to Masafuera, an island some distance west of Juan Fernandez. He considered searching for the rumoured Davis Land, but the wind was adverse, and he determined to steer north-west into the trade wind, and then westward for the Solomons, 'if there are such', or make some new discovery. The course he actually sailed was roughly west-north-west, and on the morning of 7 June he was delighted to get sight of two small islands, because

[1] The impressions of the size of these people gained by Byron and his men revived the legend of Patagonian giants, as reported so much earlier by Pigafetta, and led to much controversy and some laughter.

his best men were beginning to go down with scurvy, and the sight of coconut groves beyond the surf, and the thought of limes and bananas, were like imaginings of paradise. Byron had come in his turn to the northern fringe of the Tuamotus; the two islands were Napuka and Tepoto. There was no safe anchorage near either of them, the natives made threatening demonstrations against a boat that was sounding, and the discoverer sailed on from these 'Islands of Disappointment', with the situation of his sick becoming more deplorable every hour. Two days later land was seen again, as pleasant in appearance as the last, and with inhabitants as hostile, in spite of all attempts at friendly intercourse. Finally a landing was forced, not without the death of two or three natives, and the capture of two canoes joined together, beautifully wrought of carved planks, the seams stopped with tortoise-shell. Byron was unwilling to see the bloodshed of a second engagement at close quarters, and finally put the natives to flight with a shot over their heads. This was the island of Takaroa. Next day he obtained several boat-loads of coconuts and scurvy-grass, was able to admire the manifold uses of the coconut palm—and made the curious discovery of an old worm-eaten carved head of a rudder, which seemed to have come from a Dutch long-boat, and some small iron tools, also Dutch; they were relics of Roggeveen's *Africaansche Galey*. There were no venomous creatures, though the flies were a continuous and intolerable torment. In the woods was found a native burial-place, with many neat boxes of human bones, and the remains of turtle and fish hung on the trees around, a ghostly banquet; but no further communication having been made with the living, Byron resolved to sail next day to another island five miles to the south-westward—Takapoto. This was done, and here the natives proved more friendly, running along the beach for several miles abreast of the ship as it coasted. A midshipman who swam from a boat to the shore was obliged to retreat to avoid being stripped of his clothes, so eager were they for novelty. Pearls were the principal object of the boat's visit; they could not be obtained (apart from anything else, there was no way of mutual understanding), and though Byron was willing to remain for some weeks to trade, no anchorage could be found, and only a few trifling presents were given. To these two islands he gave the name of King George.

The westward course was pursued, and next day another island of the same group was passed, green, pleasant and apparently well populated, but with the same great surf breaking in a long line on the shore. This the loyal Byron called Prince of Wales' Island. It was Rangiroa. He then stood northwest. The disappearance of a mountainous swell from the southward and the sight of great flocks of birds flying in that direction at evening persuaded him that there, too, was land—perhaps a chain of islands reaching to a continent. The sickness of his crews prevented him from sailing to its discovery. There was indeed immediately near only the Tuamotus and the more westerly Society Islands. Another small group was seen in latitude 10° 15', on 21 June, fertile and beautiful, and swarming with people, defended in every direction by rocks and breakers —possibly part of the elusive Solomons, thought Byron, who called it the Islands of Danger. It was Pukapuka, seen so long before by Mendaña. From an uninhabited island three days later the boats were able with great difficulty to bring off two hundred coconuts, 'an inestimable treasure'. Byron's belief in the Solomons was evidently waning,[1] and this island—Atafu, most northerly of the Tokelau group—received the name of the late Duke of York. But he sailed a western course still for some days in their search till he was ten degrees west of their position as laid down in the French chart he was using, and then hauled to the northward to make the Ladrones before his water was exhausted. On 2 July Byron's Island was sighted in the south part of the Gilbert chain (we cannot identify it beyond

[1] He says, with some injustice to Mendaña, 'The only person that ever pretended to have seen them was Quiros, and I believe he left no Account behind him to direct any other person to find them by.'—R. E. Gallagher, *Byron's Journal of his Circumnavigation*, p. 109.

doubt)[1]—an island low and flat, green and delightful in appearance like so many others—like them, too, without anchorage, and surrounded with a tremendous surf. The islanders came off in hundreds, an extremely cheerful, extremely amusing and excessively thievish race, bright copper-coloured, tall and handsome, and except for ornaments of shells, all of them stark naked. Their ears were bored and hung down almost to their shoulders with the weight of the ornaments carried in them. 'We shewed them some coco nuts', said Byron, 'and made signs that we wanted some from the shore, but instead of offering to go for any, they wanted to have those we shewed them. I remarked a very dangerous weapon some of them had, it was a kind of spear, very broad at the end, which for about three feet in length was of each side stuck full of shark's teeth, which are as sharp as any lancet.' They were therefore abandoned with their fruit and their sharks' teeth and shells, and on 31 July the *Dolphin* and the *Tamar* anchored off Tinian, one of the Ladrones. It was time: the heat and constant rain had been almost unbearable, and not a man was free from scurvy. This island was not as pleasant as expected; nevertheless fresh provisions were fairly plentiful, and during a stay of nine weeks most of the sick recovered; and being by this time in known waters, the voyage proceeded without difficulty through the East Indies to Batavia, now a city populous, cosmopolitan and polyglot, teeming with fruit and vermin. Thus, leaving Batavia early in December 1765, Byron took his ships without great incident round the Cape of Good Hope, sent the *Tamar*, which near the equator had damaged its rudder, to Antigua, in the West Indies, for repairs, and anchored once more in the Downs on 9 May 1766. The voyage had occupied less than two years—a quick circumnavigation; and although Byron, apart from his partial inspection of the Falkland Islands, seems to have ignored his orders as thoroughly as possible in his hope of finding the Solomons, it evidently stirred the Admiralty to fresh investigation of the South Sea.

[1] Tabiteuea seems most likely, though Nukunau is more generally accepted.

For the *Dolphin* was not allowed to rest. In June of the same year Captain Samuel Wallis received a commission as her commander, with the object of making another—and seriously exploratory—voyage to the Pacific; with him was to sail the *Swallow*, a sloop commanded by Philip Carteret. Carteret was well fitted for such a voyage—under Byron he had been first lieutenant of the *Tamar* and then of the *Dolphin*; yet resourceful and determined as he was, on his new mission he found all his resources and determination strained. The voyage was explicitly for the discovery of the southern continent. The Atlantic was abandoned for a search west of Cape Horn for the supposed land, in longitude 100° or 120°. If it were found and sufficient provisions remained, Wallis was to return round the Horn, or if driven too far north to go to the East Indies. But if, contrary to expectation, no discovery were made, he was to stand north-west until latitude 20° in search of land and, circumstances permitting, to carry out even further exploration, retaining, however, resources enough to get to China or the East Indies, there to refit for the homeward voyage.

The *Dolphin* was filled with stores and necessaries, ordinary and medical, including 'three thousand weight of portable soup', which it was hoped would help to keep scurvy at bay, and a still for producing fresh water; but the *Swallow* was so badly fitted out, old, and so totally unequal to a long voyage, that Carteret could not believe her intended to go farther than the Falklands, where there was a frigate, copper-sheathed like the *Dolphin*, which might take her place. Nor did his application for bare necessities such as a forge, iron or a small skiff have any success. With these two vessels sailed a store-ship; the three left Plymouth Sound on 22 August 1766. They entered the Strait of Magellan on 17 December, after an Atlantic passage delayed by the wretched sailing qualities of the *Swallow*, refreshed at Port Famine with antiscorbutic berries and vegetables, trans-ferred the stores, and sent the store-ship to the Falklands with a load of wood and young trees for the improvement of Port Egmont, the British settlement there. Then followed one of the longest and most unpleasant passages of the strait of which there is record. The weather was foul, both ships were more than once in imminent peril, and once the *Swallow* was given up for lost. She steered and worked so ill that Carteret seriously asked whether she should not be sent home; for the sake of mutual help Wallis thought best to retain her as long as possible, promising to wait on her movements. They arrived at the western opening of the strait on 11 April 1767, after four months in almost perpetual danger of shipwreck—a dreary and in-hospitable region it was, said Wallis, cold, gloomy and tempestuous, a chaos rather than Nature. There was little wind at the strait's mouth, and to get through safely the *Dolphin* was compelled to carry all her sail. In the middle of the day she lost sight of the *Swallow*; fog and a fast-rising sea made it impossible to return into the strait, and Carteret was not seen again—for reasons which, on the whole, seem unsatisfactory.

Wallis now steered a course north-west and northerly. Within a month scurvy began its affliction in spite of all the measures taken to counteract it—and Wallis was a commander very careful of his men's health; and it was to the joy of all that on 6 June, Whitsun Eve, in latitude 19° 26', a low island was sighted, and shortly after another some four leagues distant. One was called Whitsun Island, and was Pinaki; the other Queen Charlotte's, and was Nukutavake. The boats could find no anchorage, and till 10 June the *Dolphin* stood off and on, while parties landed for coconuts, scurvy-grass and water. The natives proved peaceful and made no objection to these operations, while Wallis gave strict orders against molesting them. When he sailed he set up a Union Jack, with a notice that the islands now belonged to His Britannic Majesty, cut on a piece of wood and on the bark of trees, and left with some hatchets, nails, glass bottles, beads, shillings, sixpences and halfpence, 'as presents to the natives, and an atonement for the disturbance we had given them'. On this day and succeeding ones Wallis saw several small low-lying islands, which he named after the Earl of Egmont, the First Lord of the Admiralty and the planning mind of these voyages, and various members of the royal family; but so far as refreshment was concerned, they were, without exception, quite unprofitable. He was, in fact, among the Tuamotus,[1] but south of the course steered by Byron, and on 18 June sighted Otaheite, or Tahiti, the largest of a far-stretched archipelago, and as King George the Third's Island the culminating point of his loyalty. At that moment of sunset some of his men thought they saw, farther to the south still, the outline of a continental coast.

Next morning, when a mist cleared away, the *Dolphin's* company were surprised to find the ship surrounded by some hundreds of canoes, the occupants of which were gazing at her in astonishment and conferring eagerly together. The English made signs of friendship, which were returned, and at last a native came on board, followed by others. The adventure was not without its hidden dangers: as one of them was standing near the gangway, a goat belonging to the ship butted him on the haunches; 'the appearance of this animal, so different from any he had ever seen, struck him with such terror, that he instantly leaped overboard; and all the rest, upon seeing what had happened, followed his example with the utmost precipitation'. They recovered, however, and returned, and made signs that they were at least familiar with hogs and poultry, for which Wallis wished to bargain. This was not possible to any satisfactory extent till several attacks with showers of stones had been beaten off; for the only natives who seemed unequivocally friendly were the women, and when their too obvious allurements were ignored, even they pelted a watering party derisively with fruit. At last, on 23 June the ship was anchored in a convenient bay—Matavai Bay—on good holding ground, narrowly escaping destruction on a dangerous shoal in the process, and was warped up this harbour so as to command the

---

[1] Wallis's islands, after Nukutavake, were Vairaatea (Egmont, the San Miguel of Quiros); Paraoa (Duke of Gloucester's); Manuhangi (Duke of Cumberland's); Nengonengo (Prince William Henry's); Mehetia (Osnaburgh).

beach and an excellent watering place. Furneaux, the second lieutenant (both Wallis and his first lieutenant being sick), then went on shore, hoisted a pennant, turned a sod, and took possession in the name of King George III. People who were seen proved friendly, particularly one white-bearded old man through whose good offices and great influence most of the succeeding traffic was carried on. The last sign of enmity was a mass demonstration three days later, which was dispersed by the ship's guns as quickly and decisively as possible—a refreshing change from the savage massacre of earlier days. One can hardly say as much for the destruction of more than fifty canoes, some of them sixty feet long, even though little was found in them but stones and slings, the instruments of native warfare. Next day the English contrived to make it understood that they merely wished to trade for provisions, and before noon they were supplied with an ample store of hogs, fowls and fruit.

Relations being thus happily established, the sick were taken on shore. The gunner was put in charge of trade on the English side, with instructions to protect the natives from violence and fraud, while offenders were severely punished. These natives were expert pilferers, but having been thrown into panic by the ability of the surgeon in shooting duck, the pointing of a gun was sufficient to induce flight and repentance in any number of them. Nails were the articles of commerce most in demand, and herein rose an awkward complication; for the natives, it seemed, held no prejudice in favour of female chastity, and to secure the desired object the sailors took to drawing nails from the ship's timbers and even to counterfeiting them with stolen lead. This was doubly mischievous—it damaged the ship and it sent up prices. Instead of small nails for a middle-sized hog, large spikes were demanded. Yet the offenders could not be found out. Finally, towards the end of the visit, the mischief became so flagrant that in order to prevent the ship from being pulled to pieces and the price of provisions from being raised impossibly high, no man was allowed on shore except the parties sent for wood and water.

One day Wallis was visited on board by a tall, dignified woman, 'Oborea' or Purea, who seemed from the universal respect paid her to be a sort of queen. She was given a long blue cloak, a mirror and beads, and on her invitation Wallis, now fairly recovered from his sickness, agreed to visit her. He did so, on 12 July, in due state, carried by the Tahitians and followed by his own guard to a guest house, a huge and airy pavilion, more than three hundred feet long and forty wide, raised on pillars that ran thirty feet up to the ridge of the thatch. Wallis, his lieutenant and the purser, who had also been sick, were at the queen's command gently massaged by young girls—an operation, like every other, suddenly suspended in the most complete and startled amazement; for the surgeon, very warm after his walk, had removed his wig, and the sensation could have been no greater had he unscrewed a limb. The officers were clothed island fashion in 'Indian cloth', and on the return journey, as Wallis insisted on walking, Purea herself lifted him over puddles as if he were a child. Such highly agreeable contact with this lady stimulated trade in provisions, though she herself never stooped to barter; and the announcement on 21 July that the ship would be sailing in a week caused her such grief that she burst into tears.

Meanwhile at different times two parties had been sent to explore the island, one under Furneaux along the shore, the other inland under the mate. Their reports united in praise of a land where not even man seemed vile. Furneaux found it very pleasant and populous, abounding with hogs and fowls, fruit and vegetables, though the people were not immediately willing to trade. The mate's journey was a longer one. His party followed the course of a river through a wide valley of rich black earth, dotted with houses and walled gardens; when the valley became narrower and the ground rose, the water had been led off to gardens and neat plantations of fruit-trees. The sailors were treated to refreshments by a multitude of benevolent natives, who were delighted by the buttons and nails they received in exchange; and when they continued their journey up a steep mountain through heavy brushwood Tahitian guides went first, clearing a path and carrying the baggage. The top of the mountain revealed vistas of still further enchantment, hills clothed everywhere with green woods, interspersed with villages, and valleys even more fruitful and populated. No peak to its highest point was uncrowned with trees nor without its ascending smoke, while down to the ship and out to sea was a vision of beauty indeed. To the riches of vegetation the English added more, planting garden seeds, limes, lemons and oranges, and peach, cherry and plum stones. They saw no beast except hogs, nor bird besides parrots, parroquets, green doves and multitudes of ducks; and returned in the cool of the evening in very good humour with themselves and their hosts.

The people, noted Wallis, were well made, active and comely, and some of the women were extremely beautiful. They were universally tattooed about the thighs and loins, except the children, and clothed gracefully in cloth made of beaten bark, with ornaments of feathers, flowers, shell and pearls. Their food they cooked admirably in a pit with hot embers and stones, and were astonished to see the gunner boil pork in a pot, for they had no vessel which would bear contact with fire. Wallis gave away several iron pots, the use of which never failed to draw an admiring crowd. Numerous scars argued experience in warfare, and there were those expert in surgery with instruments of sharpened shell. They were dexterous canoe builders also, felling trees with stone axes, cording the planks together and caulking them with rushes; and they loved the pageantry of water processions. Their principal weapons were bludgeons and slings for stones; their bows and arrows were fit only to knock down birds. The climate was delightful, there were no vermin, nor insects except a few ants, and, so far as Wallis could see, no disease. This sublunary paradise it was which the *Dolphin* now made known to the world.

On 26 July, in spite of all the attractions of the island, Wallis got ready for sea. His visit had lasted more than a month, his sick were nearly all completely restored, and he still had a long voyage before him. Nevertheless Purea implored him to stay longer, and he was compelled to make signs that he would return; and next morning, having dispensed a number of parting presents, he sailed, not without grief himself. He steered westward, for some days still among the nearer islands, and passing several others farther off; where, having exhausted the royal family, he was obliged to fall back on the royal navy—hence, in this vicinity and much farther west, the names of Sir Charles Saunders, Lord Howe, Boscawen and Keppel.[1] Off Keppel's Island, 487 leagues from Otaheite, in the middle of August, considering further refreshment unlikely, that it was winter, that the ship was leaking and her stern shaken by the rudder, he resolved to make his way to the Ladrones and home by way of Batavia and the Cape. He therefore altered his course, and two days later passed the small group called by his officers after him the Wallis archipelago, where natives tried to seize the cutter. A current carried the ship at night out of sight of land before any provisions could be obtained. On 19 September she reached Tinian, where a beneficial stay was made till 15 October; the end of November brought her to Batavia, and after refitting at the Cape she anchored in the Downs on 20 May 1768. The voyage had lasted 637 days, a comparatively short time, especially as it had been Wallis's practice, when in unknown seas, to lie to at night and make sail only by day. It cannot be said that he in his turn had paid undue deference to his instructions; though it is true that, instructed to find 'a place of consequence' in the South Seas, he had found Tahiti.

Meanwhile, contrary to all reasonable expectation, the *Swallow*, so seriously misnamed, had survived the perils of the Strait of Magellan. Carteret had long been convinced that he had been sent on a service to which his vessel and equipment

---

[1] Tapuaemanu, Mopihaa, Niuatoputapu, Tafahi. Boscawen-Niuatoputapu was Le Maire's Verraders; Keppel-Tafahi was Le Maire's Cocos.

were quite unequal, but, he says, 'I determined at all events to perform it in the best manner I was able.' Now, on the morning of 11 April 1767, he saw the *Dolphin*'s sails disappear below the horizon, leaving him with no rendezvous or plan of operation settled, and taking all the articles of trade sent out for the use of both ships, while his lack of a forge and iron under some circumstances might quite surely mean the loss of the ship. 'I had the satisfaction, however,' he adds, 'to see no marks of despondency among my people, whom I encouraged, by telling them, that although the *Dolphin* was the best ship, I did not doubt but that I should find more than equivalent advantages in their courage, ability, and good conduct'; and with all the *Swallow*'s defects, she proved a good sea-boat.

Carteret did not get clear of the strait till 15 April, being once more in the gravest danger; and finding himself short of fresh water, decided to make for Juan Fernandez or Masafuera to replenish his supplies. He had three weeks of tempest, during which the ship was in almost continuous risk of losing her masts, or foundering, or both; sails split, rigging carried away, chain-plates (to which the shrouds were attached) broke, and the rudder-chain parted. All these things were repaired as best might be, and 8 May was a fine day. Carteret found Juan Fernandez fortified by the Spanish; but at Masafuera—after another series of unseasonable gales, during which his boats were damaged and in continual danger of being lost, and his landing parties underwent great discomfort—he managed to get a supply of water, sailing in the end on 24 May without the wood that had been cut and that it was impossible to load. He then sailed north to 26° in search of two small islands charted thereabouts, the isles of St Ambrose and St Felix, to examine their suitability as a place of refreshment for British ships, now that the Spanish had occupied Juan Fernandez; he missed them, but came to the conclusion that they and not Easter Island might be the original Davis Land which so many charts, with geographical temerity, laid down as a continent. Indeed, hauling to the south and then standing westward for forty degrees in latitude 28°, Carteret was clear that he had sailed over Davis Land, for if there was any such place he must have seen it. He continued this search for a missing continent till 17 June, though the wind and weather made it impossible to get farther southward, convinced by the rolling billows from that direction that any land that existed must be only small islands. It was now the depth of winter—the four months in the strait had retarded the expedition only too much—and the weather was extremely unpleasant, gloomy and cold, varied with thunder and lightning, rain and sleet; and for days together there was no opportunity of making an observation. Nevertheless, the ship going so badly and the voyage being so long, it was necessary to carry all the sail that could be spread, and to risk through misadventure the end which starvation would otherwise have made certain. The western course was continued till July 2, when land was discovered to the north. It was examined next day, a small island standing out from the sea like a great rock, covered with trees and with a stream of fresh water, but uninhabited. Surf prevented a landing. The island was called after the 'young gentleman' who first sighted it, 'son to Major Pitcairn of the Marines'—it is an inconsiderable speck, which was later to derive considerable notoriety from the mutineers of the *Bounty*.

The weather was again exceedingly tempestuous, while the prevailing winds kept the ship from maintaining a high latitude and drove her continually to the north. In addition, she was become 'very crazy', the sails were splitting and the men subject to scurvy. Happily, abundant rain-water was caught. Sailing now roughly north-west to longitude 165° W, the *Swallow* passed the southern fringe of the Tuamotus, and three small, low, green islands, uninhabited, and with neither vegetables nor water, were added to the numerous list named after royal dukes otherwise obscure[1]—islands probably the land seen by Quiros, guessed Carteret, on the basis of his charts, and wrongly. The

[1] Carteret actually named the first of the three (Tematangi) the Bishop of Osnaburgh's Island, after the four-year-old bishop, Frederick Augustus, second son of George III, and later the Duke of York. The other two were called the Duke of Gloucester's Islands; this name remains.

long billows from the south persuaded him as usual that there was no land near in that direction; the progress of the ship was slow, of the scurvy rapid; and he therefore bore away to the northward to get into the trade wind, hoping thus to come to some island of refreshment. If successful in this, and in putting the ship into better condition, the voyage might in the proper season be pursued to the southward, along the coast of any continent discovered that could supply provisions, till in a high latitude the return to Europe might be made round either the Cape of Good Hope or the Horn. The event, however, was somewhat different. It was not until Carteret reached latitude 16° S that he found the true trade wind, and then the weather was foul again, thick and rainy, with hard gales. Towards the end of July, in latitude 10°, he had hopes of falling in with some of the Solomons, and sailed along the parallel till he was five degrees west of their charted position, when he concluded that if they existed they must be erroneously laid down. Meanwhile there was the scurvy; the hands who had not gone down before it were exhausted by their labours; the log-lines were worn out; the ship was in so bad a condition that she would not work; and then she sprang a leak at the bows, under water and impossible to get at. Thus matters stood when, on 12 August, at daybreak, land was seen; to Carteret it was like the reprieve of a criminal on the place of execution.

This land proved to be a cluster of islands, and Carteret called them at first Queen Charlotte's Islands. The name has not survived; for, as he later made no doubt, sailing in Quiros's track he had rediscovered Quiros's Santa Cruz. He got here, however, less succour than had Mendaña and his quarrelling company. In the evening the ship anchored off the largest island, Ndeni, where black, naked and woolly-haired natives were seen; but before a boat could reach them they disappeared. The boat reported a wild, forlorn and mountainous country, with forest down to the water's edge, which would make ambush easy. Next day, therefore, the master was sent in the cutter along the coast to the west, well armed and with a few oddments for trade, and the strictest injunctions to prudence and benevolence. He returned with three arrows sticking into him and half his boat's crew desperately wounded; he had ignored both recommendations, and paid for his disobedience with his own life and those of three of the best men in the ship, who all died of their wounds. He had found a pleasant bay and a fertile settlement, with friendly and hospitable natives; had cut down a coconut-tree against all expostulation; and then, while an attack was preparing, trifled away precious time on the shore. Carteret was therefore compelled to repair the ship as best he could where she lay, and the carpenter, the only member of the crew still in tolerable health, managed to stop most of the leak. Then by a continuous discharge of muskets and guns into the woods, a watering party was enabled to work without molestation, though the master had ruined all chance of friendship or traffic with the natives. Besides this misfortune, Carteret and his lieutenant were very sick and the master was dying (these three being the only men who could navigate the ship home), seven other men were wounded, three mortally, while the gunner and thirty others were incapable of duty; it was therefore impossible to consider further discoveries to the south, and Carteret resolved to coast along to the west. He did so, naming every prominent feature, beating off an attack by armed canoes, and abandoning finally the hope of obtaining any of the hogs and poultry, fruits and vegetables, which his dispirited men saw in such plenty on the shore. This island he called Egmont; to the north-west he saw the volcano, Tinakula, which had exploded during the visit of the Spaniards.

On 18 August he turned west-north-west, and now, though this time recognition failed, he was on the verge of rediscovering a country the very existence of which geographers had begun to doubt. He had already unsuccessfully searched for the Solomons; two days after leaving Santa Cruz he sighted the two islands, Ndai, Malaita, and the islet Manaoba.[1] Off Ndai, named

---

[1] He called them Gower's, Carteret's and Simpson's. Erasmus Gower (later an admiral) was his lieutenant, Alexander Simpson the master.

Gower's, where he traded his nails for a few coconuts, natives tried to intercept the ship's boat; Carteret was forced to disperse them, and captured a canoe, a neatly built vessel adorned with shellwork—in which he found a hundred more coconuts, invaluable for his sick. Then he continued north-west, parallel to but out of sight of the group, till he picked up an atoll, then one of Le Maire's Green Islands, and then Buka, the most northern of the main Solomons, in his ignorance of their identity the victim of the Spaniards' consistent underestimation of the distance they had sailed; and on 26 August the high land of New Britain was sighted. Next day a current had set the ship into the deep gulf called by Dampier St George's Bay. A little cove was found, English Cove, where it was possible to heel the ship and stop the leak again; the sheathing of her bottom was found much decayed and worm-eaten. Here also spars were cut, and though fish could not be caught, oysters and cockles, coconuts and the boiled cabbage-top of the coconut made a change of diet that was only too urgently needed. Wood and water there was in plenty, and good ballast, but no natives were seen. Before leaving the cove, on 7 September, Carteret took possession of the country, and nailed on a high tree a leaden plate recording his visit. Then, learning of an excellent small harbour near by from a boat's crew who had been examining the coast, he took thence another load of coconuts, and regretfully continued the voyage; for it was essential to reach Batavia while the eastern monsoon still blew, and though an ordinary ship could have gone thrice the distance in the time, to the *Swallow* the least delay might be fatal.

Shortly after he left this harbour a gale and a strong current prevented any attempt to follow Dampier's course through the strait between New Britain and New Guinea; and the current setting strongly into St George's Bay, Carteret was forced to go with it, hoping that it might indicate a passage westward. Thus it proved indeed, and sailing up what had become St George's Channel, he was able to name the land on the east, now separated a further remove from its old identity with New Guinea, Nova

Hibernia or New Ireland. This strait with its many islands was cleared on 13 September; next day more islands were sighted, from which the natives twice made an attack on the ship, in spite of all signs of friendship. These natives were like those of New Ireland or Egmont Island, dark copper-coloured and naked, with woolly hair and ornaments of shell; but their faces were painted with white streaks and their lances pointed with flint. Their islands were large, lofty, verdurous, populous and well planted; further examination Carteret could not carry out. He called them the Admiralty Islands. Now in fairly well-known waters, he still found and named many smaller islets; and making his way to Mindanao, then south down the west coast of Celebes, corrected his charts frequently as he went. The Dutch at Macassar were suspicious, and sent him to the small port of Bonthain, at the south end of the island, where he was at last able to get fresh provisions—not without some trouble with the Dutch, largely his own fault: and at the end of a stay which lasted from 21 December 1767 to 22 May 1768, the season during which westward navigation was impracticable, he was glad to resume the journey to Batavia. Here he received permission to have the ship repaired; she was in inconceivably bad condition, rotten, worm-eaten and decayed, the butt-ends of the planks adjoining the stern so open that a man's hand might be thrust in between. In the middle of September, Carteret once again set sail, though the Dutch carpenters doubted the ship's ever reaching Europe, especially as he left before the proper season in order to avoid further sickness in Java. Luckily he was able to enlist a number of English seamen; of his original crew, twenty-four were dead and others so ill that seven more died on the passage to the Cape. From 28 November 1768 to 6 January 1769 he stayed at Table Bay while his men recovered. Here at least Dutchmen welcomed strangers; and Carteret commended them for their courtesy.

In the Atlantic, three weeks after leaving the island of Ascension, as the *Swallow* laboured on her tedious way, she was rapidly overhauled by a ship which hoisted French colours; and to Carteret's surprise he was hailed by name and informed that the *Dolphin* had returned to Europe, reported his probable shipwreck in the Strait of Magellan, and that two ships had been sent out to his rescue. He asked who it was that displayed such an acquaintance with him and his ship; the vessel, he was told, was in the service of the French East India Company, had been on a trading voyage from Mauritius to Sumatra, and was commanded by M. Bougainville. It offered him refreshment, and offered also to take any letters he had for France. A young officer came on board, who looked about curiously, and did his best to interrogate Carteret with tact, especially on the subject of the South Seas. He received no encouragement, but was desired to present his captain with one of the arrows from Santa Cruz, in return for his courtesies; and with that took his leave. His boat's crew had also had conversation with an English sailor who spoke French; from which it appeared that the French vessel, too, had been round the world, by way of the Strait of Magellan and Juan Fernandez,[1] though where else it had called had not been learnt. This was true: the ship was the *Boudeuse*; the Chevalier de Bougainville had just made a voyage of as much interest as that of the English, though perhaps of less discomfort. Carteret was now very anxious to speak with him again, but it was impossible; 'for though the French ship was foul from a long voyage, and we had just been cleaned, she shot by us as if we had been at anchor, notwithstanding we had a fine fresh gale and all our sails set'. The *Swallow* had still to weather a tempest in which she lost her foresail; but on 20 May 1769 she anchored at Spithead, 'to our great joy', after a voyage which, though in fruitfulness it might be exceeded, for resolution, fortitude and skill had few rivals in that century.

So we come to Bougainville, most famous of the precursors of Cook. Louis Antoine de Bougainville, who thus entered into competition with the English in the Pacific, had fought them in

---

[1] This latter, in fact, was not true (see p. 215 below); the French were for the moment anxious to conceal the details of their voyage. Hence also the story about the trading voyage.

Canada, as an aide-de-camp to the chivalrous Montcalm; the end of the war had found him eager still to serve his beloved France, and he exchanged the army for the naval service. In that age of classicism and politeness none was more classically polite than he; but he had also greater qualities—talent, a warm heart, a generous energy, enterprise, a faith in the capacities of his countrymen which defeat could not diminish. It was a time when the Falkland Islands—called by the French 'les Malouines' —was regarded by the France of de Brosses, as well as by Great Britain, as the key to the Pacific Ocean; and the French had no desire to see the British hand clasped on that key. Bougainville offered to found a settlement there at his own expense, and when Byron, in January 1765, asserted the rights of His Britannic Majesty a French colony had been already in existence for a year. The ship that Byron had encountered in the strait had been Bougainville's ship. Spain also claimed the Falklands, as geographically part of the South American continent; diplomacy was delicate, the difficulties of colonization were not small, and Bougainville received orders to hand them over to his country's allies. He was then to make a voyage to the East Indies across the South Sea. It was the desire of his heart; de Brosses had no more devoted disciple. For this expedition he was given the frigate *Boudeuse*, a newly built vessel, to be joined at the Falklands by the store-ship *Etoile*. He sailed in November 1766, with eleven officers, three volunteers and a crew of two hundred; among his company were Philibert de Commerson, a naturalist, and the young astronomer Véron, who was eager to make observations which would determine longitude at sea, and worked at this problem throughout the voyage. On 1 April 1767 the Falklands were given into Spanish keeping, and as the *Etoile* had not arrived and Bougainville was short of provisions, he was obliged to sail to meet her at Rio de Janeiro. She was damaged and leaking, and not till the middle of November could the voyage of exploration proper start, already a year after leaving France. The passage of the strait, where traces were seen of Wallis and Carteret, took fifty-two days, in December and January; and on 26 January 1768 the ships passed Cape Pillar and made into the open sea.

Bougainville had intended to call at Juan Fernandez for astronomical observations, by which he might estimate more accurately the extent of the ocean, but the winds making this impossible, he steered north-west instead for Davis Land, on still another search for the elusive continent. The *Etoile* sailed every day south of the *Boudeuse*, just within sight, joining company again at night, so that as much as possible of the ocean might be covered. This search lasted till 14 February, when Bougainville, like Carteret, concluded that he had sailed over the continent, and that the land seen by Davis must have been the isles of St Ambrose and St Felix. From that time, therefore, a more westerly course was followed, and the rest of the voyage to the East Indies lay between the equator and the Tropic of Capricorn. On 22 March the first land was seen, four islets which Bougainville called *les Quatre Facardins,* the title of a tale well known at that day—the lagoon islets of Vahitahi. Verdure, palms and hovering birds enticed the eye, but like his predecessors so often, Bougainville could find no anchorage. During the next few days other islets were encountered, low and flat like so many found by the English in the same vicinity, beaten with surf and like them without anchorage.[1] Small as they were, they were inhabited, a fact which caused Bougainville some philosophical surprise: how did these tall bronzed men—whom he at first took for European castaways—reach so insecure a home, what communications had they with other beings, and when they multiplied what became of them? And were the islands increasing in size or gradually disappearing? They were, it was certain, a peril to explorers; no wonder Bougainville thought of the collective name Dangerous Archipelago, and stood a little south to get clear of them. The southern end of this chain of islands, he thought, must have been among

[1] The islands sighted by Bougainville, between 22 and 26 March 1768, were Vahitahi, Akiaki (his Isle des Lanciers), Hao (his Isle de la Harpe, the Conversion de San Pablo of Quiros), Marokau, Hikueru, Reitoru, Haraiki, and Anaa.

those first discovered by Quiros. Bougainville, as a practical explorer, here registers his protest against the theorists. 'Upon the whole', he writes, 'I know not on what grounds our geographers lay down after these isles a beginning of land seen, as they say, by Quiros, and to which they give seventy leagues of extent. . . . If any considerable land existed hereabouts, we could not fail meeting with it; as the least latitude we were hitherto arrived at, was 17° 40′ S which is the same that Quiros observed on this very coast, whereof the geographers have been pleased to make a great continent. I agree', he adds, in memorable words, 'that it is difficult to conceive such a number of low islands, and almost drowned lands, without supposing a continent near it. But Geography is a science of facts; in studying it, authors must by no means give way to any system, formed in their studies, unless they would run the risk of being subject to very great errors, which can be rectified only at the expense of navigators.'

The *Boudeuse* and *Etoile* had been sailing, in their turn, among the islands of the Tuamotu archipelago; and now they were to be the second European visitors to Otaheite, the chief of the group called by Bougainville the Bourbon Archipelago. It was time, for though fresh water was distilled daily, and every day the sailors drank lemonade, scurvy was making its appearance, and wood and refreshment were an urgent necessity. On 2 April a high and very steep mountain was perceived, seemingly an island in itself—Mehetia, and shortly afterwards other land of indeterminate extent—Tahiti. At night the sight of fires over all the coast filled the French with joy, for fires meant inhabitants and succour. Running towards the land on the 4th, they were soon surrounded by canoes, laden with fruit, but though there was no difficulty in trade, not yet would the natives venture aboard. After plying off and on for two days the ships were able to moor safely in a fine bay and strike yards and topmasts. This was inside the reef at Hitiaa, much to the east of the *Dolphin*'s anchorage. So great was the crowd of canoes full of excited Tahitians that the French had much ado to warp in, while the presence of so many women made it no easier to keep the sailors at work. It was the English experience over again, though the pen that describes it is perhaps that of a more classically minded man than Captain Samuel Wallis—who did not find it necessary to advert to Venus and the Phrygian shepherd. Bougainville, going on shore, was met by an immense crowd, quite unarmed and inexhaustibly curious, and was entertained at the house of a chief, where an officer had his pocket very dexterously picked of a pistol. It was returned next day by Ereti, the chief, with a hog and some fowls, and relations being so good, the sick and the water-casks were landed and preparations made for the construction of an armed camp by a little brook near by. To this Ereti and his councillors displayed some opposition—the French, they made it plain, might spend all day on shore, but not the night. Bougainville nevertheless explaining that he meant to stay only eighteen days, at last prevailed upon the chief, and from that moment with hardly an interval relations were as admirable as could be desired; Ereti himself passed the first night with the French and derived a fearful pleasure from the sky-rockets which they set off at his request.

Next day a great and amicable trade began, and nails, tools, buttons and other trifles brought in the provisions that were so much needed, while women and children hastened to aid in the collection of shells and antiscorbutic plants, and the men, paid in nails, helped to get wood and water-casks to the boats. But neither guards nor friendship could prevent the filching of anything portable. Polynesian and European morality, though it was long before Europeans could allow for the fact with a calm mind, failed to coincide, and the French lost their belongings with a sort of exasperated admiration for the skill with which they were abstracted. Apart from this divergence of opinion, all was friendship: the sailors went over the island unarmed, and were entertained with food and an intimate hospitality less mercenary, it appears, than that accorded to Wallis's men—at least the ships were in no danger of falling to pieces with the disappearance of their ironwork. Bougainville indeed described his *Nouvelle Cythère* with an enthusiasm no less than his pre-decessor's, of whose visit he learnt, though his own stay was so much shorter and on a different side of the island. He walked inland, and could have thought he was wandering in a more populous Eden; the turf was covered with fruit-trees and inter-sected with cool rivulets; everywhere was ease, plenty and innocent joy. To this abundance he, like Wallis, added more, planting wheat and barley and other grains, onions and pot-herbs. And he presented Ereti with a couple of turkeys, and some ducks and drakes: 'they were to be considered as the mites of the widow'. He exchanged amiable visits with the chief of an adjoining district. Even the brutal murder of some Tahitians did not seriously interrupt the general friendship; the criminals were not identified, but four suspected soldiers were put in irons in the presence of Ereti, and Bougainville, distributing cloth and tools, made every effort to regain the natives' confidence, with happy results.

The most pressing danger came from the parting of the cables of the *Boudeuse*, which was followed by a great swell, rain and tempest. Four anchors were lost, and only on the point of disaster were the ships, after two days' anxiety, finally thought safe. This bad weather and the possibility of altered relations with the natives, moreover, made Bougainville resolve to leave the island earlier than he had planned, without surveying the coast; and as his sick were nearly recovered this could be done without grave penalty. A suitable passage through the reef was found, and on 14 April the *Etoile* moved out safely. By working all day and part of the night, the watering of the *Boudeuse* was completed; where the hospital and the camp had been set up an act of possession was buried, cut on an oak plank, and a bottle containing the names of the officers; and next morning, the wind blowing off shore, the ships prepared to sail. Ereti came in tears to say farewell, with a canoe-load of weeping wives and a parting gift of food; he received numerous presents and pre-vailed on Bougainville to take to France his brother Ahutoru, a native who wished to see the world and its arts (he did indeed develop a taste for the Paris opera-house). No sooner was the *Boudeuse* outside the reef, however, with the boats still inside securing the anchors, than the wind dropped and the tide and a great swell began to carry her rapidly on to the rocks. At the moment of imminent destruction the boats were able to take her in tow, and a westerly breeze springing up at the same time she was at last carried out of danger. The boats returned for the anchors and recovered two; but at midnight a strong gale compelled Bougainville to make sail and abandon two others. Thus, he said, for the lack of iron chains, a precaution which no navigator ought to forget, he had lost six anchors in nine days. The visit had been productive of both good and evil consequences; yet 'we considered this country as a friend, whom we must love with all his faults'.

From Tahiti the French made west, passing certain other islands of the same group. The weather was fine, and at the beginning of May still more islands were seen, surf-beaten, which Ahutoru at first took for France. Canoes came out bold enough to trade; their people were both less trusting and less honest than the Tahitians—they would not come on board, and cheated over their bargains. They were more savage and displayed no eagerness to get iron; nor did they understand Ahutoru when he spoke: accordingly he held them in the greatest contempt. But their canoes were skilfully made, with triangular sails, and followed the ships a good distance out to sea; and though the French were running at seven or eight knots, sailed round them as easily as if they had been at anchor. These islands, thought Bougainville, seemed to be in about the same longitude as Tasman's Amsterdam and Rotterdam, in which also the Solomons were laid down. They were, in fact, neither of these groups, but Manua and Tutuila in the Samoan group; or, to give them Bougainville's name, the Archipelago of the Navigators.

Then Bougainville did what so many sailors before him had refused to do—instead of considering fearfully the perils of a lee shore on the eastern coast of New Holland and changing his course accordingly to north-west, to bring him round New Guinea, he continued to the west. For a fortnight there was bad weather, calms, rain and westerly winds—the approach to land in the Pacific, generalized Bougainville (rather unsafely), was usually attended with tempests, and squally weather and thick clouds on the horizon were almost certain signs of islands. Navigation in these unknown seas through the long tropic nights, on all sides threatened with the unexpected appearance of land and shoals, was a dangerous matter, yet the shortage of water and provisions and the necessity of taking advantage of favourable winds would not allow the deliberate slowness of the prudent sailor. At this time, too, scurvy appeared again, with other maladies, and the only provisions left for general consumption were salt meat and dried pulse. On 22 May, then, the sight of four more islands was welcome—those that Bougainville called Pentecost, Aurora, Pic de l'Etoile and the Isle of Lepers; to give them their modern names, Pentecost or Raga, Maewo, Mera Lava, and Aoba. Smoke next morning argued inhabitants, and a landing-place being found, an armed party was sent on shore to get wood, some knowledge of the country, and if possible refreshment for the sick. It was at first opposed. Patience and the distribution of red cloth made the people less hostile, though they remained armed and in great numbers. They even helped to carry wood to the boats. Bougainville took possession of the group and the boats moved off before an attack could be made—followed, notwithstanding the aid already given, by a shower of stones and arrows.

The natives of the island visited, Aoba, were black or mulatto in colour, with thick lips, woolly hair and noses pierced with ornaments; short, ugly, ill proportioned and infected with what the French thought must be leprosy, but was some unpleasant island skin disease. Their weapons were bows and arrows and ironwood clubs; their huts were wretched, and they themselves seemed to be torn by war; even while the visitors were there an enemy party appeared, and the sound of a harsh drum came continually from the woods. Nor was the land itself more attractive—a mountain began its rise about twenty yards from the sea, the soil was poor and the fruit not to be compared with that of Tahiti. In the south-west was more land still, a long coast to which Bougainville made sail, impeded for a day and two nights by lack of wind and contrary currents; and on the 25th there was land on all parts of the horizon—the ships were, it might seem, shut up in a great gulf. In several places on that coast were what might be passages, or perhaps were merely large bays; to the land itself no end could be seen. The ships coasted along it, and examined a great inlet opening westward; on its northern side another inlet opened, which the boats were sent to reconnoitre. Anchorage could not be found with a two-hundred-fathom line. The reconnoitring expedition had no happy result; one boat, separated against orders from the others, had two arrows shot at her, and made this the pretext for a general and long-continued fusillade. 'The negroes howled excessively in the woods, whither they had all retired, and where we could hear their drum beating. I immediately made signal to the boat to come on board, and I took my measures to prevent our being dishonoured for the future, by such an abuse of the superiority of our power': so Bougainville, more humane than his men. Trade for provisions was now a very dubious hope; and the only possible anchorage was too far off shore for the ship to protect a landing party. The other boats found that the coast was not continuous but a series of islands. Next morning, the 27th, another fruitless attempt was made to put in, beyond a low point, where a plantation was seen with a large number of natives; once again there was no anchorage. Bougainville describes the disappointment, and a passage follows in his book which carries us back to a voyage one hundred and sixty years before, eloquent of old discovery: 'Beyond that point the land returned to N.N.W. and extended as far as the eye could reach; it was of an extraordinary height, and showed a chain of mountains above the clouds. The weather was dark, with squalls and rain at intervals. Often in day-time we thought we saw land ahead of us; mere fog banks, which

disappeared when it cleared up. . . . We saw the high mountains all day on the 28th till sunset, when they bore from E. to
N.N.E. twenty or twenty-five leagues distant.' Next morning
he was out of sight of land.

The archipelago Bougainville, still classical, called the Great
Cyclades. In spite of this name, his conviction was that he had
rediscovered Austrialia del Espiritu Santo: its appearance corre-
sponded with Quiros's account, the people were similar, and he
even thought he had entered the Bay of St Philip and St James.
He had not done so—it was not Bougainville, but Cook, who
made that final identification; but he had indeed recognized the
land of Quiros. He had sailed through the strait between
Espiritu Santo and Malekula; and now he was faced with the
problem of his next step. At first sight certainly the Archipelago
of the Great Cyclades seemed as if it might be a continent. Had
Quiros been deceived, or had he misrepresented his discovery?
What land lay still farther to the west? Geographers, if they
knew anything, knew little of Torres's voyage, and their
assumptions, like their maps, were highly contradictory.
Campbell (if we may call Campbell a geographer) regarded
Espiritu Santo as part of New Holland. The maps of de Brosses
also linked these two countries; they showed an open strait
between New Holland and New Guinea, and his text declared
the unknown to be more probably a number of large islands.
Bougainville, the first voyager since Torres, decided on investigation. To solve the problem, he said, it was necessary to sail
350 leagues farther in the same latitude. This he determined to
do, though the condition and quantity of his provisions perhaps
counselled resort to some European settlement. 'The event has
shown that little was wanting to make us the victims of our
own perseverance.'

Bougainville's purpose was to get sight of the eastern coast of
New Holland. From 29 May therefore he sailed west along the
parallel of 15°, somewhat retarded by the *Etoile*, making all
possible sail by day and running at night under reefed topsails.
The wind was favourable. On the night of 4 June the first

danger appeared—breakers on what was seen the following day to be a sandy isle hardly rising above the water, covered with birds, and called the Shoal of Diana. Next day some thought they perceived a shore with the sea breaking on it to the west; they were mistaken, but strange fruits and seaweed and pieces of wood floating by the ship, and a smooth sea, argued the nearness of land. On the afternoon of the 6th a long sand-bank ahead persuaded Bougainville that it was time to alter his course; he stood to the north and then again west. Three hours later appeared an apparently endless line of shoals and rocks, on which the sea thundered with great violence. 'This last discovery was the voice of God, and we were obedient to it.' The course was changed to north-east by north. Bougainville was already one degree farther west than Espiritu Santo extended on the chart of the French cartographer Bellin; the signs he had noted, together with the set of the currents, convinced him of the vicinity of a great land—especially to the south-east—which could only be the eastern coast of New Holland. He was, to use modern terms, on the outskirts of the Great Barrier Reef, and his convictions were sound. Less soundly, he was inclined to Dampier's opinion that New Holland must be a cluster of islands, correct though he was as to the difficulty of its approach. It would have been rashness indeed, as he said, to have risked running in with a coast from which no advantage was to be expected, and to get clear of which would mean beating against the prevailing winds. Added to this, bread remained only for two months and pulse for forty days; there was plenty of salt meat, but so noisome was it that the ships' rats were preferred.

Unluckily the favourable south-east wind now failed; but after working to the north for three days, at dawn on 10 June land was sighted, the coast of New Guinea, heralded through the night by a delicious smell. Few lands that Bougainville had seen bore a finer aspect; plains and groves along the shore rose like a magnificent amphitheatre to three successive ranges of mountains, their summits invisible in the clouds. Fertile and rich as the country seemed, interesting as perseverance to the west might be, the necessity of making some port where the wretchedness of his company could be certainly relieved prevented him from landing; prevented him, too, from adopting a course which might have made him Torres's successor. The existence of a passage opening into the Gulf of Carpentaria, and so leading to the Moluccas, was still, he thought, problematical; and as the ships were in a deep gulf running south-east, by this way, which seemed the most feasible, he determined to get out. The resolution involved a fortnight of almost despairing contention with wind and weather; for that same day a calm fell, and a great south-easterly swell hove them towards the land. This peril was averted only to be intensified on the following days, when the south-east wind returned with a great sea, rain, and a fog so thick that guns had to be fired to keep the two ships in touch. These days, said Bougainville, were dreadful; in the dark, in the midst of shoals, with the seas strewing sand and weed on the deck, even to take soundings would have been useless. Had it not been for the sight of land on the 10th, nothing could have saved them. On the 16th the weather cleared, but the wind was still contrary, and still, however much the ships worked to the south, day after day there was land to the north-east, islets, reefs, shoals, the interminable archipelago which formed the eastern extremity of New Guinea; day after day discovered the endless line of breakers. The French were paying dearly for their enterprise. Then hunger grew; the allowance of bread and pulse was reduced, pet animals were sacrificed, and Bougainville was forced to forbid the eating of the leather from the yards; almost, it seems, there is an echo of the agonies of Magellan. The masts themselves were crazy and the rigging worn, so that little sail could be made; while the ships with their foul bottoms went very ill. At last on 20 June sunrise showed high land which appeared to end in a huge cape; the ships stood north-east all day without seeing any land more easterly; and with indescribable joy it was realized that its extremity had been doubled. This gulf was called the Gulf of the Louisiade, the name given to the appalling archipelago; the cape, the Cape of

Deliverance.[1] 'I think', said Bougainville, with justice, 'we have well acquired the right of naming these parts.'

The following two days were dark and squally with a frightful sea. But on the 28th, about sixty leagues northward from Cape Deliverance, land was seen again—two islands and a long high coast. Here might be an anchorage; and at dawn on the 30th the boats were sent to examine the coast more narrowly. Later on a dozen well-built canoes came near the ship; the islanders were black and almost naked, with curled hair dyed white or yellow or red, wore bracelets and plates of shell on their necks and foreheads, and were armed with bows and lances; they seemed far from friendly. The boats reported good holding ground, but no port or river, a surf-beaten almost inaccessible shore, from which the mountains rose directly, and a country wooded all over. The natives were hostile without provoking actual conflict. On the whole the situation was hazardous, but Bougainville hoped to find a passage, his aim now being to work round the north of New Britain. Next day, 1 July, he did enter a strait four or five leagues broad, and saw a fine bay. The wind failing, the ships could not stem the tide, and night fell before they could negotiate the shoals and reefs and currents. In the meantime the boats, entering the bay to sound, had been very dexterously assailed by ten canoes, which were beaten off only by volleys from the French muskets. Two of these canoes were taken; like those previously seen, they were handsomely made, and on the raised bow of one was carved a man's head, with eyes of mother-of-pearl and ears of tortoise-shell, the lips dyed a deep red. In them was found, besides fruit and weapons and skilfully woven shields, the half-broiled jaw of a man. Again one is reminded of an earlier Spanish voyage across the Pacific, and the courageous cannibals of Mendaña, with their artistry in the crafts of life.

This island Bougainville called Choiseul. He emerged from the passage and sailing north-west passed two other islands, one very high, which now bears his own name, and another from

---

[1] Cape Deliverance is the eastern point of Rossel Island.

which canoes came alongside the ship, tempted with trifles floated to them on planks. The natives, much like those of Choiseul, though with canoes differently made, signed that they would fetch coconuts; but they had hardly gone twenty yards when one of them turned and let fly an arrow, after which they all fled as fast as they could paddle. Bougainville disdained retaliation. He named the island Bouka,[1] from a word much used by the natives; it seemed fertile and well populated. Once again a contrary wind and current forbade anchorage, and by the morning of 5 July he decided that the best hope of shelter and refreshment lay in New Britain, which could not be far away. The reception of the French, then, off these shores was more murderous than polite; but if they had been acquainted fully with the observations of Mendaña they might have solved at least one of the permanent problems of Pacific geography. For Bougainville had just sailed through the Solomon Islands, and like Carteret, who had also had trouble there, he remained sceptical of their existence.

Two days later a safe anchorage was found off the coast of New Britain. Wood and water were plentiful, there were no inhabitants, and urgent repairs could be made to the ships; accordingly yards and topmasts were struck and tents pitched on shore. The place had its disadvantages; no fruit was to be found and the sailors fished unsuccessfully, while for several days continuous rain interfered with other operations. The absence of food was serious; even when cabbage-trees were cut down they were overrun by gigantic ants, and it was not the season for turtle. Rations were again reduced. Indeed, apart from wood and water there seemed nothing plentiful but snakes, scorpions and shells—and this on a shore hailed by geographers as admirable beyond all others for European colonization! The search for curious shells led to a more extra-ordinary discovery: a sailor found buried in the sand part of a leaden plate, scratched with English words. This led to a careful examination of the whole neighbourhood, and in a bay about

[1] Now Buka.

two leagues distant were found the remains of a camp—sawn trees, a few ends of rope, and on a large tree in the middle of a space where tents had been pitched the marks of the leaden plate, quite fresh, with the nails still stuck in the trunk. It had earlier been wrenched off by natives. Fresh shoots on a cut tree indicated that the English had been there but four months earlier. It was a singular chance that brought Bougainville for refreshment so close to the camp of his predecessor. He did not yet know who that predecessor was.

Meanwhile a great storm, with repeated earthquake shocks, raged outside his harbour, and the situation daily grew worse. Not till 24 July were the ships able to get to sea. Bougainville then, with a more favourable wind than Carteret had had, although noticing the appearance of a strait, accepted the gulf for the St George's Bay which Dampier had named it. His task was now to reach the Moluccas, a part of the voyage which had its apprehensions and alarms, but was at least bound to end in a known port. Natives of New Ireland who were seen proved an unprofitable and treacherous race; nevertheless privation was still the worst enemy. The tents were cut up for clothes. The bread allowance was reduced once more. Salt meat that should have been thrown overboard was eaten, because no one knew how long the passage to the Moluccas would take. All dejection was stifled; the officers set the example, and every night the sailors danced on deck. Yet scurvy made cruel havoc, and a week more at sea would have put an end to dancing with universal sickness, when on the evening of 1 September the fires of the island of Boeroe were seen. Here the Dutch had a settlement; and the sight of a town, of ships at anchor and of cattle rambling through the meadows caused the French an indescribable joy, while their behaviour at the first meal to which they sat down so astonished the Dutchmen that 'none of them durst eat anything for fear of wronging us'. Only a sailor, said Bougainville, reduced to extremities such as theirs, could understand the emotions produced by food.

Boeroe was left after a week for the passage to Batavia, a

piece of navigation difficult indeed and made more difficult by the secrecy over its details preserved by the Dutch. French charts of the East Indies in truth might have been designed to cause the loss of ships rather than to guide them. Nevertheless on 28 September, twelve days after Carteret had sailed, the *Boudeuse* and *Etoile* anchored safely in the harbour of the Dutch capital. Bougainville was better received at Batavia than was Carteret, whose identity he could learn, and of whose voyage he learnt as much as his hosts knew, which was little enough. The sickness which Carteret had sailed to avoid fell heavily on the French— the enterprising Ahutoru called Java *enoua mate*, the land that kills.[1] Nevertheless it was not till 18 October that they could depart, when so many were down with fevers that Bougainville decided to run as speedily as possible for Mauritius, without waiting for the *Etoile*. Here he anchored on 8 November, finding his reckoning a day late, sent his sick to the hospital and had the ship overhauled. On 9 January he was at the Cape, from which Carteret had sailed three days before; he admired the colony and its little settlement of French Protestants, and left on the 17th, very eager to get sight of Carteret, who was now eleven days ahead. But Bougainville, contrary to Carteret's thought, had a newly clean ship; at Ascension he had already gained six days and sighted the *Swallow* on the evening of 25 February. He joined her next day, and offered his services with a sincerity of which Carteret was hardly aware. The circumnavigators parted, and Bougainville used Carteret's own phrase: 'His ship was very small, went very ill, and when we took leave of him, he remained as it were at anchor. How much he must have suffered in so bad a vessel may well be conceived.' Bougainville himself entered the harbour of St Malo on 16 March 1769. In spite of so much sickness he had lost in those twenty-eight months only seven men; and a number of his countrymen refused to believe that he had sailed round the world, because he had not been in China.

[1] The Tahitian *enua* (*fenua*) *mate* might also mean simply the land of sickness.

# CHAPTER X

# COOK: THE FIRST VOYAGE, 1768–1771

FOR a variety of reasons already sufficiently rehearsed, most of the expeditions of discovery recounted in the foregoing pages fell in some degree short of success. Yet in the mass their contribution to geography had been great, and when all is weighed, the failings of men as well as of ships, the short-comings of knowledge equally with the elemental obstruction of wind and sea, from that achievement it is for no man of a later age to detract. From the momentary unveiling of the Islands of Solomon and their disappearance behind the wall of legend, to the day when Dutch and English and French followed the direction of Quiros and named anew shores so often seen by him, the Pacific had been gradually taking a shape different far from the anticipated certainties of geographers and enthusiasts. Not that there was real definition, even at the end of two centuries; but the student knew more than he had known. The main island groups had been touched on, irregularly—some-times islands had been rediscovered; a number could be put on the map with some, though not great, accuracy; Australia and New Zealand, though known, presented large problems. Did the southern continent, veritable and verifiable, exist? Over an entire half of the ocean no ship had yet sailed. Was Australia, in all its amplitude, yet but an outlying sentinel of a land of boundaries almost infinite? Was New Zealand the northern limit of a coast that stretched impregnably to the Pole? Or did the south but repeat the island clusters of Capricorn and the equator? The mid-eighteenth century had still no certain responses. There were the dogmatisms of Dalrymple, high flights of other geographical theoreticians, the doubts of

Carteret and Bougainville; there remained yet the vision of Quiros, however attenuated and transformed. Within seven years of Carteret's return to England the questions had been answered. For the practical analysis which resolved into ascertained and exact knowledge so much of the structure of theory the world is indebted to Cook.

To treat summarily of the voyages which Cook made with such signal results is inevitably to commit injustice; yet the injustice must be done. Indeed, his career is one of which the justification lies not so much in the underlining of its detail as in the comparison of the map of the Pacific before his first voyage with that at the end of the century. For his was a life consistent and integrated; to a passion for scientific precision he added the inexhaustible effort of the dedicated discoverer; and his own devotion was matched, as nearly as any leader could hope, by the allegiance which was rendered him by his men. James Cook was born a Yorkshireman, the son of a day-labourer of the village of Marton-in-Cleveland, on 27 October 1728. He displayed enough promise as a child for his father's employer to pay for his early schooling; and as a youth, enough passion for the sea to evade the respectable career of a shopkeeper which opened before him. Apprenticed to John Walker, a prominent coal shipper of Whitby, in the hard training of the North Sea he rapidly rose to skill in his craft and to the prospect of commanding a ship. But in 1755 there broke out that informal series of naval actions which merged into the Seven Years' War; the navy needed sailors, and Cook, with an eye to a more varied experience than that of the coal trade, volunteered as an able seaman. Within a month he was master's mate. He saw service in the Channel and the Bay of Biscay, he earned promotion, he was present at the siege and capture of Louisburg; and in the survey of the St Lawrence River which preceded the capture of Quebec he took full part. There followed his first notable piece of independent work, a detailed charting of the St Lawrence, which made his reputation as a skilful marine surveyor, surveys of part of the Newfoundland and Nova Scotian coasts, and further studies in the mathematical and astronomical sciences which he loved so well. Newfoundland was deemed of the highest importance by both English and French, and indeed for a century and a half remained a fruitful source of dispute; and in 1763 Cook was sent out to make a systematic survey of its difficult and comparatively unknown coast. Here, in his first command, he did work remarkably accurate, rapid and persistent, and the published collection of his charts of Newfoundland and Labrador remained not wholly superseded till a very recent period. More, in 1766 he observed an eclipse of the sun; his results were communicated to the Royal Society, and in two important quarters—by the Society and at the Admiralty—his name was now favourably known. To this conjunction of Cook's own talents and of circumstance was due the decisive step which made him the greatest of Pacific explorers.

Scientific men all over Europe were anticipating, not without excitement, the transit of the planet Venus over the disc of the sun which was to occur on 3 June 1769. The phenomenon was important for astronomy, and it would not take place again for another hundred and five years. Several different nations were actively preparing to observe it. A committee of the Royal Society advised that Great Britain should send two observers to Hudson's Bay, two to the North Cape of Lapland, and two to some suitable island in the South Pacific—for in relation to the transit the southern hemisphere was more favourably situated than the northern. The British nation, held the Society, would be dishonoured should they neglect the phenomenon; and accordingly the Crown agreed to provide the expenses of observation and the Admiralty a ship. Dalrymple was recommended by the committee as an observer for the South Seas, by reason of his general talents, and also as 'having a particular turn for discoveries'; but Mr Dalrymple, with a very lively appreciation of those talents, announced that he would go to the Pacific for the Society only if placed in entire control of the ship. This, held the Admiralty, would be quite repugnant to the regulations of the navy; and Dalrymple, with a resentment that did not easily perish, maintained a stubborn front. In the event the choice fell upon Cook, who was promoted in May 1768 from master to lieutenant, and given command of a specially purchased vessel, the *Endeavour Bark*. He was near forty years old, in the full maturity of his mind and capable beyond other men, and his rise from the lower deck had been meritorious and surprising enough; but no one as yet suspected that in him was a principal genius of the age.

The *Endeavour*, which thus became one of the celebrated ships of discovery, was a cat-built[1] bark of 368 tons, a typical East Coast collier from the shipyards of Whitby, less than four years old, and from her roominess and excellent quality as a sea-boat peculiarly well fitted for the work of exploration. She was now given an extra sheathing of wood filled with nails as a protection against the ravages of the tropical teredo worm, and fitted out for a voyage that, it was estimated, would occupy two years at least. She was victualled for nearly eighteen months, and when she sailed had a complement of ninety-four. Of this company, besides Cook, the most prominent was Mr Joseph Banks, a young gentleman of large fortune and a Fellow of the Royal Society, who, a botanist of some accomplishment, had already been to Newfoundland and was eager to make the voyage with a retinue of naturalists, artists and servants. To the reception of Banks and his company the Admiralty raised no objection; and to the observations of himself and Solander, his principal naturalist and a pupil of Linnaeus, the voyage owed the fame it justly obtained in spheres beyond those of astronomy and geography. Banks indeed out of his fortune spent with a lavish generosity—'No people ever went to sea better fitted out for the purpose of Natural History, nor more elegantly',[2] it was reported; and between Banks and Cook there sprang up

[1] A ship with round bluff bows and wide deep waist, tapering towards the stern. She was called the *Endeavour Bark* to distinguish her from another *Endeavour* already in the Royal Navy.

[2] Letter from John Ellis to Linnaeus, quoted in *The 'Endeavour' Journal of Joseph Banks*, I, p. 30.

immediately a just estimate of worth and a mutual and lasting friendship. For the primary purpose of the voyage, the observation of the transit, Cook himself was appointed to act together with Charles Green, one of the assistants at Greenwich Observatory. On the advice of Wallis, who returned to England in May, it was determined that no station could be more suitable for the operation than the paradisal island of Otaheite.

The primary purpose was not the only one, nor in the end did it prove the most important. The eighteenth century was an age of reason and an age of science—it was also the age of the Seven Years' War and a bellicose economic imperialism; while Great Britain was busy losing one empire she was with equal industry laying the foundation of another. Wallis's instructions to search for the southern continent will be remembered, and no less the fortification of Juan Fernandez and the competition for the rather barren prize—but how potentially valuable as a base!—of the Falkland Islands. Cook's instructions followed as a logical step in this international rivalry; if his voyage proved also a cardinal step in the advancement of geography, its intention was largely but to continue the main line of national policy. Of this a scrutiny of the successive secret orders given to the exploring captains of the century will exclude all doubt. 'And whereas', ran Cook's instructions, 'there is reason to imagine that a continent, or land of great extent, may be found to the southward of the tract lately made by Captain Wallis in His Majesty's ship the *Dolphin* (of which you will herewith receive a copy) or of the tract of any former navigators in pursuits of the like kind; you are therefore . . . required and directed to put to sea with the bark you command, so soon as the observation of the transit of the planet Venus shall be finished, and observe the following instructions'. He was to proceed to the southward as far as latitude 40°, in order to discover the continent, unless it was sooner met with. As great an extent of the coast as possible was to be explored and its peculiarities noted; together with the nature of the soil and all its products, of which, where possible, specimens were to be brought back. The nature of the people, if people there should be, was also to be carefully examined, their friendship and alliance cultivated, and trade opened. Furthermore, with their consent, Cook was to take possession of convenient situations, or if the land was uninhabited, to annex it in due form. But if neither the continent nor indications of it were encountered, he was to sail westward between the latitudes of 40° and 35° till he fell in with the eastern side of Tasman's New Zealand. This he was to explore so far as circumstances admitted, taking account of the necessities of return either round the Cape of Good Hope or the Horn, as he himself judged best. The main object was the 'discovery of the Southern Continent so often mentioned', and from this end there was to be no diversion; yet the situation of newly discovered islands was to be carefully fixed, and surveys made and possession taken of any which appeared important. Emergencies were left to Cook in consultation with his officers. On return, all log-books and journals kept by officers were to be surrendered; nor, until official permission had been granted, were they or any of the crew to divulge where they had been.

It has already been remarked that Banks's contribution to the scientific resources of the expedition was very great, and no less comprehensive was the Royal Society's care for the instruments needed for its observations. The Admiralty was less enterprising. In 1765, John Harrison had been awarded £10,000 on the successful trial of his chronometer, an invention which was to bring into navigation a precision it had never had before. In spite of this, there was no chronometer in the *Endeavour*, and it was the task of Cook and Green to fix their position by means of lunars—a laborious and unreliable method for the mathematically ungifted, but one in which they reached an astonishing measure of accuracy.[1] Cook, however, was thoroughly acquainted with what scholarship could tell him of his pre-

[1] In this connection should be noted also as extremely important the first publication, in 1767, of the *Nautical Almanac*, largely owing to the energy of Nevil Maskelyne, the astronomer-royal. Maskelyne was a fervent lunarian, and bitterly opposed to the claims of the chronometer-makers. Harrison claimed the full reward of £20,000, but the second half was not paid till 1773.

decessors in the Pacific—there were on board the learned and enthusiastic volumes of de Brosses, the English abstract of part of Tasman's journal, and, even more important for the outcome, Dalrymple's little book of 1767 with its chart of the track of Torres, a copy of which, sense of insult overborne by scientific passion, the author presented to Banks. But if Cook had, in some sort, the advantages of foreknowledge, far more important were his own reserves of acquired skill and natural genius—his deliberate boldness and calculated caution, his freedom from prejudice, his humaneness and his extraordinary technical accomplishment. It may be added that he was over six feet in height, was by nature affable but short-tempered, direct in speech, of a determination which verged on obstinacy, and as he spared not his own energies, spared no more those of his men.

The *Endeavour* sailed from Plymouth on 26 August 1768.

Cook called at Madeira for water, wine and provisions, and was able to distribute a large quantity of onions among his men —no trivial detail on such a voyage; he also had two men flogged for refusing to eat their allowance of fresh meat. Scurvy, it is evident, was to be fought from the start with the weapons of extremity. At Rio de Janeiro, reached on 13 November, there was difficulty with the viceroy, as a result of which Cook stayed on board ship and exchanged a long series of memorials with the obstructive official, employing his leisure in drawing a plan of the harbour. The viceroy insisted that the ship was a smuggler, and imagined that the transit of Venus was 'the North Star passing through the South Pole'. On 7 December the voyage was resumed, at first through bad weather; luckily it cleared by Christmas Day, when the whole crew got drunk. Cook was entering the Pacific through the Strait of Le Maire (for which he left sailing directions still used in the twentieth century) and round the Horn; Tierra del Fuego was sighted on 11 December, and on the 15th he anchored in the Bay of Success for wood and water. Here Banks, Solander,

Green and others went on shore to climb a range of hills and botanize, with melancholy consequences—they were overtaken by night and a heavy snowstorm, wherein Banks's two negro servants were frozen to death and Solander was with difficulty kept from a fatal sleep. Yet next day the vegetation was a delight, and wild celery and scurvy-grass were collected in great quantities for the general benefit.

Cape Horn was passed on 27 January 1769, when fog and a contrary wind prevented the fixing of its exact position. Farthest south was reached on the 30th, in 60° 4′ S, 74° 10′ W, and the course was altered to west by north to bring them as directly as possible to Tahiti. It brought them incidentally over a part of the southern continent which had not hitherto been traversed (for preceding expeditions had taken a more northerly course to Juan Fernandez or Masafuera), and by 1 March they were in latitude 38° 30′ and 560 leagues directly west of Chile, where the sea showed no trace even of currents—a sure sign, thought Cook, that there was no great land-mass near. Banks, who evidently disapproved of theorists, was extremely pleased, and not even the necessity of balancing the globe could shake his scepticism: until we know how the globe was fixed in the position assigned to it since creation, he remarked, we need not be over-anxious about its balance. These first weeks in the Pacific were uneventful—Pitcairn was passed without being seen; and on the morning of 4 April the first lagoon with its surrounding reef and coconut palms was sighted—Vahitahi in the Tuamotus. Further islands were now encountered nearly every day,[1] though as usual there was no anchorage. The variously named Tahiti rose over the horizon on the 11th; natives came out with green branches, the signs of friendship; a trade in vegetables and fruit at once began, and on the 13th the *Endeavour* lay in Wallis's anchorage in Matavai Bay.

At Tahiti a stay was made longer than that of earlier visitors—from April to July. An observatory was erected and a fort built

[1] Akiaki, Hao, Marokau and Ravahere, Reitoru, Anaa—all in the Tuamotus; then Mehetia, then Tahiti.

at 'Point Venus', somewhat to the alarm of the Tahitians, who, having no warlike intention themselves, were unprepared for such an elaboration of defence. The necessary observations were made on 3 June in a cloudless sky, with a temperature of 119°, two other parties being sent out as a safeguard to observe independently. The remainder of the time was filled with the necessary preparations, with trade, and with scientific observation of a kind hardly less important than that of astronomy. Banks, who was greatly gifted in the management of natives, was put in sole charge of the trade, while Cook, in the effort to assure a constant friendship, ordered that the islanders were to be treated 'with every imaginable humanity'. The naturalists were in heaven, while the high-spirited enthusiasm of Banks and the universal curiosity of Cook elaborated a fuller and more accurate description of the country than any Pacific island had yet received. In the study of native ceremony, Banks went so far as to strip off his clothes and be blackened with charcoal and water; and Cook's journal is a model of scientific detail and exact statement. The first noticed and most prominent characteristic of the Tahitians was, of course, their ability as thieves—they were, said Cook, 'prodigious expert'. They invited a party to dinner, and stole Solander's opera-glass and Banks's snuff-box; they stole Cook's stockings from under his head, though he swore he had not been asleep; they stole a sentry's musket, and a quadrant —a very serious loss—within five yards of which another sentry had been stationed the whole night; they stole iron in any shape or form; when a party slept on shore they stole something from nearly every man—entertaining the victims in return with an unappreciated concert of drums and flutes and singing. Fortunately, essential instruments were later returned, not in the case of the quadrant before Banks had exhausted himself in a hot and breathless pursuit. The only other disadvantage of the island was the flies, which were so pestiferous that they even ate the colours off drawings while the artists were at work.

Of those personalities whom Wallis had remarked, the 'queen', Purea, seemed to have fallen from her high estate. A youth who was carried on a man's back and treated with great reverence was pointed out, so the English wrongly thought, as the king of the whole island, but they had most to do with two friendly chieftains whom Banks (more classical even than Bougainville) nicknamed Lycurgus and Hercules, and with Tupaia, a man who made himself exceedingly useful in all respects. The natives took almost equal liberties with the names of the visitors, and at the banquet which Cook gave on the king's birthday they toasted 'Kilnargo', or King George, with disastrous enthusiasm. Lycurgus also complained that he had been poisoned and in the extremity of illness sent for Banks; he had, it appeared, swallowed a quid of tobacco begged from a sailor, but was restored through the agency of large quantities of coconut milk. Cook's care made these almost the only misfortunes from which the Tahitians suffered; a thief was shot dead, unhappily, on the third day, but this was smoothed over. He even took the body of one of Banks's artists, who had died of a fit, out to sea for burial, lest he should offend religious susceptibilities. There was the usual commerce between the sailors and the island women— and the attractive Banks himself was mightily struck by 'a very pretty girl with a fire in her eyes'; and during the observations, when the officers were all employed, a great number of nails were stolen from the store, for which the only man who could be convicted was flogged.

When the astronomical work had been finished, the ship and its contents were overhauled; meanwhile Cook travelled with Banks round the island and charted its coast in detail. Other anchorages were found, including Bougainville's, of whose visit there remained at Hitiaa traces in the axes the natives brought to be sharpened. Excursions were made on shore, and Cook gives a detailed description of a great *marae*, or 'temple' and burial-place, the enormous stonework of which had excited his curiosity. It had been built by Purea and her husband Amo in honour of their young son, and was the cause of their fall from power; for the pretensions and arrogance that accompanied its completion had led to a war and the final passing of their glory, already undermined by Wallis's guns. Of the native religion Cook could learn little; it seemed to have decayed from its primitive vigour, like its more civilized parallel. 'The misteries of most religions are very dark and not easily understud even by those who profess them', he wrote. The very remark, in its measured hesitation, is an index of the passage of centuries of exploration. Even for such studies, however, the visit could not be indefinitely prolonged, and on 13 July sail was made for other islands of the group. With the ship went the native Tupaia, who had learnt some English and was anxious to travel, and a boy, his servant, both added to Banks's following. Tupaia was a chief and a principal priest, his capacity as such being exercised in the *Endeavour* in prayers for wind, perhaps after due perception of its likelihood. A more useful accomplishment was his skill as a pilot. The islands visited were Huahine, which was surveyed, and where a good trade in provisions was carried on; Ataha or Tahaa, and Ulietea or Raiatea, where a leak in the ship was mended and the visitors were entertained with music, dancing and a dramatic performance. At Raiatea, Cook hoisted a flag and took possession of the whole group, which, apart from Tahiti, he called the Society Islands, 'as they lay contigious to one another'. Up to this time seventeen islands had been seen, and Tupaia was able to enumerate nearly one hundred and thirty in the vicinity, of seventy-four of which Cook drew a sketch map. That there must be at least this number of islands and probably a great many more lying somewhere unvisited in the Great South Sea, he was quite certain. Meanwhile the ship had been very well off for fresh provisions, and its company, though nearly twelve months out from England, were all in good health. On 9 August, Cook left the islands and sailed south.

The task that now lay before him was to find either the great southern continent or the eastern coast of New Zealand. He therefore made to the south till 2 September, when he was in latitude 40° 22′, and the continent should punctually have appeared. There was not the least visible sign of land; nor did the continuous swell rolling up from the south argue its existence. The search was not exhaustive: there might still be land somewhere to the south-east of Tahiti, but the evidence was so far negative. Cook was certainly convinced that hanging clouds and a thick horizon were no infallible indications of a continent. Bad weather discouraged any further progress south, and he determined to turn north again in the hope of something better, making to the west whenever possible. Towards the end of September, after stretching successively north-west and south-west, he was aware of seaweed and floating wood, and a difference in the birds flying round the ship—all signs of land; and on 6 October a boy, Nicholas Young, earned an extra gallon of rum by sighting the northern island of New Zealand. 'All hands seem to agree that this is certainly the continent we are in search of', wrote Banks in his journal. On the 8th the ship sailed into a bay, where quantities of smoke showed that the country was inhabited, and anchored near a small river. In the evening Cook landed without opposition, but four boys who were left in the boat were threatened with attack by a band of natives, one of whom was killed. Next morning he landed again with Tupaia, but again the natives were aggressive, in spite of presents given, and Cook felt forced to order one who had snatched Green's hanger to be shot, when the others retreated. It was an unfortunate beginning, lightened, however, by the welcome fact that Tupaia's tongue was understood by these Maoris. In the afternoon the surf was too heavy for landing, and Cook tried to intercept two canoes, with the object of giving presents, making friends of the occupants, and letting them go again. He failed miserably: a musket fired over the canoes (which might have succeeded in its object in Tahiti) merely caused a fierce attack on the nearest ship's boat; and her crew, firing in self-defence, killed or wounded three or four men. Cook and Banks alike expressed the bitterest regret. Three young Maoris at least who jumped overboard and were picked up soon overcame their fear in the delights of eating and drinking, singing and dancing; and next day they were landed without any further conflict, though in the neighbourhood of about two hundred armed men. It was evident now and later that the New Zealanders were both war-like and brave.

Cook, unable to get any refreshment, called this first landing-place Poverty Bay—a name, unjust indeed, which it still possesses. His plan was to coast southwards till about 40°, and then, if there seemed no better prospect, to turn once again north. Thus he passed the wide bay called after Sir Edward Hawke of the Admiralty, where the natives sold him bad fish; Cape Kidnappers, where they tried to abduct the boy servant of Tupaia; and at Cape Turnagain in 40° 34′ altered his course once more to the north. At intervals it was possible to buy fresh food, or to gather wild celery, and Banks and Solander collected with vigour whenever they were on shore. The valleys were well timbered, with trees unknown in Europe. As the ship sailed round East Cape and the Bay of Plenty, the country improved in appearance and became more cultivated—though the people remained impolite, breaking off trading to steal Cook's sheets, towing behind in the wash, shouting defiance and throwing stones. Ten days were spent at Mercury Bay, so called because there, on 9 November, Cook and Green observed the transit of Mercury. Here they made good friends, after some preliminary doubt on the native side; for what sort of beings, it was asked, were these new-comers? Was their ship a great bird, with its white wings? Were they goblins, or otherwise super-natural, who paddled their boat backwards? They killed birds from a distance with thunderbolts; if they looked fixedly at an ordinary mortal he felt ill. Yet they were generous, and their chief was obviously a great man. So there was good trade in fish; good water, wood, wild fowl and green vegetables were found on shore; and the officers were able to look a little more closely at the country. The people showed the visitors over one of their villages, a *pa* fortified with amazing skill—a post indeed, noted Cook, 'where a small number of resolute men might de-fend themselves a long time against a vast superior force, arm'd in the manner as these people are'. Time was to prove the justice of his observation, even when the assailants brought artillery. The impression Cook himself made was very favourable; as late as the mid-nineteenth century an old chief remembered with pride being patted on the head as a child by the explorer, and would imitate his peculiarities of gait and gesture. At this bay Cook had the name of the ship and the date carved on a tree, and took formal possession of the place.

Still running close to the land, he hauled round a prominent cape to explore a deep gulf and the river at its head, called the Thames from some resemblance in size to its namesake, while with the neighbouring Maoris a very cordial trade was established. Indeed, one unfortunate who was caught in theft was beaten by English and natives alike. The weather then became very squally, and it was some time before Cook could find an anchorage in the magnificent harbour of the Bay of Islands. The country hereabout was fertile, well planted with sweet potatoes; but the natives once again threatened attack. They tried to steal an anchor buoy and mobbed Cook and Banks, till they were stampeded by shots fired over their heads, when Tupaia's mediation was invaluable. Nor did they harbour resentment. At the same time sailors were punished for raiding native plantations. Shortly afterwards, on 13 December, a gale blew the ship out of sight of the coast for the first time since Cook had made his landfall, and two days later, seeing land to the south-west, with a great swell coming from the west, he concluded he had come to the northernmost point of the country. There were westerly winds and a strong current, and after Christmas (when all hands piously got drunk again) the wind freshened to a hurricane, with heavy rain and a 'prodidgeous high sea'. Yet, running some distance to the north out of sight of land and back again Cook was able to identify Tasman's Three Kings, and working under extraordinary difficulties fixed the position of Cape Maria van Diemen, to which he was never close, with only two minutes of error in latitude and four in longitude. This was after weathering 'a gale of wind . . . which for its strength and continuence was such as I hardly was ever in before'.

Curiously enough, it was at some time during this bad weather in the second half of December that Cook passed another ship that was on the New Zealand coast, the French *St Jean Baptiste*, commanded by Jean François Marie de Surville. Neither saw the other. Surville's expedition, a private commercial one, had not had New Zealand for its objective, but, probably, Tahiti—it was an attempt to anticipate the British there, though it did not leave its port of departure, Pondicherry in India, until six weeks after Cook had actually landed at Matavai Bay. Surville had sailed by way of the Philippines, the Bashi Islands and the Solomons (which he did not recognize) as far as latitude 14° S, and then decided that the bad health of his crew made it necessary to call at the land which Tasman had discovered. He steered south down to latitude 35° and then east, sighting New Zealand on 12 December just south of what is now known as Hokianga Harbour. On that day Cook, on the east side of the island, was nearly opposite, in latitude 35° 37', half a league from the shore. Surville turned north in the gale that blew Cook out of sight of land, rounded Cape Maria van Diemen on the 16th, saw the Three Kings and came to the eastern coast. He had some trade with the natives, by whom he was received with great honour, and on the 17th anchored in the port which Cook called Doubtless Bay. So frightful had been the ravages of scurvy that since leaving Port Praslin, in the Solomons, two months before, sixty of his crew had died, and a few days more without sight of land would have spelt utter disaster. At Doubtless Bay the sick were taken ashore, and the antiscorbutic vegetables there gathered being of immediate benefit, Surville remained throughout the rest of the month, giving the natives pigs and fowls and various seeds. Then after Christmas came the hurricane which Cook also experienced, and in which Surville's ship was with difficulty extricated from danger. During this bad weather a dinghy sank, and when the natives were seen dragging it away, Surville, in spite of the friendly treatment he had had from them, drove them off, burnt their canoes, captured a chief, and placed him in irons. It was foolish, for now the French could expect no help and could only depart. A third of Surville's crew were dead, he had lost four anchors, four cables, and a boat, had only one anchor left, and his rigging was in a ruinous state. He therefore called a council and, the wind being favourable, it was resolved to sail to Peru forthwith; the unfortunate chief was taken (Surville had a habit of kidnapping ethnological specimens) to die miserably at sea, and on 8 April 1770 Surville, attempting to enter the harbour of Chilca on the coast of Peru in a small boat, was capsized on the bar and himself drowned with two companions.

At the beginning of January, having survived the elemental onset of the weather, Cook, however, was sailing down the western coast, a dangerous coast which at first showed nothing but the desolation of long sand-hills. During all these weeks he was making a chart that for its accuracy remains one of the major achievements of the century. He saw the noble snow-crowned peak of Taranaki that Tasman had not seen, and named it Mount Egmont after the First Lord of the Admiralty; he noticed the fires of men once again. Then on the 14th he came to a 'very broad and deep bay or inlet', on the southern shore of which appeared a number of smaller bays where work might be carried out on the ship. She was by this time very foul and in need of overhauling, while wood and fresh water were running short. A very convenient place was found in Ship Cove in the long inlet called by Cook Queen Charlotte's Sound. In this cove, which became one of his favourite harbours, he was excellently situated for all he needed. The surrounding country was thickly timbered, the water was good and abundant. Banks and Solander were overjoyed at their opportunities. The ship was anchored not a quarter of a mile from the shore, and in the mornings its company was awakened by the singing of an innumerable host of birds: 'who seemd to strain their throats with emulation perhaps', wrote Banks in his journal; 'their voices were certainly the most melodious wild musick I have ever heard, almost imitating small bells but with the most tuneable silver sound imaginable to which maybe the distance was no small addition.' The people of the Sound, who began an immediate acquaintance by 'heaving a few stones against the ship', quickly turned exceedingly friendly, trading without cheat or fraud. They were cannibals, it was found, and the neighbourhood was strewn with the bony relics of departed feasting, when the captured in war or hapless strangers had been knocked on the head and committed to the admirable Maori oven. Banks was able to buy the head of a recent victim. Murderers' Bay, where Tasman's men had suffered, was only seventy miles away. Cook could learn no tradition of that earlier unfortunate visit.

While work was going forward on the ship boats were continually out surveying. Thick forest hampered any view of the surrounding country. One day, therefore, while Banks and Solander busily botanized, Cook and a sailor climbed a hill to get a sight, if possible, of the end of the inlet. This was intercepted by still higher hills, but Cook came down in high spirits. The view was open to the eastward, and they had seen that the 'deep bay or inlet' was no bay, but the great strait that Tasman and Visscher had suspected. There, in fact, was the eastern sea, and there went the last thread of supposition that the northern part of New Zealand at least was a continent. Furthermore, from an old Maori Cook learnt that neither was the land of the strait continental, but islands. He took possession of the sound, drank Queen Charlotte's health, and as his ship was now in good shape again, on 6 February made out into the strait that bears his name, where the treacherous currents which are one of its characteristics almost at once threatened to carry the Endeavour ashore. They changed just in time and the eastward passage was made in a tide which roared like a mill-stream. In spite of all indications, some of the officers were still unsatisfied that the northern island did not form part of a continent; there were indeed on board two parties, one of which desired a continent (including Banks, in spite of his scepticism), the other which did not—or, according to Banks's genial gibe, began 'to sigh for roast beef'. To set the matter at rest, Cook sailed north to Cape Turnagain, called his officers on deck to receive their admission and then turned south.

The coasting and survey of this southern island was made difficult by adverse and squally weather, which blew the ship four times out of sight of land and split several sails, and gave some peculiarities to the subsequent chart. Nevertheless, by 13 March the *Endeavour* had rounded the southernmost point of the land and was working up the western coast, and Banks had seen 'the total demolition of our aerial fabrick calld continent'. What promised to be a good harbour was noted in the opening Cook called Dusky Bay, passed as night fell, from which the coast trended away to the east and the north. The land had at first a rugged and barren aspect, then the great mountains of the Southern Alps were seen, and then the fertile bush-covered strip of shore that lay still farther to the north. It was the coast that Tasman had sighted, seemingly uninhabited as he had found it. On 24 March, Cook, like Tasman, rounded the north-west point of the island and came again into the strait. Circumnavigation was complete, and he began to think it was time to depart. Two days were spent in Admiralty Bay overhauling the sails and obtaining wood and water, and by the end of the month the *Endeavour* was ready to leave New Zealand on her homeward voyage.

Cook's instructions, so far as they were explicit, had now been converted into solid and brilliant achievement. He had given New Zealand a sure and defined outline; in less than six months he had charted 2400 miles of coast in a manner as accurate as it was unprecedented. His mistakes were not great ones: he thought that Banks Peninsula, on the east coast of the South Island, was an island. He thought that Stewart Island in the south was a peninsula. He certainly disclaimed minute accuracy. But all the questions which Tasman left open had been answered, and a mass of information accumulated about the country itself, its products and its inhabitants. It was a land ideally suited for European settlement, of soil seemingly for the most part rich, and of bewildering beauty. The timber was magnificent, the promise of grain and fruits considerable, fish was abundant, and there were no animals larger or more threatening than dogs and rats. Few native races were of finer appearance than the Maori or of more supple intelligence, or were more versed in all the skills of life—the making and management of canoes, the building of forts, the preparation of flax and the weaving of garments, an elaborate and spirited carving, the decorative use of feather and shell. Fond of battle they were, it was evident, courageous and merciless in victory, with many customs strikingly similar to those of Tahiti and a language almost identical. It was in the warmer north that the population was greatest and the people seemed most intelligent. The southern island was obviously almost empty of inhabitants, and those there were seemed poorer than the northern tribes, cultivated the ground but little, and lived on fern roots and fish; nor were their canoes as ornate and cunningly contrived. Yet if ever it were decided to settle a colony in New Zealand, now numbered among the possessions of His Britannic Majesty, the most suitable place, thought Cook, would be in the north, either on the River Thames or the Bay of Islands. With the fertility of such a land an industrious people would quickly muster not merely the necessities but the luxuries of life; for the native tribes appeared to be too greatly divided among themselves to oppose unitedly the settlement of newcomers. There was justice in Cook's observation; nevertheless, both he and Banks underestimated the force of resistance that lay in the complex economy and war-toughened fibre of those very intelligent cannibals.

It was now the end of March 1770, and there lay before Cook the choice of route by which he should return home. His instructions directed him to take that round either Cape Horn or the Cape of Good Hope, while allowing much to his own discretion. There were objections to either course—the southern summer was drawing to its close; the ship, though refitted as well as might be, was not in first-rate condition; to sail to the west by the Cape of Good Hope would preclude any further discovery; on the other hand, to make directly across the southern Pacific to the Horn, in a necessarily high latitude, though it might dissipate finally the continental theory, would be to sail too close to disaster. This last alternative lay very near Cook's heart; but he had the prudence as well as the logic of the discoverer, and he decided against it. He might, again, follow the example of so many of his predecessors, notably of Tasman, and without incurring the blame that was so gratuitously Tasman's, take the shortest route to the East Indies for the supplies and repairs that would surely be necessary. There was a fourth possibility. A council of officers was held from which emerged a unanimous decision. It was resolved, says Cook, 'to return by way of the East Indies by the following rout: upon leaving this coast to steer to the westward untill we fall in with the East coast of New Holland and than to follow the direction of that Coast to the northward or what other direction it may take us untill we arrive at its northern extremity, and if this should be found impractical than to endeavour to fall in with the lands or Islands discover'd by Quiros'. The resolution was significant, and it was to bring the *Endeavour* into perils which even Cook, could he have foreseen them, would have hesitated to incur; but in ignorance of this danger-ridden future he weighed at daylight on 31 March and with a favourable wind steered west.

Sixteen days out birds were seen that were found only near land; next day there was a south-westerly gale which forced the ship off her course; and on the morning of 19 April Lieutenant Hicks saw land five or six leagues distant, running north-east to west. Cook had wished to fall in with Van Diemen's Land as nearly as possible at the place where Tasman had left it, to see if it were, in fact, joined to New Holland; and if it had not been for the gale he would probably have discovered Bass Strait. He was now north of the desired landfall, and though he could see no land to the south, he was compelled to leave the question unresolved. The land seen by Hicks was one of sloping hills partly covered with trees and bushes, and large tracts of sand; later it improved in appearance, and smoke showed that it was inhabited. Cook sailed north seeking a harbour, but more than once heavy surf and a contrary wind prevented a landing. It was not till 29 April in latitude 34°, on a coastline now much more barren, that a sheltered bay was seen where he was able to anchor. Cook, Banks and a party went ashore. A few naked savages had been sighted, armed with long spears and throwing-sticks. Their bodies were painted with broad white streaks; others, in the worst canoes Cook had ever seen, were so busy fishing that they scarcely seemed to notice the advent of the *Endeavour*. Two men came down resolute to dispute the landing of the thirty or forty Englishmen, and all parley was useless. Finally a charge or two of small shot was fired, and they retreated. From some small huts near by, poorly made, a bundle of spears was taken away, and beads, ribbons and nails left in return; next morning they were found untouched.

The main difficulty was the obtaining of water, though in the end more than enough was found, while there was wood for fuel everywhere. Cook surveyed the harbour, and shore parties inspected the country. The soil was by turns sandy and swampy, lightly timbered, free from undergrowth, and bearing a sort of coarse grass; inland was found much richer soil and even lush meadows (for which the first unfortunate Australian colonists, twenty years later, looked in vain, becoming somewhat embittered by their disillusionment) broken by expanses of rock. Banks and Solander collected numberless specimens, unperturbed by the occasional spear thrown by a fleeing aborigine—enough indeed to give new limits to the whole science of botany. As abundantly found, almost, by the fishermen, was the great sting-ray, so abundantly that the bay was called Stingray Harbour, a name altered later, apparently as Banks's enthusiasm over his collections grew, to Botany Bay. Transportation to the Pacific was not yet, however, suggested, and Cook sailed north again with no foreshadowing of the future, to come abreast a few hours later of another bay wherein good anchorage seemed likely, which without entering he called Port Jackson, after one of the Admiralty secretaries—a bay discovered

later to be among the finest harbours of the world. Progress was
slow, currents were swift and variable; nevertheless, day by day
the coast was accurately charted, that coast of bay and promon-
tory with its inland hills, ridges and valleys and wooded plains,
giving place to barren sand and the plants of the tropical zone;
and always rose the columns of smoke by which the 'Indians'
warned their fellows of the portent visible at sea. Cook
anchored again on 23 May in a large open bay with a stream of
fresh water—Bustard Bay, in honour of the large and excellent
table-bird shot there. The ants and mosquitoes in their turn
found Banks a source of nourishment not to be despised, as he
ruefully records. This was a short distance north of Moreton
Bay where Brisbane now stands.

North of Bustard Bay, the sea was broken by awkward
shoals, outside which and through islands and reefs Cook
groped in unsuccessful search of water, into his Thirsty Sound,
where he stayed two days. Not only did he need water, but the
ship's bottom was again foul, and he was anxious to scrape it
clean as soon as he should find a good harbour. The coast now
rarely showed signs of fertility, and except for one or two fruitless landings he pressed on, at night as well as by day, for the
light of the moon was clear and brilliant. So near was the
*Endeavour* to the land that she had sailed right inside the Great
Barrier Reef and its formidable hazards without Cook's being
aware of it; and now the reef began to close in upon him. On
10 June, at sunset, a coral shoal was seen, and he resolved to
stretch off all night, both to avoid such dangers and to see if any
islands lay near—perhaps some of Quiros's, which were supposed to be in this latitude, about 16°S. The wind was gentle,
the moon bright, the sea smooth, but its depth began to vary
with abnormal suddenness. Soundings were made constantly.
Then danger seemed past, and all except the watch had turned
in, including Cook. Just before eleven o'clock they were in
seventeen fathoms; and then before the lead could be heaved
again, the ship struck. She was beating violently on a coral reef
of terrifying sharpness, and it was high water.

Cook was on deck at the second blow, cool and precise. He was not given to overstatement, but he had no doubt of the crisis. Even if the ship were got off with a large leak, she might sink at once, the boats would not take her whole company, and the land which could be seen six or seven leagues away held nothing of promise. She was, however, making little water and might get off at the next high tide. Anchors were carried out and a vain attempt made to haul her off. Then forty or fifty tons of ballast, decayed stores and guns were flung overboard, still without success; and the tide ebbed. It rose again, and the pumps could not keep down the leak. 'This was an alarming and I may say terrible circumstance and threatend immidiate destruction to us as soon as the ship was afloat', wrote Cook. He determined to heave her off, whatever the risk might be. To stay would no less be fatal. Every possible hand was sent to the capstan and the windlass, and at last, after twenty-three hours, she floated in deep water, so far from sinking that the pumps even gained on the leak. It was decided to 'fother' the ship—that is, to lower over her bows a sail on which oakum and wool were sewn, covered with dirt, and drag it along the bottom, so that this mixture would be sucked into the hole and close it. Jonathan Monkhouse, a midshipman who had seen the operation performed, was put in charge, and so successful was the result that in a quarter of an hour she was pumped dry. The ship had already stood in for the land, and a boat was sent off to look for some place where she could be safely beached. A small river was found, and by the second evening after the shock she was moored within twenty feet of the shore and was being emptied of her contents.

When Cook praised he did so with the moderation that was part of his character, but in this instance at least moderation was justly exceeded. No men, he said of his ship's company, ever behaved better than they had done; while Banks, remarking on the absence of apparent emotion in the officers, testified also not merely to the cheerfulness and alacrity of the seamen, but even to their extraordinary abstention from oaths. Certainly the exertions of all, including the scientific supernumeraries, aided by good fortune, had saved the ship; and now a hospital tent having been erected on shore for the few sick, she was warped farther up the river and beached. The damage was serious, for the coral had cut straight through the bottom with scarcely a splinter, as if an axe had been employed. Luckily a piece had broken off, and remaining stuck in the hole, had helped materially to reduce the leak. It was not till 4 July that the *Endeavour* could be floated again, fairly securely patched, though nothing could be done to repair the sheathing, seriously damaged as it was. Meanwhile the men were allowed all possible freedom, and the fresh fish and vegetables, turtles and enormous shellfish that were obtained did much to improve the general health. Cook fixed the longitude astronomically with great exactitude; Banks and Solander collected with vigour; and parties went walking and hunting. They even shot three kangaroos, the appearance of which had caused vast excitement. Coconuts were picked up on the beach encrusted with barnacles, a sure sign of a sea-passage —perhaps from the land of Quiros, which land, Cook was convinced, could certainly not be any part of New Holland.

An attempt was made at this river to arrive at good terms with the natives, the first seen, except at a great distance, since Botany Bay. A shy race, Cook's cautious tempting nevertheless brought them near, to carry on a long attempt at communication with Tupaia, who on this occasion exhausted his linguistic faculties in vain. These people were obviously unrelated either to Tahitian or to Maori: they differed also from the natives of the west coast, described by Dampier with such detail and distaste. The hair of these was not woolly but straight; their colour, when Banks spat on his finger and got beneath the outer covering of dirt, seemed to be chocolate rather than black. Their noses were pierced for ornaments; but on the whole their features were not disagreeable, nor their soft voices unpleasant. They were as ignorant and savage in their life as their fellows in other parts of New Holland, cultivating no ground and knowing no metal; they were also as naked. Their acquaintance, once made, was tenuously maintained; and when they were prevented from carrying off turtles they saw on the deck of the ship they set fire to the undergrowth all round the camp.

These investigations were the employments of an enforced idleness; for though the repairs to the *Endeavour* had not taken long, not till 6 August did the wind allow Cook to put to sea and continue the voyage. It was not a continuation that promised to be pleasant. From a hill he climbed he could see nothing in any direction but shoals, and the master, looking for a passage with the pinnace, had reported as unfavourably. A constant look-out was kept from the mast-head and the pinnace went ahead to sound; and thus the *Endeavour*, with her insecure bottom and barely three months' provisions, crept on 'the most dangerous navigation that perhaps ever ship was in'. Cook and Banks landed on a high island in hopes of better observation, and in the east saw the sea breaking on the outside of the interminable reef. There were openings in the reef, and after consultation with the officers Cook resolved to sail through, for he was anxious to reach the East Indies. The result was viewed with a modified pleasure: when they were once more in the open sea, after being entangled since the middle of May and sailing 360 leagues with the leadsman never out of the chains, the ship made more water than before, and a pump had to be kept going continually. Nor was it possible to survey the coast closely enough. One of the tasks Cook had set before himself was to determine finally whether New Guinea and New Holland were joined or not, and he stood now in danger of missing a passage to the west. Danger was not confined to this chance. On the night of 14 August he shortened sail lest he should overshoot the strait, and next day sighted land again which was obviously still New Holland. The wind went round to the east, and to avoid being carried on to the reef he changed course to north and then at dark to south. Shortly afterwards it fell quite calm; and at day-break the next morning the reef was seen not a mile away, smitten by tremendous breakers. Towards this reef, rising perpendicularly from a fathomless ocean, and these breakers the

*Endeavour* was rapidly drifting. The boats were sent off to tow, and when the ship was within eighty or a hundred yards of disaster she was headed to the north. Yet disaster seemed certain: 'the same sea that washed the sides of the ship rose in a breaker prodigiously high the very next time it did rise, so that between us and distruction was only a dismal vally the breadth of one wave and even now no ground could be felt with 120 fathoms.' Once again there was complete absence of panic; and Green the astronomer, Clerke, the master's mate, and the gunner went on taking a lunar to determine the longitude, with as much self-possession as if they had been safely moored in harbour. At the moment of losing hope a small breath of air enabled them to increase their distance to two hundred yards before it fell calm again. Then a narrow opening was seen in the reef, through which it was resolved to go; but the ebb tide gushing out carried them a quarter of a mile away. A second opening was noticed which appeared practicable; the ship was headed for it, and with a light easterly breeze and the help of the flood tide she was hurried through this 'Providential Channel' into a safe anchorage.

The *Endeavour* was once again surrounded with shoals and islands, but the other danger had been so great that these now caused Cook less concern. The prospect to the north did not seem quite so bad as the labyrinth through which he had already passed. While the pinnace was being repaired the other boats were sent out fishing, and the ship crept north again by a route of dangers never followed since, the boats constantly sounding ahead. If there were no strait to the westward, this painful progress would be succeeded by the necessity of beating out of the great gulf south of New Guinea against the trade wind as Bougainville had done; and the ship was in no state for such a contest. But Cook was convinced, if not of the existence of the strait, at least of its strong probability, and he was determined to give an exact answer to the ancient question. On 21 August the land began to look very narrow, and at noon the opening of the passage was seen. It was a passage much broken by islands, and after the boats had found rocks and shoals in the channel nearest the mainland, the ship followed them through the next one to the north. Before sunset a party landed on a small island —Possession Island—where, as there could be no new discoveries farther west, Cook formally took possession of the whole eastern coast of New Holland from 38° northwards under the name of New Wales or New South Wales. Almost the whole of this coast—2000 miles—during the last four months had been surveyed and charted. From a hill-top, islands were seen in the north-west, but to the west and south-west was the open sea. Danger, however, was not yet finished with. Through Endeavour Strait the ship groped after her pinnace, once nearly losing an anchor, and a little later in a nasty sea coming close to running on a reef again. At length on 29 August the coast of New Guinea was sighted, and exploration, though not the voyage, was at an end. The passage the *Endeavour* had sailed through was south of that used by Torres, who had coasted New Guinea; nor did Cook doubt that a better one might be discovered among the islands farther to the north. Nevertheless the achievement gave him, he said, 'no small satisfaction not only because the dangers and fatigues of the voyage were drawing to an end, but by being able to prove that New-Holland and New-Guinea are two seperate lands or islands, which untill this day hath been a doubtfull point with geographers'. The brevity of the comment is a summary of the man.

The charts of de Brosses were fairly satisfactory for the New Guinea coast, but shoals remained a difficulty, and the ship had still another narrow escape from striking. A landing was made, however, before she left a shore where Cook could only duplicate work already done. There was a sudden ineffectual attack by a few natives, but he refused to have coconut trees cut down which would have provided refreshment for his crew only at the cost of a further attack and consequent bloodshed. The decision to make for civilization without more delay was received with enthusiasm and even an improvement in the general health. On 17 September the island of Savu was made, an island where fresh food could be obtained, even if Indian beef and mutton were not particularly appetizing. In the mouth of the Strait of Sunda the first European news the ship had had for two years was given by a Dutchman; and Cook learned that Carteret had reached England in safety with the *Swallow*. On 10 October the *Endeavour* anchored at Batavia.

It was clear that the ship must be thoroughly overhauled. The sails split in the slightest puff of wind, the pumps were in bad order and the hull was so damaged that it made upwards of a foot of water an hour. Cook was hardly prepared, however, for what he now learnt from the Dutch shipwrights. In one place the planking, cut down by the coral, was no more than an eighth of an inch thick, and worms had so eaten the timbers that the mere fact that the ship floated was amazing. The false keel was gone to within twenty feet of the sternpost. It was in a happy ignorance that those desperate leagues from the Endeavour River had been sailed. But the workmen were adept and quick, and by 14 November the hull was fit for sea again, rigging went forward, stores and water were got on board. Yet Cook could not leave before 26 December; and the interval was appalling. The regimen enforced on board all through the voyage had brought the ship to Batavia without the loss of a single life through sickness, nor with one man then sick; and, a phenomenon in that age almost incredible, not more than four or five had even been touched by scurvy. Certainly on leaving England the *Endeavour* had received a supply of all the antiscorbutics then known; but of much more effect had been Cook's insistence on the preventive measures systematized by himself. No commander before had been so particular about the diet of his men —the allowance of salt beef and pork was reduced almost from the beginning of the voyage; he forbade the sailors to mix the salt beef fat with their flour, and instead of pickled suet issued raisins; butter and cheese were banned after leaving England; sour-krout, mustard, vinegar, wheat, orange and lemon juice, saloop and portable soup were used regularly, and every chance of obtaining fresh vegetables and 'scurvy-grass' was eagerly seized. Even when there was no shortage of water, old supplies were emptied out and the casks refilled. Cold bathing was encouraged by exhortation and example; a scrupulous and unusual cleanliness was observed throughout the ship and the lower decks were dried regularly with stoves. But at Batavia the season was exceptionally bad: nothing could stay the fever of the East Indies. By the end of November scarcely a dozen hands could be mustered for duty; when the ship left seven had died, more than forty were sick, and the rest were all weak from the terrible onset of malaria and dysentery. Tupaia and his boy were dead, as was Monkhouse the surgeon; Banks and Solander survived by an uncomfortably narrow margin. The *Endeavour* was like a hospital ship; yet the Dutch captains remarked how lucky the English had been. Nor was the tale complete. Between Batavia and the Cape, before the healthy south-east trade began to blow, and at the Cape itself, there died twenty-two men more, including Green the astronomer and Monkhouse the midshipman who had fothered the ship. Hicks, the lieutenant, died later in the Atlantic from consumption, which had been with him all the voyage. The Cape was sighted on 10 March and a stay of a month made; on 1 May the ship was at St Helena; on 10 July the sharp eye of Nicholas Young made out Land's End; and three days later, 13 July 1771, the *Endeavour* anchored in the Downs and Cook left for London to report.

It was a report of a type to which the Admiralty was scarcely accustomed. In spite of the comprehensive nature of the secret instructions bestowed on Pacific voyagers, they were perhaps not expected to convert themselves into encyclopaedias. Nor did Cook do this; but he did something not unlike it. His achievement, soberly estimated, was already after this one voyage the greatest which the history of discovery could record. True, he had not set out blindly into the void; he was endowed with advantages unknown to most of his predecessors; he had fellow workers of uncommon talent; he was faced with a definite task. But the greatest of his advantages was himself, and only on that condition are the results of his first circumnavigation explicable. He had charted upwards of 5,000 miles of coastline, of no ordinary difficulty for the surveyor; he had fixed the position of most of that coastline with a precision which was absent in a great part even of the civilized world; and he had done this under difficulties for retreating from which no man could have given him blame. Those stormy weeks off Cape Maria van Diemen and the passage through the appalling dangers of the Great Barrier Reef are an index of scientific passion no less than of the resolution and technical skill of the sailor. Great error in calculation, the accepted inevitable among navigators, became with him the regretted exception. One of the worst longitudes of the voyage was that of Cape Cornwall in Torres Strait, 70' too far to the west, after days of dead reckoning among that tangle of shoals, when observations had been impossible. In the Strait of Sunda again his longitude was wrong by three degrees. The fact measures the inadequacy of technical resource even at that period; the rarity of serious error is a measure of Cook's own mind. He had taken a bay, a landfall, a vague strip of coast, and presented to geography an outline, clear and defined, set and proportioned in the general scheme of knowledge. Nor was that outline the bare abstraction of the map. There was in his journal the statement of winds and seas, tides and sunken rocks, of the character of lands, the habits of men, such as no sailor had yet given the world. He had not discovered the great southern continent, but he had more than any other man made doubtful the thesis of its existence. He had not discovered Tahiti, but he gave that island of Venus and of George III a complete and rounded existence. He had not discovered New Zealand, but he had brilliantly reduced it to the dimensions of fact. He had not discovered New Holland, but he had from a vague obscure crystallized New South Wales; and he had shown that this eastern coast at least was no archipelago, but continuous land. He was the second and not the first captain to sail between Australia and New Guinea; but the act had both the force and the effect of a new discovery. He had pursued these objects with a sure and astonishing tenacity, a capacity to make fruitful every league of a voyage, which compelled a positive and considerable result. That result had been attained with an accompaniment which amazed his expert contemporaries as much as did his additions to geography. Scurvy had been the familiar spirit of Pacific voyages, of Bougainville and of Carteret no less than of Magellan; more than shipwreck and storm had its agonies imperilled the lives of seafaring men. Yet in those three years, as has been already recorded, the *Endeavour* had borne on her sick-list no more than five scurvy cases; and of these not one was mortal. Had it not been for the imperative necessity of calling at Batavia, Cook might have reached England with the loss of those few men only who died from accident, or who joined the ship, like Lieutenant Hicks, already stricken with fatal disease. But Batavia, as Bougainville's Ahutoru had remarked, was *fenua mate*, the land that kills; and it had exacted its sacrifice.

There were limits to Cook's achievement, as he had pointed out. The New Zealand coast in some respects had been dubiously defined; it was still uncertain whether Van Diemen's Land were part of New Holland or not; and most vital of all, in the eyes of one school of geographers, it was still arguable that the disproof of the continental hypothesis was far from final. Cook's own estimate of his accomplishment may indeed be given, for it is part of the quality of his genius. 'Altho' the discoveries made in this voyage are not great,' he wrote from Batavia to the secretary of the Admiralty, 'yet I flatter my self that they are such as may merit the attention of their Lordships, and altho' I have faild in discovering the so much talk'd of southern continent (which perhaps do not exist) and which I my self had much at heart, yet I am confident that no part of the failure of such discovery can be laid to my charge. . . . Had we been so fortunate not to have run ashore much more would have been done in the latter part of the voyage than what was, but as it is I presume this voyage will be found as compleat as any before made to the South Seas, on the same account.'

No discoverer ever measured his claims with more moderation. Certainly, whatever the completeness of this voyage, the Pacific still harboured secrets which were to give employment to many navigators. The arch-problem, that of the continent, Cook thought might be solved in one voyage more. On the method of that solution he, the most methodical of men, contributed a brief postscript to the journal he wrote while in the *Endeavour*. How, then, could further discoveries in the South Sea most feasibly be made? This latest expedition had entered the Pacific round Cape Horn: let the next do so by way of the Cape of Good Hope and sail west to east rather than east to west, south of New Holland to Queen Charlotte's Sound. Here 'again refresh wood and water; takeing care to be ready to leave that place by the latter end of September or beginning of October at farthest, when you would have the whole summer before you and after geting through the Straight might, with the prevailing westerly winds, run to the eastward in as high a latitude as you please and, if you met with no lands, would have time enough to get round Cape Horne before the summer was too far spent, but if after meeting with no continent and you had other objects in view, than haul to the northward and after visiting some of the islands already discovered . . . proceed with the trade wind back to the westward in search of those before mintioned—thus the discoveries in the South Sea would be compleat.' Thus, vividly enough if not with a final elegance, Cook sketched a plan bold, lucid and simple in design. He had in his mind a base; and he could rest his strategy on a knowledge of the winds of the southern hemisphere that was becoming mature. The execution of the plan—this he could not see—would be made complex by perils hitherto unguessed. Granting the necessity for such a voyage, for its commander there was one possible choice.

# CHAPTER XI

# COOK: THE SECOND VOYAGE, 1772–1775

COOK was promoted commander and began to move in the society of the learned and the great. But the interval at home in London was short; both Cook himself and Banks had urged another voyage; the continental theorists were loud that their thesis had not been disproved; and scientific curiosity and national rivalry combined to emphasize the necessity. For the study of geography, as we have seen, flourished as much in France as in England. Frenchmen had already experienced the storms of the New Zealand coast; Bougainville had despatched Ahutoru on his way back to Tahiti, much polished after a year in Paris;[1] while in 1771 Marion du Fresne and Kerguelen, both French commanders, had sailed in search of the land of de Gonneville. Nor could the Spanish regard themselves as relieved from the ownership of the Pacific by the officious intrusion of British voyages of 'curiosity'—they formally annexed Easter Island, sent missionaries to Tahiti, and indignantly imagined British settlements all over the ocean. This excitement, however, deterred neither the Admiralty nor science, and the decision for another voyage being taken, Cook was inevitably nominated to command it. With him was to go once again the enthusiastic and generous Banks.

The hazards of the Great Barrier Reef had convinced Cook of the desirability of a consort on such expeditions, and it was determined this time to send two ships, specially purchased. Nothing could be more proper for the purpose, went Cook's opinion, than vessels of the type of the *Endeavour*: 'The ship

[1] He never reached Tahiti, but died at Madagascar in the course of his journey.

must not be of great draught but of sufficient capacity to carry
a proper quantity of provisions and stores for the crew, and of
such construction that she will bear to take the ground, and of
such a size that she can be conveniently laid on shore if necessary
for repairing any damage or defects, and these qualities are to
be found in North Country built ships, such as are built for the
coal trade, and in none other.' Accordingly two recently built
Whitby ships were bought, the *Resolution*, 462 tons, and the
*Adventure*, 340 tons. They were fitted out with a generosity
totally unusual in the navy. It is quite evident that for once at
least the emergence of a born explorer was regarded as a piece
of sublime good fortune. He was given able officers: some of
them had been with him before and others were men of proved
abilities. Cook himself took the *Resolution*, while to the command of the *Adventure* was appointed Tobias Furneaux, who
had sailed with Wallis in the *Dolphin*. Banks lavished expense
on his own preparations, engaging Solander once more, Zoffany
the portrait-painter, and a train of others, draughtsmen, horn-
players and servants—a total of fifteen besides himself. Unfortunately the *Resolution* provided no accommodation for such a
number of supernumeraries and their baggage, and considerable
alterations had to be made to the ship. Banks indeed had favoured
the employment of a large East Indiaman, the claims of science in
Cook's ideal vessel being too lightly regarded. The alterations
made the ship so crank that Cook and his officers considered her
unsafe, and she was therefore restored to her original condition:
this made her 'the properest ship for the service she is intended
for of any I ever saw', said Cook; but Banks, regarding the
accommodation as impossible, abandoned the expedition in indignation, in spite of the money he had spent, and took his party
to Iceland. Whatever the personal motives involved his decision
must be regretted. For though Cook and Banks did not cease to
be friends, it ended in the appointment as naturalists to the
voyage of John Reinhold Forster, a German of some reputation
and ability but more self-regard, of infinite querulousness, quite
unused to the sea or sailors, and his son John George Adam, a

pleasant youth, though much under the thumb of his father. At the Cape, Forster was to engage the additional help of the Swede Anders Sparrman. Other expert assistants were more agreeable. Wales and Bayly, who were appointed by the Board of Longitude as astronomers, one to each ship, were excellent workmen in their science—of Wales, in the *Resolution*, Cook spoke with great appreciation. Four chronometers were sent on the voyage. Only one made on John Harrison's model was to prove successful: 'our never-failing guide', 'our trusty friend the Watch', were the phrases Cook was to bestow upon it before the end. At Plymouth, Wales and Bayly made careful observations of the latitude and longitude on which to start these 'watch machines'; and from that port on 13 July 1772 the vessels sailed.

The instructions for the voyage were modelled on the lines already sketched by Cook and in close consultation with him. Leaving the Cape at the beginning of the southern summer, he was to sail south and try to fall in with the 'Cape Circumcision' reported by Bouvet in 1739, said to lie in latitude 54° S, longitude 10° 20′ E; and if this was discovered, to find out whether it was part of the southern continent or merely an island. If it was part of the continent, there were to be the usual investigations and surveys, convenient situations were to be annexed and medals distributed among the inhabitants. This being done, further discovery was to be prosecuted to the east or west as seemed most fitting and as near to the South Pole as possible. If, on the other hand, the cape was an island or impossible to find, Cook was to stand to the south as long as he saw any likelihood of falling in with a continent; if in this he was unsuccessful, he was to turn eastward on the same quest in as high a latitude as possible and thus to circumnavigate the globe—on the completion of which operation he was to return to England by way of the Cape. When it was unsafe to stay in high latitudes he was to retire to some known place to refit; if any disabling accident happened to the *Resolution*, he was to pursue the given plan in the *Adventure*. New islands discovered were to be surveyed and taken possession of; and on the return to England secrecy was to be enjoined on officers and crews. These instructions,[1] indeed, were extremely well calculated to attain the highest scientific results, to deprive the French of the honour of a great deal of first-rate original discovery, and if the Spanish had only been acquainted with their text, to confirm and amplify the darkest of suspicions. In their amazingly triumphant prosecution the benefits, it is pleasant to add, were mainly to geographical and other science.

Madeira was reached before the end of July and once again Cook purchased quantities of onions. A few days later, at Port Praya in the island of St Jago, he was able to get pigs, goats and fowls, and fresh fruits and water. The material details are important; for another successful assault on scurvy would be proof that the system pursued in the *Endeavour* had permanent value. There were heavy rains at the end of August, and the *Resolution* was constantly fumigated, washed and dried with stoves. Furneaux's precautions throughout the voyage were somewhat less immaculate. On 30 October the ships arrived at the Cape, where Cook learnt from the governor that he had been visited by other explorers. These were Kerguelen and Marion, each with two ships—Kerguelen had mentioned the discovery of land in latitude 48°, near the longitude of Mauritius (not a very good calculation), along the coast of which he had sailed for forty miles before being blown off by a gale; Marion was bound on a voyage of discovery to the South Pacific. The chronometers were corrected by observations on shore, and the one made to Harrison's design was found to be working excellently. The crew were allowed as much freedom as possible and fresh food in abundance, so that when on 22 November the voyage south was resumed they were all as healthy as when they had left England.

The task was now the discovery of Cape Circumcision. As

---

[1] The instruction about secrecy was standard on these voyages, and all logs and journals were confiscated before the ships arrived home. Nevertheless there were many unofficial, 'surreptitious', and wildly inaccurate accounts published before the official ones saw the light.

the latitude got higher the air became much colder, while for a week a gale raged, so heavy that for some time neither ship was able to carry any sail. Extra clothes were served out as they worked steadily towards the Antarctic ice and the livestock died of cold and wet. But the gale blew them out of their course so far to the east that the search for Bouvet's cape had temporarily to be abandoned. On 10 December, in latitude 50° 40', ice was met, and somewhat farther south a field of ice so large that no end could be seen to it east, west or south; Cook searched for an opening to the south-east for several days, in danger from bergs and floating blocks, but finding none, resolved reluctantly to make north again. Signs of scurvy, evident in the middle of the month in both ships, were checked by wort and preparations of oranges and lemons. Meanwhile the ice-field had been left out of sight and once more Cook turned south, until on 26 December in latitude 58° 31' and longitude 27° 37' E he steered west, working gradually southward. The ships were encompassed by large masses of ice, some of them two miles round, and sometimes inevitably mistaken at first for land—an appalling danger to any ship on their weather side in a high sea. In latitude 60° they were in the longitude given by Bouvet as that of Cape Circumcision but ninety-five leagues farther south; there were no signs of land, and it seemed that Bouvet must have been deceived by the ice. For only the second time since leaving the Cape the moon was seen and Wales was able to fix their position. At the beginning of January 1773, Cook turned east and then again began to work to the south, in foggy weather and in such great cold that the rigging was coated with ice. Happily the ice when melted provided excellent fresh water, and thus one great anxiety was removed. On 17 January the Antarctic Circle was crossed, for the first time in history, but by evening the ships were blocked beyond all possibility of progress by an immense ice-field, and from a latitude of almost 67°, a little to the west of what is now Enderby Land, they were forced to retreat. No ship had ever before suffered such danger from the southern pack ice and floating ice islands—how different from the coral islands of the north with their lavish coconuts!—and it was time to think of the refreshment of Queen Charlotte's Sound. Cook sailed north-east to look for the land sighted by Kerguelen, and looked in vain—he was about ten degrees west of it—and then south-east till he was again past the sixtieth parallel. On 8 February in a gale and foggy weather the ships parted, and could not rejoin: as there was a rendezvous in New Zealand the *Resolution* continued her course, for, the south-west swell arguing an absence of land in that direction, any continental mass must lie to the east. This easterly course was followed, in cold and stormy weather with only one pleasant break, till 16 March, when it was altered to north-east and the coast of New Zealand. Cook had again intended to touch at Van Diemen's Land, to discover its true relation to Australia, but the wind being hostile, he abandoned the problem in the hope that Furneaux would have solved it. Land was sighted on 25 March, and next day the *Resolution* put into Dusky Sound. She had been out of sight of land for 117 days, in which she had sailed 3660 leagues; one man was sick.

Dusky Sound and the delightful harbour within it called after Lieutenant Pickersgill provided safe anchorage and pictur-esque scenery, though rainy weather. An observatory and the forge were set up, and abundant wildfowl, seals and fish, together with a spruce beer now brewed, all fortified the general health. The water was good, and still today there may be seen the great creeper-covered stumps of the trees which Cook's men felled. European seeds were planted, a pair of geese left to breed. Few natives were seen. Presents were left in a deserted camp and amicable relations established with one family; the neighbour-hood, however, did not seem to be well populated. Inland barren and precipitous mountains closed the view. Possibly, thought Cook, Dusky Sound, remote as it was from Europe, with its timber large enough for the mainmast of a fifty-gun ship, might some day in the inscrutable future be a thriving centre of British commerce. Thus speculating, and with his men refreshed, he left after seven weeks for Queen Charlotte's

Sound. Here on 18 May he found the *Adventure*, and immediately sent the boats on shore for scurvy-grass—for though Furneaux had been at the rendezvous for six weeks, he had men sick. After parting in the fog and trying in vain to rejoin the *Resolution*, he had, as Cook hoped, made for Van Diemen's Land, coasted it eastwards, and anchored for five days in Adventure Bay, taking in wood and water. Then he had intended to sail north as far as Point Hicks, Cook's first Australian landfall, a course which would probably have solved his problem; he came to the islands now called after him, and finding that the land trended away to the west, into what he thought was a deep bay, was persuaded by wind and weather to make for New Zealand, convinced that Van Diemen's Land and New Holland were one.

Furneaux had made preparations for wintering at Queen Charlotte's Sound; Cook was not yet ready to rest. He was inclined to cross the Tasman Sea to Van Diemen's Land himself; the winds being contrary, however, he accepted Furneaux's opinion and ordered him to refit for a continued voyage eastward, though it was not before 7 June—the middle of the southern winter—that the ships could put to sea. With the Maoris who were seen in the interval there was peaceful intercourse, some of it of a kind that Cook considered no improvement to native morals; and before he left he landed goats, pigs and sheep to breed (the sheep died overnight). His plan was now to run eastward between latitudes 41° and 46° once more in search of the continent, to about longitude 135° W; then, if it had not been found, to make for Tahiti; whence, after provisioning, he would return to Queen Charlotte's Sound for wood and water, and traverse the whole width of ocean between New Zealand and Cape Horn. Furneaux was given rendezvous at Tahiti and New Zealand, with directions, in case the ships were finally parted, to follow out the general orders for the voyage as well as he could. The plan, though it might not bring a continent to light, would at least discover the possibility of winter voyaging. This, in fact, was all that was discovered during the first part of the programme.

There was rough weather all through June, but by 17 July longitude 133° W was reached without any sign of land. Possibly there might be some between the northern and southern courses of the *Endeavour* in 1769, and Cook turned north to answer that question. Land there was none. Scurvy had again made some inroads on the crew of the *Adventure* and one man had died: extra measures were immediately taken to allay the disease, with fairly satisfactory results; in the meantime Cook's anxiety had kept him from delaying to fix the position of Pitcairn, a short distance to the east of his course. By 13 August he was among the Tuamotu islets and their reefs and at night a precautionary boat was sent ahead. Five days later he was off Tahiti and, wishing to get fresh provisions as soon as possible, he approached it on the south-east side, narrowly escaping the joint dangers of the reef and a strong tide. At Vaitepiha Bay, on the north-east corner of the island, coconuts and bananas were plentiful, but pigs were few; and the natives had hit on the stratagem of fastening up coconuts from which the sailors had drunk the milk and selling them again. Nor, for some unexplained reason, was there much better trade at week later at Matavai Bay—possibly, it was thought, owing to the advice of a white man said to be on the island, perhaps a Spaniard, as a Spanish vessel had visited Tahiti. Nevertheless Cook was eagerly welcomed by the people who crowded the deck, remembering the *Endeavour* and enquiring after Banks and Solander; Point Venus was reoccupied, the sick taken on shore, the observatory set up. Of all the vegetables planted in 1769, only pumpkins had flourished, and for these the natives showed no taste (neither did Cook). At Huahine and other smaller islands the welcome received was of more material satisfaction. Cook was not allowed to land at Huahine except with great ceremony and the elaborate interchange of presents, while the chief wept tears of affection. Food was abundant and nearly four hundred hogs were bought. The only untoward accident was the stripping of Dr Sparrman, when botanizing, of all his clothes except his trousers—an assault that may have been due to his unwitting infringement of

some native *tapu*; and the chief willingly becoming a hostage,
the garments were returned. At Raiatea there was a dramatic
performance, partly describing a robbery, and acted, says Cook,
'in such a manner as sufficiently desplayed the genius of the
people in this art'. A sufficiency of fruit was obtained from a
neighbouring island—not indeed before the bag containing all
the articles of trade had been stolen and recovered. This interval
at the Society Islands was, on the whole, satisfactory both to
Cook and to the islanders—men from the *Adventure* who caused
a disturbance were punished, and Cook increased his reputation
in those seas for fair-minded humanity. He set sail again on
17 September, taking with him an adventurous young Raiatean,
'Odiddy', who was returned on his next visit. Furneaux took
another young man, called Omai, from Huahine; Omai was to
go farther, to England indeed, and there as an example of mild
savagery give great joy to Mr Banks and Dr Solander and the
less scientific social world.

The course was now to the south of west; Cook wished to
touch at Amsterdam and Middelburg, those islands where
Tasman had obtained refreshments so long before, without
sailing over tracks already known. At night the ships lay to, lest
any island should be passed unseen. Hervey's island, or Manuae,
was sighted and named after one of the Lords of the Admiralty
(it and its neighbours now more commonly bear Cook's own
name); and on 1 October Middelburg, or Eua, was rediscovered
after 130 years. No suitable landing-place was noticed, and the
ships bore up for Amsterdam—Tongatapu. They had been seen,
however; canoes came off, the coast appeared more promising,
and they ran in again to find good anchorage and an unarmed
people so numerous and so eager to trade that those who could
not get near flung their goods into the boats over the heads of
their friends in front. The chief, 'Tioony', entertained a party in
his house with fruit and the harmonious singing of girls, to
which Cook retaliated with the ships' bagpipes, much to the
pleasure of his hosts. This island had well-kept plantations, but no

food for sale, and next day the ships crossed over to Tongatapu and Tasman's old anchorage. Here the islanders were as enthusiastic in their welcome, though at first no more willing it seemed to part with their provisions—only native cloth was offered, and to prevent the sailors from bartering their own clothing Cook forbade the purchase of curiosities. The next day pigs, fowls and fruit were produced in sufficient supply and trade went forward as usual. A quantity of red feathers was also obtained, which were to cause some excitement elsewhere in the Pacific. The people were as great thieves as their fellows in other parts, and added cunning to thievery; one who stole some books from a cabin and was chased in a boat exchanged his canoe for the water and, when almost caught, dived straight under the boat, unshipped the rudder and got clear away. Some stolen articles were afterwards returned. The tongue spoken was much akin to that of the Society group. One peculiarity, nevertheless, the natives displayed that had not been previously encountered: many of them were without the top joint of a finger, sometimes on both hands—a sacrifice, as it was later found, in propitiation of a god. This group, Tonga, where Cook had been received with such pleasantness, he called the Friendly Islands.

He sailed for New Zealand on 7 October, and after being delayed by contrary winds sighted land on the 21st. He stood close in to the coast near Poverty Bay in the hope of giving stock and seeds to any natives who might come off. He saw none there; but farther south, off Cape Kidnappers, the ship was visited by two chiefs, to whom were presented boars and sows, cocks and hens, and many different vegetable seeds. Then came heavy squalls, which developed into a week-long gale, moderating only to rage with a greater fury; and in this gale the two ships parted company for the second time and finally. Nevertheless, at the beginning of November the *Resolution* was safely lying at her old anchorage in Ship Cove, and Cook was preparing her and his men with all speed for another plunge into the Antarctic. Of the ship's stores, 7000 pounds of bread were unfit to eat; it was a blessing that scurvy-grass and wild

celery could be gathered in plenty, together with some vegetables from the gardens that had been planted. To improve the
resources of the country, and in spite of the varied misfortunes
of the stock already set on shore, cocks and hens and more pigs
were hopefully presented to friendly natives. There were fresh
studies in ethnology. Some sceptics in England had doubted the
fact of Maori cannibalism. All doubt could now be answered by
a party who, seeing the remains of a youth lately killed, bought
the head and took it on board, where a man eagerly devoured a
piece broiled and offered to him. Cook was then on shore; when
he returned to the ship curiosity got the better of his indignation; another piece was broiled, and the performance was
repeated for his benefit on the quarter-deck, 'where one of these
canibals eat it with a seeming good relish before the whole ships
company'. It was not shortage of food which had led to this
custom, thought Cook; for only enemies slain in battle appeared
to be eaten. He was coming to know the Maori with, if not
intimacy, some familiarity. His summarized conclusion as to
their character is not without interest, nor indeed justice: 'few
considers what a savage man is in his original state', he wrote,
'and even after he is in some degree civilized, the New Zealanders are certainly in a state of civilization, their behavour to
us has been manly and mild, shewing allways a readiness to
oblige us; they have some arts among them which they execute
with great judgement and unwearied patience; they are far less
addicted to thieving than the other islanders and are I believe
strictly honist among themselves.' Their habit of eating their
enemies had probably been handed down from ancient times;
and from traditional customs a nation, especially one so remote
and unvisited, was with difficulty weaned. Civilization lay in the
commerce of goods and learning: 'an intercourse with foreigners
would reform their manners and polish their savage minds'.

    At the end of three weeks there was still no sign of the
*Adventure*, and as the summer was passing Cook resolved to
embark on the next part of his voyage, the investigation of the
ocean to the south between New Zealand and Cape Horn.

Leaving necessary information for Furneaux in a bottle buried beneath a marked tree in the vegetable garden, on 25 November he sailed; during the passage of the strait guns were fired in case his consort were near, then abandoning hope of meeting her again he turned south-east. A few days later the *Adventure* arrived in Ship Cove; but it is Cook's voyage which must now be followed. On 6 December his calculations showed that the ship was at the very antipodes of England, and the usual south-west swell seemed to deny the existence of land in that quarter. The first iceberg was encountered after another six days, and in three more, in latitude 66°, bergs and loose ice surrounded the ship. She edged north out of the fog and then eastwards for a few days till the weather improved, when Cook turned south again over the Antarctic Circle, to reach 67° 31', beyond the southernmost limit of the previous summer. The cold was frightful, the sails like plates of metal, the rigging so coated with ice that the ship was worked with difficulty, and the men cased in frozen snow as if in armour. Yet there was no scurvy, nor indeed any sickness but that arising from exposure, a slight fever which was easily cured. Christmas Day the *Resolution* spent drifting along with great masses of ice, kept clear of them by light airs, and luckily saved from destruction by continual daylight and clear weather. From this position Cook struck north and north-east—he was covering the ocean in a series of immense zigzags—till 11 January 1774, when he was in latitude 47° 51' S, longitude 122° 12' W; and then again south-east, where by the last day of the month he had reached the highest of his own latitudes, far beyond that which any other sailor had ever attempted, 71° 10' S.[1] The longitude was 106° 54' W, a great distance west of the present Graham Land, and much south of its northern extremity. Here progress was stopped, finally and absolutely, by an immense field of ice, solid and forbidding.

[1] Vancouver, Cook's great disciple on the north-west coast of America, used to claim that he had been nearer to the South Pole than any other man; for as a young midshipman in the *Resolution* he had at this moment made his way to the very end of her bowsprit, just as Cook was prepared to tack about to the north again, and waving his hat, cried out *Ne plus ultra!*

Petrels were seen, arguing the presence of land somewhere. But it was unattainable, of that Cook was satisfied. If a continent did exist in the South Pacific, it lay so far south as to be cut off entirely by the ice. 'I will not say it was impossible any where to get farther to the South', he wrote with his characteristic lack of dogma; 'but the attempting it would have been a dangerous and rash enterprise and what I believe no man in my situation would have thought of. It was indeed my opinion as well as the opinion of most on board, that this ice extended quite to the Pole or perhaps joins to some land, to which it had been fixed from the creation. . . . As we drew near this ice some penguins were heard but none seen, and but few other birds or any other thing that could induce us to think any land was near; indeed if there was any land behind this ice it could afford no better retreat for birds or any other animals, than the ice it self, with which it must have been wholly covered. I who had ambition not only to go farther than any one had been before, but as far as it was possible for man to go, was not sorry at meeting with this interruption, as it in some measure relieved us, at least shortned the dangers and hardships inseparable with the navigation of the southern polar rigions.' So it remained to turn once more north—but where? Cook's original instructions had directed him to circumnavigate the globe and return home by way of the Cape of Good Hope; and that circumnavigation, between the Horn and the Cape, he might now certainly have completed. He discussed the alternatives in his journal, in a passage of classical content. Undoubtedly, he said, he might have reached the Cape in April, with the first object of the voyage faithfully carried out. 'But for me at this time to have quited this Southern Pacific Ocean, with a good ship, expressly sent out on discoveries, a healthy crew and not in want of either stores or provisions, would have been betraying not only a want of perseverance, but judgement, in supposeing the South Pacific Ocean to have been so well explored that nothing remained to be done in it, which however was not my opinion at this time; for although I had proved there was no continent, there remained nevertheless room for very large islands in places wholy unexplored and many of those which were formerly discovered, are but imperfectly explored and there situations as imperfectly known; I was of opinion that my remaining in this sea some time longer would be productive of some improvements to navigation and geography as well as other sciences.'

His plan was, in fact, to reduce to order the chaos of assertion, myth and unidentified discovery that still brooded over a large part of the ocean: by observation and the verified certainties of the chart to give to undisciplined tradition definite relation and form. He would first search for the great land Juan Fernandez was said to have discovered in latitude 38° S; then if unsuccessful, find and fix the position of Easter Island; then make for Tahiti to refresh his men and perhaps gather some knowledge of the *Adventure*; then sail to the west to settle the position of the land of Quiros, Austrialia del Espiritu Santo; and then turn south-east again so as to reach Cape Horn in November, with a whole summer before him in which to complete the exploration of the South Atlantic. The design was great, but he thought it was possible; his officers were heartily agreed in its favour; and his men, faced with another year's absence from home, rejoiced at the prospect of a milder climate and the pleasant ways of Otaheite.

The *Resolution* therefore stood away north, through a storm that would have been disastrous among the ice and did prove destructive to her sails and running rigging. On 17 February she crossed the outward track of the *Endeavour* in 1769, and reaching the supposed position of Juan Fernandez's land, cruised in search of it, with a natural lack of success. No continent ever had credentials more inadequate. Birds there were, but birds were becoming discredited witnesses: 'I do not believe there is one in the whole tribe that one can rely on in pointing out the vicinity of land', Cook wrote. Then for some time he himself was very seriously ill with a 'Billious colick', to the great grief and alarm of the whole ship's company. James Patten the surgeon worked devotedly; Forster's dog, the only fresh meat on board, was converted into soup for the patient, and by 4 March Cook was on deck again, amid general joy. In a week more the great statues of Easter Island were sighted; canoes came off with plantains, and two mornings later, while the ship was working back to the anchorage off which she had been blown, Cook landed, to be immediately surrounded by eager natives. Some of them had European hats and handkerchiefs, the fruits of a Spanish visit of 1770; they, too, spoke a language allied to Tahitian—a fact which seemed to point to great migrations of the same primitive people over the whole of the settled Pacific. Roggeveen in his day had described the fertile appearance of the island, but in the fifty years' interval a change had come: to Cook it seemed parched and dreary, with only a few plantations visible, and no trees more than ten feet high. The enigmatic statues, it seemed, were not now worshipped by the natives; did they perhaps mark certain *marae*, burying-places for tribes or families? Whatever they might be, they did not make up for an inadequate water supply and shortage of food. Cook sailed again after a few days, on 16 March.

He steered a course for Tahiti round by the north-east, and on 6 April, after a relapse into sickness—luckily not serious—made another rediscovery of great interest. This, unseen since that fatal second voyage of Mendaña, was the Marquesas group, the settling of the exact position of which cast great light on the geography of the older chapter of exploration. In a sudden squall the ship had a narrow escape from dangerous rocks, but good anchorage was found in what was named Resolution Bay—the port Madre de Dios of Mendaña's island of Santa Cristina. Except for their thieving and some cheating, Cook admired the Marquesans, as fair almost as Europeans and in physique without exception the finest race of people in the South Sea. Their clubs and spears were neatly made, and they used slings. They were attracted by nails, and were at first eager to get them in exchange for their fruit and fish and pigs—regrettably small animals, of which it took about fifty to give the crew one meal. Water was obtained, little fresh provision else; and finally trade was brought to a stop when a midshipman gave a few of the red feathers from Tonga for a pig, after which no other payment would be accepted. Cook was forced to take his departure in extreme annoyance, for though his men were not at all sick, they needed a change of diet; and in that respect the Marquesas were an unprofitable archipelago. He sailed on 11 April, touched at Takaroa, one of the two small islands which Byron had named after George III; discovered that other little group of atolls he himself called the Palliser islands;[1] and on the morning of the 22nd was in the old anchorage at Matavai Bay. The camp was reoccupied, the observatory erected, but the hospital was not needed, for there were no sick. Cook, somewhat discouraged by the material failure of his last visit to Tahiti, did not intend to remain long; so great, however, was the warmth of his reception and so plentiful were supplies that he made it his base for re-fitting. The whole island seemed more prosperous than it had been the year before—new houses and canoes were being built on every side, and the stay here and at the adjacent islands lengthened to six weeks. Indeed, when Cook first went to visit the *arii rahi* or great chief Tu he was almost torn to pieces in the exuberance of welcome. As at Port Resolution, great store was set upon red feathers, and the ordinary articles of trade running short, no investment could have been of greater profit. The ship's stores were overhauled, and island vegetables compensated for uneatable bread. There was the usual irritation: in spite of all amiability, thieving flourished as much as ever. At Huahine a shooting party was robbed of all its trade goods, and three officers, the next day, of their very clothes. Cook had lost clothes, too, at Tahiti. He gave deep consideration to the necessary counter-measures; for if the offenders were exasperating,

[1] They were Arutua, Apataki, Kaukura and Toau, latitude 15°–16° S, all close to longitude 146° W. They were called after Cook's friend Sir Hugh Palliser. Palliser commanded H.M.S. *Eagle*, in which Cook served in 1756–7; was governor of Newfoundland during part of the time of Cook's survey; and as Comptroller of the Navy had much to do with the fitting-out of his ships. Cape Palliser and Palliser Bay, on the New Zealand coast, are also named after him.

they were certainly not vicious, and in the depth of turpitude there was no ill feeling. Once an armed party was landed, by invitation, to pursue a band of marauders; whenever possible, hostages or houses were seized as security for the return of anything valuable; and when one native had been caught in the act of carrying off a small water-cask, Cook resolved on a grand ceremonial punishment by way of warning. The miscreant was sentenced to two dozen lashes; there were speeches on the nature and necessity of equal justice for all men, Tahitian and English alike; a native chief formally accepted the principle involved; the marines went through their drill; and Cook retired quite uncertain whether he had supplied Tahiti with a salutary deterrent or merely an agreeable diversion.

The other main excitement of the time was the preparation of a great war fleet to sail against the nearby island of Eimeo, or Moorea, the chief of which had come into conflict with some of the Tahitian magnates. Between three and four hundred double canoes were afloat, great and small, decorated with flags and streamers and manned by nearly 8000 warriors, their leaders swathed in splendid garments of war. Cook, seeing some of the manoeuvres, was greatly impressed by the skill with which they were managed; and would have liked to have witnessed the fate of Eimeo. But it was obvious that during his visit there would be no assault made; he therefore left Tahiti on 14 May, to spend his remaining time at Huahine and Raiatea; and on 4 June sailed west for Espiritu Santo. No explorer was ever on better terms with native peoples than Cook with these Tahitians and Society islanders, and none ever exercised a wiser restraint in his relations with them. Observation convinced him that their women in general moved on a higher moral plane than he and his predecessors had first reported; and the rights of both women and men, so far as he could see to it, were rigidly respected. He refused to take with him to England any of the young Tahitians who wished to join the ship, seeing no possibility of returning them to the island; and he writes of individual persons with insight and admiration. One asked him to come back again, and learning that this was the last visit, enquired the name of Cook's *marae*—which Cook thought meant burying-place. Cook told him Stepney, the parish where he lived in London, repeating the word till they could pronounce it, whereupon they all shouted 'Stepney *marae* no Toote'! In Cook's meaning of the word, this was a prophecy sadly false, but the trivial incident illuminates a hidden depth of humanity.

On the passage to Espiritu Santo other islands were sighted; Lord Howe, or Mopihaa, discovered by Wallis, which seemed uninhabited; Palmerston, a lagoon surrounded by sand-banks and islets; and on 20 June, Savage Island, or Niue, where the natives were hostile and Cook narrowly dodged a spear thrown at his party. The ship was at the Tongan island of Nomuka from 26 to 29 June, and was well supplied with food even before she had anchored; but friendly as the island might be, the theft of muskets and an adze, and even an attempt to steal the lead off the line while it was actually being used in sounding, was carrying friendship too far, and when the epidemic grew worse Cook seized two canoes as security. The stolen articles were nearly all returned, and watering went forward unimpeded. At this island a 'leprous' disease was much noticed—the distressing yaws.

From Nomuka a roughly north-west course was sailed. Aurora island, the one discovered in Quiros's group by Bougainville, was sighted on 16 July, and in a hard gale Cook tacked between it and the Isle of Lepers or Aoba and over to Malekula, where he anchored in Port Sandwich. Bougainville, it will be remembered, had passed through the group convinced that it was the land of Quiros, but for sufficient reasons had made only a short visit; nor did he know the real extent of the Austrialian 'continent'. It was Cook's work to remain a fortnight, to explore and circumnavigate the whole archipelago, stretched out in a line of 350 miles, to identify Quiros's harbour, to fix the position of the islands with great accuracy, to make a chart which was used to correct later casual observations up to the end of the nineteenth century, and to give them their modern name of the

New Hebrides. At Malekula satisfactory relations with the natives were impossible. They were a race not allied to any hitherto encountered, were to Cook's eye ugly and ill proportioned, and spoke a language without affinity to Tahitian; for he had passed beyond Polynesia. The first day they were well received, and on the morrow swarmed over the vessel; one of them, quarrelling with a boat-keeper, aimed an arrow first at him and then at Cook, other arrows were discharged and only a shot fired over the crowd cleared the ship. When an armed party went on shore for wood and water it was met by a crowd fully accoutred with spears and clubs and bows and arrows; and though the green boughs of peace were exchanged and permission given to cut down trees, while a pig and a piece of cloth passed as presents and there was a little trade in arrows and coconuts, no watering-place could be found, the natives seemed opposed to exploration, and Cook weighed for some better position.

He made south, not before many of the ship's company had eaten of a poisonous fish—perhaps the same that had caused such havoc among Quiros's men; for they suffered similar agonies. After a week or ten days, however, all recovered. In the meantime, proceeding through these unknown waters with great caution, standing off and on at night and sailing ahead only by day, Cook found islands both large and small; several seemed inhabited, but no favourable opportunity of landing presented itself. On 4 August he attempted to land on Eromanga, one of the most southerly of the group. Near the shore a few yams and coconuts were traded, and the natives urged the boats in, when Cook, who had stepped ashore, was visited by suspicion and embarked again, making signs at the same time that he would return. This was the signal for the people to rush at the boats and try to drag them on land, seizing two oars and hailing stones, spears and arrows on the crews. Several men were wounded; Cook's musket, loaded with small shot, missed fire, and he was obliged to order his marines to shoot. Several natives in their turn were wounded; and regarding friendship now as out of the question, he made immediately for the island of Tanna, twelve leagues to the south, where the night before the flames of a volcano had been seen.

Here a good anchorage was found, Port Resolution, and the ship was warped close in. The natives came with coconuts and departed with anything they could seize—even trying to make away with the anchor buoys—and it was not till guns were fired in their near neighbourhood that they would leave the ship temporarily in peace. In provisions, however, the island did not prove profitable. One friendly old man several times brought yams and coconuts to the ship to exchange for whatever was offered him, and a strong party was landed under his guidance in the hope of getting water. A little was obtained, together with wood and coconuts in exchange for presents; but when three boats went ashore next day the Tannese, in great numbers, appeared very threatening. Efforts to make peace failing, they were stampeded by the firing of the *Resolution*'s guns; following which permission was given for the taking of wood, water and ballast. Later, when the ship's tiller-head was found to have sprung and a new one had to be made, the price of the necessary tree rose to a dog and some cloth. Although excellent plantations of yams, plantains and sugar-cane were seen, little could be bought, because articles of exchange dear to other peoples had no appeal to these. They wore hardly a garment and in general set no store on cloth; they were so primitive as to see no use for iron. Cook understood that they were cannibals. The only gift the island afforded indeed was that of hot sulphurous springs, which proved beneficial to the rheumatism of one of the crew.

Cook therefore bore away to the south-west, in case the group was continued in that direction. Clearly it was not, and rounding Tanna he followed the western coasts of the islands north to Bougainville's Passage, and so reached Espiritu Santo. On 25 August he entered a long deep harbour, the veritable Bay of St Philip and St James, and knew he was on the scene of the tribulations of the great visionary. The wind was light and variable, and the passage up the bay was not made without some trouble; here was the extraordinary deepening of the water which had proved the destruction of all Quiros's hopes—that water of three fathoms close to the beach, fifty and fifty-five at a distance of two cables' length, with no soundings at all two miles out; here was the sudden change of weather—this time fortunately in Cook's favour—which relieved him 'from the apprehensions of being forced to an anchor in a great depth on a lee shore and in a dark and obscure night'. Here were the two rivers, and Cook's men landed near that up which Quiros's boats had gone. Here was the luxuriant vegetation, the hills and plantations, the valleys with their streams, the crowded coconuts, the smoke by day and the fires by night of a large population. Certainly Quiros was justified in some degree at least. And Cook understood the confidence of the dawning seventeenth century in its continent; his eyes, too, saw no end to that far-stretched land.

The identification was made, but the time for remaining so far north was passing rapidly. A few fishing canoes came near enough to the ship for presents to be thrown to their occupants, and then Cook, giving the eastern point of the bay the name of Cape Quiros, took advantage of a favourable wind to set sail for New Zealand and the refreshment of Ship Cove. Land was sighted, however, as early as 4 September—it was the northern coast of the large island called New Caledonia, in appearance, so Cook thought, resembling no country so closely as New South Wales. The *Resolution* was taken through the reef, and anchoring was surrounded by canoes. The people here were unarmed and timid, gaining courage with the presents given them; they were a well-made race, good-natured (even if cannibals), and intelligent enough to appreciate both red cloth and nails; they possessed also the incredible virtue of stealing nothing. Their land was well planted and carefully watered (though the island on the whole seemed barren except for good timber), but as they possessed no animals of any sort, not even pigs, Cook left them a boar and a sow, and presented a pair of dogs to a delighted chief. Water was obtained for the ship, but Cook and the Forsters were poisoned once more by a hitherto unknown fish, purchased from natives who had given no warning. Wales was able to observe an eclipse of the sun and thus fix the position of the island, and the boats were sent along the coast to the northward. Unfortunately there was little time for further investigation, and Cook left his anchorage on 13 September. Until the end of the month he was on the north-eastern side of New Caledonia and at its southern end, where he found the Isle of Pines—the great araucarias that Forster took for pillars of basalt—and had one night of frightful peril amid reefs and breakers as he tried, unsuccessfully, to get round to the other side of the island. At last, on 3 October, he decided he could stay no longer, compelled 'for the first time to leave a coast I had discovered before it was fully explored'. Possibly, he thought, the western side had some communication with New Holland through isles and sand-banks—a guess already disproved by the voyage of Surville. Standing south, he discovered and was able to land briefly on Norfolk Island—small, attractive, uninhabited—where the vegetation was much like that of New Zealand, and a welcome supply of fish, birds and cabbage-palms was obtained. On 17 October the white cone of Mount Egmont rose above the sea, and next morning the ship was anchored in Queen Charlotte's Sound again.

The bottle left for Furneaux had gone, trees had been cut and there were signs of the erection of an observatory; and from the natives, who in their delight at seeing Cook jumped and skipped about like madmen, he got confirmation of the visit of the *Adventure*. She had arrived shortly after his own departure and stayed two or three weeks. There was also a somewhat confused story of the loss of a ship on the other side of the strait and the massacre of those of her people who reached the shore, a story so lacking in circumstance that Cook put little credence in it; nor indeed was he to learn the truth till much later. New observations had rectified his chart of New Zealand in one or two respects, scurvy-grass and wild celery now refreshed the crew—the vegetable gardens had been neglected by the natives

—the ship was refitted as well as possible; and on 11 November the *Resolution* left the Sound for the final stage of her discovery. Cook's intention was to cut across his tracks of the preceding summer in a straight line to South America, in latitude 54° or 55°, lest he should have left any land after all undiscovered in that region, and then to complete his circumnavigation of the southern hemisphere between the Horn and the Cape of Good Hope. He sighted Cape Deseado, the western limit of the Strait of Magellan, on 17 December; certainly on the track he had sailed there was no land, and no likelihood of any near by. The South Pacific had been as thoroughly combed as one man could do it, and there could be no possible denial of his conclusion. It remained to follow the coast of Tierra del Fuego round to the south, surveying when practicable, and obtaining what fresh food there was—and it was a desolate and barren country enough. Christmas, however, went very cheerfully with goose pie and Madeira wine, the Horn was passed on 28 December, and the New Year was spent in observations of the coast of Staten Island, though thick and foggy weather precluded accurate surveying. Then on 3 January 1775 Cook sailed into the South Atlantic. The unfortunate Dalrymple, so much of whose geographical structure had now been dissipated, had placed on his chart in this vicinity a long coastline, including a Gulf of St Sebastian in latitude 58° 9' S, longitude 53° 14' W. That point the *Resolution* reached with the usual negative result. She then bore up north and east, and on 14 January sighted South Georgia, an island pardonably first believed to be an immense iceberg, so covered was it with snow. Cook landed and took possession of it, though doubtful if his country would derive any pleasure from the acquisition; he himself found that its seals and birds were welcome substitutes for salt meat.

As Cook had mistaken South Georgia for ice, he thought, equally he might have passed some other island, the original of Bouvet's Cape Circumcision, under the same impression; and the hypothetical injustice must if possible be repaired. He made south to the sixtieth parallel, then east amid fog and ice, convinced by the swell that Dalrymple's land at least did not exist. The misty islands of the South Sandwich group, called by Cook Southern Thule, were sighted at the end of the month, and through the first three weeks of February he followed his eastern course, making gradually northwards, and passing a little to the south of the land actually seen by Bouvet, the island named after him. Cook crossed his own outward track of December 1772, and abandoning finally the unprofitable search for Cape Circumcision changed course for the Cape of Good Hope. His task in the southern hemisphere was done. In the middle of March ships were met, whence came to the *Resolution* both fresh provisions and some news. The *Adventure* was home; she had called at the Cape twelve months before with a story of a boat's crew massacred and eaten in New Zealand by those same natives whose disposition and humanity Cook had been wont to praise. To gain an authentic account he must wait till he met Furneaux; in the meantime, on 21 March, the *Resolution* herself anchored in Table Bay and the necessary refitting went forward. Only the rigging had suffered severely; the ship was otherwise in a very satisfactory condition. At the Cape, Cook met Crozet, the lieutenant of Marion, who had been killed on the coast of New Zealand in 1772; he heard of islands discovered by Marion south-east of the Cape, and heard also for the first time of Surville's voyage. By 27 April his own voyage could be resumed; he called at St Helena and Ascension, and then made for the island of Fernando de Noronha, off the Brazilian coast, the position of which he was anxious to fix exactly. He came to the Azores in July, sighted England on the 29th of that month and anchored next day off Spithead.

This voyage lasted three years and eighteen days, during which Cook sailed upwards of 70,000 miles; and of all his crew he lost four men, three by accident and one by disease. Not one died of scurvy.

# CHAPTER XII

# COOK: THE THIRD VOYAGE, 1776-1780

In spite of the fact that Great Britain was in the midst of the excitement which attended the opening of the American War of Independence, Cook's return created some noise. He himself was promoted post-captain and had a long conversation with George III; his officers also were promoted; while Wales the astronomer became mathematical master at Christ's Hospital, and therein attained a double immortality, his memory embalmed not only by Cook but by Elia. An appointment to Greenwich Hospital falling vacant, Cook applied for it and was installed, with the proviso, made by himself, that whenever there was work to do for which he was specially fitted his retirement from active service might be cancelled. His time was occupied in preparing for publication an account of the voyage. In February 1776 he was unanimously elected a Fellow of the Royal Society, and to its proceedings contributed a paper on his methods of combating scurvy. The Society gave him the Copley medal; and certainly no paper ever systematized a more arduous experience or a more successful result. If Rome decreed the *Civic Crown* to him who saved the life of a single citizen, what wreaths, oratorically enquired the President of the Society, were due to that man who perpetuated the means of preserving on distant voyages so many of Britain's intrepid sons, her *Mariners*? Eminence, too, brought Cook, though not the wreaths at least the attentions of Mr James Boswell: 'While I was with the Captain, I catched the enthusiasm of curiosity and adventure, and felt a strong inclination to go with him on his next voyage.' To which replied the ungeographical Johnson: 'Why, sir, a man *does* feel so, till he considers how very little he can learn from such voyages.'

Meanwhile Cook had gathered from Furneaux's journal the history of the *Adventure* after the two ships finally parted company. Furneaux, it will be recollected, had been blown off the New Zealand coast early in November 1773. He had got back to it near Cape Palliser on the 4th, obtained some fish from the natives, and been blown out once more. This gale damaged his sails and rigging, his decks were leaking and the ship was short of water; he therefore put into Tolaga Bay, a little north of Poverty Bay, and managed to collect supplies of wood, water, fish and vegetables, only to run still again into bad weather. Not till the 16th could he at last start south, and even then it was the 30th before he reached Queen Charlotte's Sound, its tree-trunk carved with the words 'Look underneath', and Cook's bottle. The *Resolution* had been gone six days; Furneaux began to refit as fast as possible, delayed by the necessity of baking anew a large proportion of his bread. He was ready to sail by 17 December and sent out a boat with ten men to gather vegetables, intending to depart next day. The boat did not return; the launch was sent off to search for it, and found the remains of its crew, all of whom had been killed and cooked for eating. Beyond firing on the natives who had these remains with them, nothing useful could be done; for the population near by was great and hitherto had been perfectly friendly. Furneaux could only guess that there had been some sudden quarrel, and that his men had omitted necessary precautions. This, then, was the basis of the garbled story told to Cook at the Sound ten months after the tragedy; like Furneaux, he could only suppose an explanation, nor could he think less of the essential virtue of the New Zealanders. The truth was in detail much as Furneaux had guessed, so Cook learnt later on. The boat's crew had been carelessly at dinner, when a quarrel arose over food snatched by attendant natives; tempers flared, two Maoris were shot by the only man who had his musket by him, their fellows rushed the party and massacred them all. Care, or moderation, or both, might have obviated this fierce bloodshed.

It was not till 23 December that Furneaux sailed, and when

after some days he got away from the coast he stood south-east, according to his instructions. In latitude 56° the cold was intense and, with high seas breaking continually over the ship, he resolved to make for Cape Horn; this he did, though he incidentally reached the latitude of 61°. No more than Cook did he see any sign of land. By this time he was short of stores, the ship was not in good condition and his men were becoming sickly; he therefore judged it advisable to cross the South Atlantic to the Cape of Good Hope to refit, and thence return directly to England. He made a fresh search for Cape Circumcision, but finding nothing beyond the masses of floating ice which made navigation in those latitudes so hazardous, he concluded that Bouvet had been deceived, and that the French continent was either a small island or evanescent ice. He came to Table Bay in March, spent a month there and arrived in England on 14 July 1774. The *Adventure* had had thirteen deaths, one from scurvy; and the scurvy from which its crew suffered might very probably with better care have been largely reduced. Not all commanders, however efficient, even though they sail with Cook, have the habitual and urgent conscience of a Cook. Geographically, at any rate, the independent voyaging of Furneaux had done something to reinforce the conclusions to which Cook himself had come with a more exhaustive finality.

The South Pacific might be explored: it was still possible that fruitful discovery lay elsewhere unachieved. In August 1775, Cook was writing to a friend a very favourable report on the *Resolution*, 'so little injured by the voyage that she will soon be sent out again, but I shall not command her, my fate drives me from one extream to another; a few months ago the whole southern hemisphere was hardly big enough for me and now I am going to be confined within the limits of Greenwich Hospital, which are far too small for an active mind like mine.' Greenwich was a fine retreat and a pretty income, but whether Cook could bring himself to like ease and retirement, time would show. Time showed indeed; if Omai, who had made a great hit in London, were to be sent home, that in itself would occasion another voyage. But there was a much greater purpose in view, decided on in fact months before Cook's return. The *Resolution* was dismantled only to the extent required for going into dock, where she was to be refitted for a further expedition. There were again to be two ships, and in the choice and preparation of the second, once again a Whitby-built vessel, the *Discovery*, 298 tons, Cook was actively concerned. A commander was not to be chosen with the same comparative readiness; one man was naturally and pre-eminently designate, were it not for the leisure he had earned and the brevity of the time since his return to England, after seven years of singularly arduous labour. In February 1776, Cook was taken into consultation by the Admiralty; it became clear to him that Greenwich was in truth too small for an active mind, that ease and retirement could not be his, and he declared that he would go. The offer was immediately accepted, and he at once took command of his old ship and began to enter men. His first lieutenant was John Gore, who had been with Wallis in the *Dolphin* and Cook himself in the *Endeavour*; and in the *Resolution* also sailed one who was to reach fame, not altogether untarnished—the master, William Bligh, against whom both the crew of the *Bounty* and his subordinates in New South Wales were to mutiny. The command of the *Discovery* was given to Charles Clerke, whose lot had lain with Cook from the day he sailed as able seaman in the *Endeavour*. Clerke's first lieutenant was James Burney, a lieutenant under Furneaux, later to become the historian of Pacific discovery; a midshipman was Vancouver, who was himself to command a famous expedition to the Pacific and the North American coast. There were indeed in those ships a dozen men destined for future distinction. Bayly the astronomer went with Clerke, no independent astronomer with Cook, to whom himself and to James King, his young second lieutenant, were entrusted the observations. He had an excellent natural historian in his surgeon William Anderson. Among his scientific instruments he took his trusty friend, the chronometer of the previous voyage.

What was the great purpose that the Admiralty now wished to consummate? It was the discovery of the North-West Passage, from its supposed Pacific outlet—a return to the abortive proposal for Byron in 1764, the plan for the command of the ocean from the north. Independent of strategic concern, it was a purpose fostered by the Royal Society: 'a voyage to make discoveries on the Northern coasts of the Pacific Ocean would contribute to the promotion of Science in general, and more particularly that of Geography', the Council of the Society held; and such a voyage the Society had taken the lead in urging upon British ministers. Taking into account geographical knowledge, economic ambition and national policy, it was the logical next step in exploration, as well as the revivification of old endeavour. Cook's instructions included other things. He was to go first from the Cape of Good Hope and spend the early part of the summer looking for the islands of Marion and Kerguelen, which if found might provide a port, or at least shelter, wood and water, of great future advantage. This search was not to occupy too much time, for it was essential to land the returning Omai at the Society Islands. Leaving these about the beginning of February 1777, Cook was to make a passage as direct as possible to New Albion, in about 45° north latitude; he was to recruit at the first convenient port, and then to coast north to 65°, arriving in that latitude about June. From there he was to explore all large rivers and inlets which might extend towards Hudson or Baffin Bay; if a passage seemed certain or even probable, he was to do his best to get through it. Other measures were left to his discretion. If he could find no sufficient strait, he was to winter at Petropavlovsk in Kamchatka, or anywhere else more favourable. The following spring, the search for a passage into the Atlantic either east or west was to be continued north as far as was prudent; the return to England might then be made by whatever route promised most for the improvement of geography and navigation.

These instructions were accompanied by an Eskimo

vocabulary; and on 12 July 1776 Cook sailed. It was virtually the anniversary of the beginning of his second voyage, and the sailors who had been with him then regarded it as a lucky day. 'I imbark on as fair a prospect as I can wish', he wrote himself. Clerke was detained in London, having become entangled in the financial misfortunes of a brother; it seems that in the Fleet prison or somewhere about it he picked up the tubercular infection that destroyed him before the end of the voyage. The *Discovery* therefore could not sail till 1 August.

It may be here noted that on the outbreak of war between Great Britain and her old enemies France and Spain, the latter countries issued general orders to their fleets not to interfere in any way with Cook's vessels. He was prosecuting the general interests of mankind, they held, and he was to be treated as neutral in its wars. Benjamin Franklin, the American minister in Paris, made the same request to American ships. No recognition of scientific achievement could signify more greatly.

On the passage to the Cape it grew clear that the *Resolution* was no longer the admirable instrument of discovery that she had been. Badly caulked at the dockyard, her seams opened so much that in a few days hardly a man could lie dry in his bed, while the sails in the sail-room suffered great damage; long before she came to the Arctic her leaks had given continual trouble. She reached Table Bay, however, on 18 October with little greater incident than this discomfort, being overtaken there by the *Discovery* early in November. Provisioning was completed for two years, and so much stock added to the cows, horses and sheep brought from England for the islands that the *Resolution* left the Cape more like a Noah's ark than an exploring vessel. Both ships sailed together on 30 November and made south-east, in accordance with their instructions, for the identification of the recent French discoveries. Cold weather and gales were fatal to several sheep and goats, and in a sudden squall the *Resolution* lost her mizen-topmast—not a serious loss, as the stick was already suspected and could be replaced. Early in December two barren rocky islands were sighted, apparently those reported by Marion and Crozet, and as they had no name on a chart given to Cook by the latter, they were called Prince Edward Islands. Nor did they have harbours, and the course was changed to east to pick up Kerguelen's discovery. A further small group of islands discovered by Marion and Crozet, now avoided by Cook, he named after them, and on 24 December in latitude 48° 30′ the island twice visited by Kerguelen was sighted. There was good anchorage in a bay Cook called Christmas Harbour; water was found in plenty, but no wood; and although fish were scarce, birds and seals provided a welcome change of diet. The ships ran along the rugged coast to the south-east; so bare of vegetation was it that it was called the Island of Desolation, a name changed after the voyage to Kerguelen's Land; and on 30 December Cook left it and made for his familiar base in New Zealand.

January 1777 began with dark fog, and in a squall the masts of the *Resolution* suffered fresh damage. This was not completely remedied till the ships reached Van Diemen's Land, where they anchored in Adventure Bay on 26 January. There also was plenty of fish and some poor grass for the cattle. The few naked aborigines found displayed no interest in presents; bread they threw away, and when Omai, in his civilized pride, fired a musket they disappeared precipitately into the bush. Pigs were left in the hope that they might breed: here Cook's benevolence was doomed to be without result. This was the first time he himself had been on the coast of Van Diemen's Land, and he might, if he had had more time, have taken the chance to verify Furneaux's report as to its connection with Australia; but he saw no reason for rejecting this, and at the end of the month departed without further delay, to anchor in Queen Charlotte's Sound on 12 February. During a fortnight there was the usual salutary change of diet; some of the vegetables planted on the preceding voyage were found to have survived; and the brewing of spruce beer, in which Cook had great faith as a counter to scurvy, was put in train. When the ships first appeared very few natives would come on board, out of all those whom Cook recognized and who remembered him; and not for some time could they be persuaded that he was not an instrument of vengeance for the slaughtered boat's crew, or that he put no delight in their own wild justice. And this generosity, noted Lieutenant Burney, seemed to earn not so much gratitude as a certain contempt.

Enquiry, however, convinced Cook that the quarrel was unpremeditated: that if the natives had been savage, the English had not been without fault, and that punishment of a people whose life was so largely passed in the practice of revenge could be wisely overlooked. Beyond guarding his working parties carefully, therefore, he took no step which could impair good relations; and when Omai wanted to take a New Zealander to Tahiti with him there was no opposition, while a father presented his son for a servant to the volunteer traveller with complete indifference.

Cook left Ship Cove for the last time on 25 February; a course to the east and then north brought him a month later to Mangaia, one of the Cook Islands, where there was no safe landing, and the only native who came on board fell over a goat and was far too terrified to give much information. Other islands of the group were visited, and some coconuts, scurvy-grass and fodder obtained; water was running short and thunderstorms were welcome for the rain that was caught. As March went on Cook was more and more worried by the contrary winds that afflicted him, and his consequent slow passage; early in April he decided that he must abandon his time-table and turn to Tonga for refreshment, calling at Tahiti later. On the islets round the Palmerston lagoon a little more food was collected, though it had to be carried half a mile along the reef through water waist-high. It was the end of April when the ships at last reached the Friendly Islands, and in this fruitful archipelago they remained till the middle of July. Arrangements for trade were systematized, the cattle were landed to recruit their strength, and an observatory and camp set up under the command of

King, the man on this voyage who, besides Cook, showed most talent for dealing with native peoples. Management was no less needed than before; thieving was rife and ingenious, and Cook, at his wits' end to find a deterrent, once or twice seemed to his officers to be more harsh than he should have been. Finally, Clerke evolved the method of shaving the heads of guilty parties, which was effective as a mark of infamy—though of ambiguous value for those Englishmen who had the misfortune to be bald.

The length of the visits both to Tonga and later to the Society Islands afforded opportunities for observation of native life greater than had ever been hitherto given, for the exchange of gifts on a lavish scale, and, in Tonga, for some confusion to arise in regard to native dignitaries. The disentangling of princes and kings and superior kings took some time; but as each fresh acquaintance involved the formal presentation of large quantities of yams, coconuts, plantains, hogs, fowls, sugar-cane and bread-fruit, these chiefly friendships provoked no regret. Cook replied with the usual articles of trade, and presented European seeds for the native plantations. Wherever he went, he was entertained with music and dancing, wrestling and boxing matches—in return for which the marines went through their rather inefficient drill, and there were displays of fireworks which stimulated the highest ecstasy of astonishment and delight. In spite of all the friendliness, it is said that at Lifuka, one of the more northern islands, there was a plot to murder all the visitors and take the ships, which luckily broke down. After a number of short but dangerous passages through reefs and shoals, Cook came at last to Tongatapu, the largest island, the fertile residence of Paulaho, king of all Tonga. Here the cattle were landed and the observatory and camp set up again, constant trade made the shore like a fair, valuable red feathers were acquired, and an eclipse of the sun was observed. Paulaho dined on board the *Resolution* every day, developed a taste for wine, and was as cheerful over his bottle as the most civilized of monarchs. To obviate the stealing of livestock, a number of cattle, goats, sheep and horses were presented to the chiefs. Other thefts went on, till the king and other notables were taken as hostages—a method of securing the return of important articles which again proved successful. Cook witnessed and reported in invaluable detail the important ceremony celebrating the coming of age of Paulaho's son; unfortunately, before a great chiefly funeral could take place he had to depart. He also learnt of the existence of Fiji and Samoa. He left Tongatapu on 10 July, visited old friends at Eua for a few days, had some trouble over the stripping of a waylaid sailor, and finally sailed for Tahiti on 17 July. The visit had been well rewarded, for it had conserved the ships' stores and improved the general health, and relations with the natives, in spite of their passion for theft, had on the whole been good.

A heavy squall did some damage to masts and sails and both ships were leaky, but on 12 August Cook was once again anchored at Vaitepiha Bay and Omai reunited to his friends: he was immediately popular, much more for the red feathers he had brought from Tonga than for his own vain and foolish sake. Red feathers, indeed, became the staple currency; nails and beads were no longer the object of the economic enthusiasm of Wallis's day. Ships from Peru, Cook found, had twice been to the island since his last visit; had left, and taken away, a mission; had raised a cross, built a house and buried their commander there. They had also warned the Tahitians against Cook, to whom, however, the whole district was now formally made over; of which the acknowledgment was a very successful firework display. At Matavai Bay the usual camp was established, a garden planted, and the friendliest relations at once resumed. Most of the remaining stock was landed, and the ships were rid of a great deal of vexatious trouble; recompensed, said Cook, by the satisfaction felt 'in having been so fortunate as to fulfill His Majestys design in sending such usefull animals to two worthy nations'. More astonishing even than fireworks was the horseback exercise of Cook and Clerke, though Omai's equestrian attempts were undoubtedly more entertaining. Cook's interest on his previous voyage in the war fleet prepared to subjugate Moorea will be remembered—this visit found the war still in progress, and he had to decline to give his aid. He did not decline, however, to attend the last of the great ceremonies he was to witness in the South Pacific, that of a human sacrifice in the cause of Tu and his uneasily allied chiefs. This complex and lengthy ritual was the subject of one of the most thorough of all Cook's descriptions of Polynesian custom. Interested as he was, when his opinion was asked on the procedure, he felt bound to answer that in England it would have meant the hanging of even the greatest chief who thus disposed of his people—an attitude which, however pleasing to ordinary Tahitians, was to the magnate who had supplied the victim vile beyond contempt. The ceremony, moreover, had only a modified success—the utmost the *atua*, or god, would vouchsafe in answer was a patched-up truce.

Refitting was completed by 21 September. Cook was cured of a severe attack of rheumatism, native fashion, by being squeezed and pummelled from head to foot—a remedy painful but triumphant; and he regretfully had to decline a present from Tu to the King of England of a beautifully made double canoe, for which he had no room in either ship. On 29 September he sailed for Moorea. Friendship and trade here were broken for a while by the destruction of a number of houses and canoes, so strong was Cook's determination to get back a stolen goat. He was, it seems plain, becoming a rather exasperated man; at Huahine, where the ships next went, a 'hardened scoundrel' who had stolen a sextant had his ears cropped. On this island Omai finally made his home, a house was built for him and a garden planted, and an assortment of European goods—pots and pans, plates and glasses as well as a hand-organ, a globe of the world, a musket and a horse—left with him. The two young Maoris were left with him, too, though if Cook had seen any possibility of returning them to their own country he would have carried them on. From Huahine the ships crossed to Raiatea, where three men tried to desert, and were not all recovered until after the seizure of hostages and the miscarriage of a counterplot to seize

Cook himself and Clerke while they were ashore bathing. The natives next day had no hesitation in discussing their plan and its failure—an innocency that, however irritating, at least displays no great depth of vice. Nor was there further untoward incident; the month at Raiatea reinforced the health of all on board the ships, and on 7 December Cook left harbour. He obtained from a neighbouring chief one of the anchors abandoned by Bougainville, to make into hatchets for trade, and then steered north for the prosecution of the most arduous part of his voyage.

The most arduous: and certainly, in the hopes of many, it might prove the most important and the most fruitful; for a northern passage between Atlantic and Pacific would have meant not merely an alternative route to the east but a revolution in the trade of the world. Cook, as he sailed north, might very well have seemed to some ardent economic philosopher to hold the future of that trade between his hands. He harboured no rash views himself—in the matter of his work he ever fell short of too much belief; but having given Clerke the necessary orders for independent cruising in case of a separation, he took his ships with a minimum of delay towards New Albion. On 24 December a small low island was seen—Christmas Island—where a few days were spent in getting turtle and observing an eclipse of the sun. Fish were caught and coconuts, yams and melons planted. He departed on 2 January 1778, and on the 18th, in about latitude 21°, sighted land again—the first time European eyes had rested on the Hawaiian islands.[1] The wind prevented a near approach to the first island seen, but from the second, Atoui or Kauai, canoes paddled with a cargo of stones, thrown overboard when found not to be needed, and occupants who resembled the Tahitians and spoke their language. No anchorage at once presenting itself, Cook sailed along the south-eastern coast, while

[1] Reference has already been made in Chapter III to the Hawaiian tradition of the wrecking of a ship with white men in the sixteenth century. A later claim that the group was discovered by a Spaniard, Juan Gaytano or Gaetan, in 1555 is now disallowed.

natives crowded to see the wonder and a constant succession of canoes brought out pigs and potatoes to trade for nails. The fresh food was exceedingly welcome—not so the thieving, the immediate sequel of inducing the boldest among the savages to come on board. Anchorage was found at last, and Cook landed to investigate the water and the inhabitants, who to his surprise threw themselves face-down to the ground. When he could get them to rise they brought a multitude of small pigs, with no hint of payment; but presents were distributed, the water found to be good, and next day trade and watering went forward with brisk good nature on both sides. 'No people could trade with more honisty than these people', wrote Cook, with great satisfaction all too prematurely. He took a walk on shore, and was able to put into his journal an excellent description of the people, their houses and artifacts, and the place of worship, with its grinning carved figures, that he called a *marae* and the Hawaiians a *heiau*. He thought of Tahiti and New Zealand, and again asked himself the question that was never far from his mind: 'How shall we account for this nation spreading itself so far over this vast ocean?' Strong winds drove the *Resolution* across to the neighbouring island of Niihau, where good yams, salt and water were found, and goats, pigs and seeds left, before the ship's anchor dragged, and the passage north was resumed.

This was on 2 February; a few days before reaching the fortieth parallel Cook adopted a more easterly course, and on 7 March New Albion was sighted in latitude 44° 33' N. It was the shore of what is now the state of Oregon; and here began the remarkable coasting voyage to the north and through Bering Strait, which, while not totally disproving the existence of the passage Cook was in search of, at least ruled it out in navigable waters. Vitus Bering, that unfortunate Dane, had in the Russian service in 1728 sailed from the south through the strait named after him, and in 1741 had managed to cross the ocean from Kamchatka south of the Aleutian islands to the American coast at about latitude 58° 30'. One or two Russians had passed the Bering Sea to America without realizing it was

America; a Spanish captain on a voyage of reconnaissance from Mexico in 1775 had coasted north to 58°. But the coastlines of Canada and Alaska were virtually unknown. Here it was that Cook's charts were to throw a light sufficient to define them with something near the accuracy of the modern map. The land first sighted was tree-grown and moderately high, but as the ships made slowly north in stormy weather the hills and wooded valleys were backed by the snow-covered slopes and peaks of great mountains. Cook's maps indicated the existence of at least two straits, those of Juan de Fuca and an imaginary Admiral de Fonte; on the actual coast he saw no sign of them, but did find an inlet which provided a good harbour. This wild and picturesque place was King George's or Nootka Sound. The surrounding country was inhabited by Indians who put off immediately to trade, and did so without fear or remorse—for so far from re-sembling the Sandwich islanders they not merely stole anything metal that seemed movable, from fish-hooks to candlesticks, but even added water to the bladders of oil they sold. 'These people', said Cook, at the end of a descriptive passage of some eloquence, 'got a greater middly and variety of things from us than any other people we had visited.'

They were a swarthy race, with flat broad faces and high cheek-bones, black hair long and straight, and all exceedingly dirty; in disposition good-natured though hot-tempered, with a miscellany of weapons—bows and arrows, slings, spears, clubs and stone tomahawks. Their houses were large buildings of split trees, much more substantial than the airy dwellings of Polynesia. In the villages was no domestic animal or vegetable; many berry-producing bushes grew about the forest edge, how-ever, and there was plenty of fish. Furs were the principal articles of trade; of these a surprising number was obtained. The main necessities to Cook were water, which was plentiful, and timber for the repair of his masts, which was even more abun-dant in the immense forest all about him. By 26 April the ships could leave, in threatening weather which led on a two days' hurricane, during which the *Resolution* sprank a leak, and there was no observation of the coast. Later on they could run closer in, though for a time, when the land trended to the west and there was also a westerly wind, progress was slow. Near Cape Hinchinbroke, early in May, they put into Prince William Sound, where natives, in anticipation of easy booty, poured on to the *Discovery* with drawn knives. The crew produced their cutlasses, the invaders were driven off in confusion, no harm or damage done, and Cook congratulating himself that he could leave the inlet without firing a shot. These people were different from those of Nootka Sound. They were much like Eskimos in dress, arms and canoes, with peculiarities of their own. While waiting for the weather outside to clear, the *Resolution* was heeled and her leak repaired; it was found that in some places the oakum had entirely gone from the seams. This operation was completed by 17 May; then a fortnight was spent exploring the great 'river' later called Cook Inlet, in the hope that it would give a direct passage to the Bering Sea and the northern coast at latitude 65°. The hope was vain, and Cook turned south-west down the line of the Alaskan peninsula and the Aleutian islands till at the end of June he found a passage through. Perils were thick, from mist, fog, shoals, rocks and tides. Fish was obtained from natives or caught by the men, a few herbs were gathered, the possibilities of a fur trade were clearly inviting. Several natives who came on board had obviously met Europeans before, probably Russian traders.

Through July Cook followed the American coast as nearly as he could northwards, and on 9 August, Cape Prince of Wales, its westernmost point, in latitude 65° 38′, was sighted. Next day he landed on the opposite shore of Asia, where the natives seemed a fine race physically and not unfriendly, though a little timid. The country was desolate. Passing through the strait and over to America again, he came in a week more to the first floating ice, earlier than it had been expected, and impeded by this as well as by fog, he pushed on slowly but steadily till the middle of the month. The ice meant danger, for the ships might at any time be caught and crushed; but it also provided a supply of fresh food from 'sea-horses', or walruses. On 18 August he was in latitude 70° 44', his farthest north, close to the edge of ice ten or twelve feet high and as compact as a wall, stretching impenetrably from west to east as far as the eye could reach. There was nothing to do therefore but turn south-west. Eleven days later, in about latitude 69°, longitude 179° W, all attempts to get through the ice proving vain, and the season being too far advanced for the prospect to improve, the search was abandoned till the next summer. Water and wood were again needed, and Cook resolved to run down the Asiatic shore in hope of meeting with supplies. It was destitute of timber, and he crossed to Alaska once again, where in Norton Sound drift-wood was obtained, but no water. While Cook was walking on shore indeed he met with the first growing wood he had seen for nearly three months. The ground also produced heath and berries; from a family of natives he obtained 400 pounds of fish, the price of which was four knives made from an old iron hoop. A few beads presented to a child sent the whole family into tears of joy.

Farther south dangerous shoals guarded the coast. Cook therefore laid a course for Unalaska, one of the Aleutian islands, where he had already found a harbour, reaching it on 3 October after a very heavy gale in which the *Resolution* again began to leak badly. Here he remained for three weeks, while the leak was repaired, the ships were watered, and the men were employed in picking berries and catching fish. Here also he met the chief of the Russian traders in the islands, one Ismailov, who discussed their geography with Cook so far as mutual linguistic difficulties would permit, and allowed the English to copy his manuscript charts. He gave Cook letters for Russian officials; and to him Cook presented an octant, with a letter and chart for the Admiralty to be forwarded through Siberia. In the meantime some of the officers had visited the Russian settlement, where they were well received. On 26 October the ships sailed, not for a port in Kamchatka where wintering would mean six or seven months' idleness, but for the Sandwich Islands. It was among these islands that Cook decided to recruit his men. His exploration of the North American coast, as far as the main object of his search was concerned, had revealed nothing. Yet he had already made vast additions to the map, while there remained the succeeding summer in which to reinforce or modify his conclusions, before in compliance with his instructions he turned his face homeward.

The passage south began in storm, but with November the weather moderated, and on the 26th land was sighted, the rocky and surf-beaten coast of the pleasant island of Maui. Cook did not stop here, or indeed come to an anchorage for almost eight weeks, during which his men suffered the extremes of frustration. At sea, he felt, he could regulate trade better, and the less contact sailors had with the islanders the better. As the vessels coasted the northern side of the island canoes brought off needed provisions, trading without suspicion or deceit, nor attempting to steal. On the last day of the month Hawaii, the Owhyhee of Cook's journal, was sighted and the ships slowly sailed down its north-eastern and south-eastern coasts—coasts which appeared more abrupt and rocky than grateful to the land-hungry eye. A heavy gale off the eastern point of the island played havoc with the *Resolution*'s rigging and blew three sails to pieces, and for a time, till a lull occurred and fresh sails could be set, the ship was in some jeopardy; then at night the *Discovery* parted company and the two ships did not rejoin until 6 January 1779. Cook worked along the coast, trading, and rounded the southern point on the 5th. When Clerke rejoined him they stood off and on for ten days, till at daybreak on the 17th, on the west side of the island, a promising bay was seen; it afforded safe anchorage, and here, after that tedious time, Cook at last resolved to refresh and refit. The native population was great; nearly 800 canoes swarmed round the ships as they moved to their anchorage; men and women crowded on board and swam off from the shore. Unlike their fellows of Maui, they were accomplished and persistent thieves, and only the efforts of a friendly chief, who now and then drove them off the ships, allowed order to be kept. It was time for both ships to make harbour: the *Resolution* was in bad case, the sails and rigging of the *Discovery* also greatly needed repair, and her decks were so leaky that through the whole three weeks preceding they could not be washed. This harbour was 'Karakakooa' or Kealakekua Bay.

In the afternoon Cook, King and some others landed to inspect the place, accompanied by a chief and a man named Touahah, or Koa, who had visited the ship earlier and, it was soon found, 'belonged to the Church'. Prostration in Cook's honour had been the rule at Kauai the previous January: here still greater honour was paid him. Koa had come on board with much ceremony, covering Cook with a piece of red cloth in addition to making formal gifts of a pig and coconuts; and now on shore he conducted him with great state to a rather grisly *heiau* close by, a place of skulls and hideous images. Here took place a ceremony of considerable length and some embarrassment—prayers, orations and presentations; Cook was invited to climb with Koa half-way up a rickety scaffold, a procession of ten men with a live hog and a large piece of red cloth prostrated themselves before him, the hog was offered to him, and as he clung to his precarious perch he was wrapped in the cloth. Descending he was taken to another part of the *heiau*, and seated between two images with his arms outstretched and supported by Koa and King. Another procession then brought a baked hog and other food; Cook was rubbed with a piece of well-chewed coconut, kava was tasted, and pieces of the hog put into the mouths of Cook and King alike—Cook's piece already chewed according to native notions of honour. At this Cook brought the proceedings to an end by distributing a few presents and returning to the ship, he and his officers all somewhat mystified, but judging that there had at least been good evidence of friendship and respect. On Cook in addition had been conferred the name or title of 'Orono'; when he again landed he was clothed as before in red cloth and presented with a pig and kava, while a priest constantly attended him to see that he was paid proper respect.

The ceremonies, wrote King, so far as Cook was concerned, approached adoration—and that, as the Hawaiians later made clear, was their exact nature. Cook in truth had been deemed a god, and for a human being to assume the status of divinity, however unconsciously, is a difficult and ambiguous task—even in a society where the greatest chiefs are regarded as sacred beings. The god for whom Cook was taken, 'Orono', or Lono, was the mildest of the Hawaiian deities, the god of the *makahiki* season, when war and hard work were forbidden, and men rejoiced in the produce of the earth: Lono the divine chief who had left the country long ages before, prophesying his return in a great ship bearing gifts. Cook had come twice at the right time, his sails were like the banner of Lono, he brought gifts. The identification was complete. There seemed no end to the supplies that were laid at his feet.

During the remainder of January relations with the Hawaiians were excellent. The ships were refitted, the observatory set up on shore in a sweet-potato field made *tapu* for the purpose; trade was good, food was plentiful, and a large quantity sent off to the ship was presented, said Koa the priest, by him as a free gift. Trade was interrupted on 24 January, as 'Terreeoboo', or Kalei'opu'u, the 'king', was about to return from Maui, and the bay was under *tapu*. Next day it was resumed, and this very great chief visited the *Resolution*. The day after that three canoes containing himself and other richly dressed chiefs, Koa, his fellow priests carrying representations of important gods, and a load of pigs and vegetables, paddled round the ships while the priests chanted with great solemnity. As no one came on board, Cook immediately went on shore, where King turned out the guard from the observatory in honour of Kalei'opu'u, and the chief dressed Cook in his own magnificent feather cloak and helmet, laying other beautiful cloaks at his feet. Then they exchanged names, and Cook was presented with the food. A number of chiefs were taken out to the *Resolution*, where Cook in his turn made presents. All through these ceremonies not a canoe was to be seen in the bay except those used by the participants, and the people remained either in their houses or prostrate on the ground.

While the ships were in the bay more than one party made an excursion up into the forested heights of the island, country so difficult that twenty miles was the limit of exploration; and they, too, had been kindly treated. As the visit drew to a close firewood ran short, but the priests, much to King's surprise, readily gave him the outer fence of the *heiau*, together with most of the carved images which formed part of it. There was a further proof of friendship when an old seaman who died from a stroke was buried in the *heiau* at the chiefs' special request, his funeral followed by three nights of sacrifice and ceremony by the priests themselves. Nevertheless several enquiries were made as to when the ships were going, for supplies on the island were becoming scarce, though they would again be plentiful at the next bread-fruit season. Cook therefore prepared to leave in two days; an enormous quantity of vegetables and a whole herd of pigs were collected from the unfortunate people for a final gift (of which Kalei'opu'u himself retained a share), the camp was broken up, and all made ready for departure. It may be noted that King's faculty for personal friendship with the natives was so great that they urged him to remain, offering to hide him till the ships were gone. On 4 February they sailed north to survey the coast and look for a better anchorage, followed by a great train of canoes and a still further gift of provisions from Kalei'opu'u.

The wind was at first very light, but in the night a gale sprang up, so strong that sails were split; the next night there was another, and in the morning the foremast of the *Resolution* was found so seriously sprung that it would have to be un-stepped for repair. Cook was in a quandary: no other anchorage had been found, and it seemed that he must return to Keala-kekua Bay. In that harbour, already so thoroughly denuded of supplies, he could hardly expect his first flattering welcome to be renewed. With that foremast, on the other hand, he could not proceed, and after some hesitation he resolved to accept the lesser evil and go back. On 11 February therefore the ships anchored in their old station, in a bay strangely quiet and empty. Questions brought the answer that Kaleiʻopuʻu had gone away and had placed the district under *tapu*; the priests, however, were benevolently inclined; the mast was taken on shore, and as the work was likely to last some time the astronomical instruments were landed and set up on the *heiau*. For two days matters went smoothly, though when Kaleiʻopuʻu came back he did not seem wholly satisfied. After that a series of irritating thefts led to angry expostulation; the work of the watering party was impeded; expostulation was met by stone-throwing. The hostility of the natives seemed to be increasing; and Cook, returning baffled and annoyed from fruitless search for one thief, began to contemplate the use of force. All natives were ordered off the *Resolution* and King doubled the sentries round the observatory. In the night between the 13th and the 14th the petty pilfering that had been going on culminated in the theft of the *Discovery*'s cutter—not apparently for the sake of the boat, for it was afterwards found to have been broken up, but for the iron which it contained.

Fate now moved swiftly. Cook resolved to go ashore and seize Kaleiʻopuʻu as a hostage for the cutter's return, and a landing party of marines was ordered. It was the sort of stratagem that had succeeded before, and there was no reason this time to fear its failure. Boats were stationed at each end of the bay to prevent canoes from escaping; and just before eight in the morning of 14 February Cook left the ship with Lieutenant Phillips and nine marines for the village of Kaawaloa, where Kaleiʻopuʻu was. King was to reassure the people near the observatory and guard against any outbreak there. He warned his men, and explained to the priests, to their apparent satisfaction, that no injury was intended against the chief himself. Cook marched into the village, where he was received with the customary respect, and asked for Kaleiʻopuʻu. Kaleiʻopuʻu was plainly not concerned in the theft of the cutter, and was quite willing to go on board the *Resolution* with his two young sons; close to the beach, however, his wife and some of the chiefs remonstrated and kept him back. A large crowd was gathering, and began to arm, and Phillips, as a precaution, drew up his marines in a line on the rocky shore. Cook, finding that Kalei'opu'u's friends would not allow him to go, and not wanting the bloodshed which would have attended force, abandoned the plan; unfortunately at that moment a messenger rushed up with fatal news—shots had been fired on the other side of the bay to stop a canoe, and an important chief, Kalimu, had been killed. To the Hawaiians this seemed open and cruel warfare; their excitement boiled over and stones flew. As Cook and Phillips walked towards their boat one man threatened Cook with a stone and a large iron spike; he replied with a charge of small shot. It did no harm, as the man was protected by his thick war mat; but the stones were hailing on the marines and a chief attempted to stab Phillips, who gave him a blow with the butt of his musket. It is possible that in this crisis Cook's hot temper rose, for he was unaware of the death of Kalimu, as of the whole foundation of native feeling towards him and his men. He fired again from his second barrel, loaded with ball, and killed a man. The marines fired; before they could reload, the crowd fell on them, killing four and wounding others. Phillips was stabbed, but shot his assailant; the boats opened fire. Cook had reached the water's edge safely and waved to the boats to pull in, and at that moment he was struck down and stabbed from behind. He fell forward with his face in the water, and the yelling people rushed to keep him under and finish him off with clubs and daggers. Phillips and his surviving marines struggled to safety and the boats returned immediately to the ships. It was barely an hour since they had rowed to the shore.

In both vessels there was a stunned silence. To imagine Cook dead was to advance to the incredible; the ships became suddenly strange. But the work could not stop; Clerke took command, while King was at once reinforced and told to get the foremast back on board. This was done and the camp broken up by one o'clock. Later on King was sent to try to recover the bodies, without success, and learnt only that they had been cut to pieces. The next night a priest whose friendship had not wavered came off with a bundle containing some parts of Cook's body. On the 20th and 21st his bones were brought to Clerke by another priest, and at sunset, while the guns fired in naval salute, they were given to the waters of the bay. Cook had been honoured like the greatest of dead Hawaiian chiefs: his flesh scraped from the bones and burnt, his bones preserved as sacred relics. During the intervening days sufficient water had been obtained for the ships, at first in the face of considerable opposition, which added to the savagery of the sailors, already thirsting for revenge, and gave excuse for the firing of a village; then peace was made at Kaleiʻopuʻu's request and there was little molestation. Nor did Clerke exact any further vengeance for what had happened, bitter to him above all Cook's men as it must have seemed; for the tragedy was clearly not one deliberately prepared; the Hawaiians mourned Cook equally with the English, and in the chain of circumstance the first deadly shot had been fired by an English hand. The man who succeeded Cook in command was as humane as Cook. The foremast was in place and its rigging completed by 22 February, and on that day the anchors were weighed and Kealakekua Bay was left for the last time.

Clerke's task was to complete the work laid down in Cook's instructions, and the remainder of the voyage may be briefly recounted, for in its object it was predestined to failure. It saw the loss of another leader. The ships steered north, touching at some of the other islands of the group and getting supplies at Kauai and Niihau, and sailing finally from the Sandwich Islands on 15 March. Kamchatka was sighted on 23 April; the vessels had been separated more than once in thick weather, and were covered in snow and ice; the *Resolution* needed constant pumping to keep her clear of water. There was little refreshment at Petropavlovsk, named in the instructions; stores were therefore obtained through the good offices of the Russian governor at Bolsheretsk, on the other side of the peninsula, to whose generosity little return could be made. It was learnt, however, that a tribe on the shores of the northern Bering Sea, long hostile to the Russians but visited by Cook in the preceding summer, had been so touched by his kindness that, taking him for Russian, they had entered into a league of friendship and had sent a deputation to ratify it. The northern voyage was resumed on 13 June up the Asiatic coast, through Bering Strait; but the summer was a bad one, on both coasts there were fogs and floating ice, and the ships could penetrate no farther than a point five leagues short of the previous year's limit. They suffered badly from the ice, and by 27 July Clerke had realized anew the hopelessness of his mission. He determined to return to Petropavlovsk to refit and then to sail for England. His own malady had advanced from the day he left home, and on 22 August he died. He was only thirty-eight, and the experience and devotion of which his life was an epitome lends something more than pathos to his early death.

Gore, the first lieutenant of the *Resolution*, now took command of the expedition, and King became captain of the *Discovery*. On the necessity of bringing the voyage to a close, considering the state of the ships and their supplies, the officers were all agreed; what repairs were possible, therefore, were made at Petropavlovsk, the stores ordered on the previous visit were collected, and the harbour left on 9 October. They followed down the coasts of the Kurile Islands and of Japan, were driven to the east by bad weather, were more than once in danger, and on 4 December anchored at Macao on the Chinese coast. Logs and journals of the voyage were surrendered; the seamen disposed so profitably of the furs they had collected that some of them wished to go back for more; and the ships were refitted. They got clear of Macao Roads on 14 January 1780, passed through the Strait of Sunda, made Simon's Bay at the Cape with a very healthy company, sailed again on 9 May and sighted the Irish coast three months later. Stormy southerly winds drove them north, so that their first anchorage after leaving the Cape was Stromness harbour, in the Orkney islands.

King was sent overland from Stromness with letters for the Admiralty, and on 4 October, after rounding Scotland, the ships anchored off the Nore. They returned after four years and nearly three months; but they returned without Cook.

The study of Cook is the illumination of all discovery. His voyages in result destroyed a whole geographical philosophy; although their motive was in part the enlargement of empire, he conferred upon them the neutral and unslaked intent of science; in method he raised his calling to the stature of science. To geography as a science of facts he gave more detail and more order than the whole of the effort that had preceded him since the cardinal voyages of the Renaissance. To the great questions which geography asked as a science his answers were negative; but to these fundamental denials he added a wealth of exact and detailed affirmation that changed signally the aspect of the problems not of geography alone. To dogma he opposed experience; to the largeness of faith the hesitations of the enforced sceptic; to enthusiasm he presented the cool passion of unsatisfied enquiry. The results of his eleven years' devotion to discovery need be no further emphasized: to elaborate the intention of the scientific mind would be a superfluity. Yet result is so entirely the child of method, intention so often the shuttlecock of circumstance, that the logic of the mind of Cook may yet be the subject of summary.

No man ever understood better the conditions of success. The care he gave to the detail no less than to the fundamentals of preparation was in itself a revolution in discovery; and he realized as no other captain had done that each day of a voyage was a preparation for the next. Discovery at sea meant the ability to keep the sea for lengthy periods; navigation was useless without administration. On the necessary qualities of his ship he was insistent—had other discoverers had better ships, he said, they might have had better results. The extraordinary pains lavished on the equipment of the second voyage were founded in the extraordinary experiences of the first; yet the foresight which watched over the progress of the *Endeavour* and marked its every stage with fresh accomplishment surely lay in a reason which fringed the intuitive. Cook was learning his trade as an explorer on that voyage, we must remember; he made mistakes; more than once luck was with him. More than once luck was with him at later times; but of the gratuitous triumphs of good fortune there were in his career not many. All discovery depends on elemental forces; all experiment is carried on under conditions; given the conditions, Cook left little to chance. His mind had unusual scope; it did not bow to the visitations of an inspired madness. He was the genius of the matter-of-fact. That with this care for every material and human factor the disaster of his death can be made accountable to a faulty ship, as well as—one is compelled to believe—to a faulty temper, is the ultimate irony. The defects of the *Resolution* on the last voyage have been traversed, yet not with fullness, and they are to be contrasted with her perfection for her purpose on the second. The truth may be that no vessel of that century could experience the rigours of two such voyages without giving way. Between them she had gone into dock for refitting, and Cook contrasts the equipment of the navy with that of the merchant service. The standing rigging and some of the other equipment had been bought with the ship, and though already in use for more than a year, it outlasted that taken new from the king's stores; some of it survived even the ship's second voyage. Naval stores, in fact, were usually condemned before they were half worn; merchant ships were rigged without this extravagance, but for a long term. The hull and masts also suffered: we can blame the dockyard, reflecting still that the strain to which they were subjected in all climates and under every possible condition may be very considerable explanation. Yet Cook never lost a ship, he himself never directly lost a man through the defects of his ship, nor did any ship under his command, except once the *Discovery*. Nor through such defects was he ever reduced to that exigence which had been the commonplace of exploration.

His care for detail was not confined to initial preparation.

The remarkable reduction in sickness on his first two voyages has been noticed; on the last and longest of all the *Resolution* lost only five men through this means, three of whom were in a precarious state when they left England: the *Discovery* not a single man. His water was rarely rationed; his men never drank it stale; on longer voyages that most made before they had more fresh food. To these two facts may be chiefly owing the absence of scurvy in those arduous years, yet also to a multiplicity of precautions systematically enforced. The achievement, in the eyes of contemporaries, was astounding; certainly if Cook had done nothing else, it would be title to memory among navigators. But in the application of more abstract science there was an equal presence of pains. Allowance must be made for the general advancement of astronomy and navigation, for the devotion of Banks and Solander the naturalists, of Wales and Bayly the astronomers, for the invention and improvement of the chronometer, to which Cook paid full tribute. Nevertheless it is his work that lies at the foundation of modern marine surveying, they were his charts that remained standards of accuracy for a hundred years and more, it was his insistence on the precision of a finished task that held his ship cruising through weeks of storm off some uncertain coast. To no single instrument, furthermore, did he trust the requirements of exactness. He had the chronometer at Nootka Sound, but he checked its results by no fewer than one hundred and thirty-seven lunar observations. It must be remembered that though the *Discovery* had Bayly, in the *Resolution* astronomy was the department of Cook and King. For them it was a fundamentally navigational thing. Apart from such specialized devotion, we can see in Cook also a continuously growing appreciation of all the natural sciences with which he came in contact, whether they were matters of detail or not. His own reasoning and reports on the formation of oceanic ice, as he faced it in the Antarctic, show a mind that rested firmly on fact, whatever damage that might entail to the conventional physics of the time.

Able in his technical sciences, Cook was also no mean practical psychologist. He knew how to command: he knew, almost always, how to humour. On his own leisure he set little store, and no officers and men laboured harder than his; but there was purpose in the labour, and the measure of the affection he drew is the willingness of many to sail again with him, the silence that fell on the ships when it was known that he was dead. Nor was the command, much less the persuasion, of the eighteenth-century seaman a gift vouchsafed to every officer. A passage from Cook's journal in the *Endeavour* epitomizes his attitude: 'The Sour Krout, the men at first would not eate untill I put in practice a method I never once knew to fail with seamen, and this was to have some of it dress'd every day for the cabbin table, and permitted all the officers without exception to make use of it and left it to the option of the men either to take as much as they pleased or none at all; but this practice was not continued above a week before I found it necessary to put every one on board to an allowance, for such are the tempers and dis-posissions of seamen in general that whatever you give them out of the common way, altho it be ever so much for their good yet it will not go down with them and you will hear nothing but murmurings gainest the man that first invented it; but the moment they see their superiors set a value upon it, it becomes the finest stuff in the world and the inventer an honest fellow.' This was not the last instance of intractable material successfully managed—as the record was not the last of Cook's meditations over the character of the British seaman.

His perception of human nature was not confined to his own sailors. His studies of native peoples have a permanent life; his conclusions as to their essential character remain valid. This psychological ability was part of the humane tenor of his own mind; in an age when the noble savage was a literary convention and the deserving poor the object of a charity not unmixed with self-righteousness, Cook's humanity has a grateful air of un-patronizing common sense. True, men were flogged in his ships, but, in comparison with contemporary naval practice, not with great severity. Where indiscriminate murder was still the treatment accorded by most sailors to savage races, he found the secret of good understanding, certainly in an apparent superiority of force, but more prominently in strict honesty and gentle treatment. 'It has ever been a maxim with me', he wrote, 'to punish the least crimes any of my people have comited against these uncivilized nations, their robbing us with impunity is by no means a sufficient reason why we should treat them in the same manner.' He did not hesitate as a man of peaceful intent to expose himself to risks. Nor was this all: the continual necessity for recruiting the health of his crews was joined with a constant regard for the health of others. To the stringent efforts made by Cook to prevent the spreading of disease through the islands there is testimony both by his surgeons and by his men; that the task was impossible may be laid to the account not of those men alone but of the islanders—and to the contemporary short-comings of scientific medicine. Yet where discipline was so strict and relief from discipline so inviting, the number of attempted desertions from his ships could be counted on the fingers. In an environment where the history of cruelty is so constant that the mind takes no impression of it, the individual instances of hasty passion on Cook's part shock from their very infrequency; and Cook by his nature was a passionate man. He was not slow himself to deplore those lapses. His last lapse he did not live to deplore.

No man concerned in Pacific navigation more than he could have known the satisfaction of the achieved result; and no man viewed it with more moderation. But if he knew the exaltation of discovery, he knew also its weariness of mind—though that he was unaccustomed to reveal. Once or twice, indeed, as in the desolating reaction from crisis on the Australian coast, his pen escaped its stoic control. 'Such', runs the journal, 'is the vicissitudes attending this kind of service, and must always attend an unknown navigation where one steers wholy in the dark without any manner of guide whatever. Was it not for the pleasure which naturly results to a man from his being the first discoverer even was it nothing more than sand or shoals, this kind of service would be insupportable especially in far distant parts like this, short of provisions and almost every other necessary.' The world, he laments, would hardly admit excuse for the man who left unexplored a coast once discovered. If he enlarged on its dangers, he was charged with timidity and want of perseverance; if he went forward boldly and met disaster, with temerity and want of conduct. With timidity he himself could never be charged; with temerity he would not be if he escaped with safety; yet considering his single ship and the other circumstances he must own he had engaged among islands and shoals more than perhaps he ought to have done. 'But if I had not I should not have been able to give any better account of the one half of it, than if I had never seen it, at best, I should not have been able to say wether it was main land or islands and as to its produce, that we should have been totally ignorant of as being inseparable with the other and in this case it would have been far more satisfaction to me never to have discover'd it, but it is time I should have done with this subject, which at best is but disagreeable and which I was lead into on reflecting on our late danger.' Revelation in such rare moments is complete.

Of such a man legend inevitably grew. To the peoples of the Pacific, whether they recognized in him the aspect of deity or not, he was and remained a fabulous figure, alike in the power he personified and in his benevolence. His sailors related that he would come up on deck, even from sleep, when no one else suspected land, and change the course; for them, too, he took on legend. To King, temperance in Cook was scarcely a virtue, so great was the indifference with which he submitted to self-denial—it was a characteristic contested, however, by Samwell, the surgeon, who noted the temperance, but lauded the virtue. Cook, he said, always when possible kept a good table; and who, reading the painstaking detail with which the circumnavigator registered the recipe of a Tahitian pudding—'I seldom or never dined without one when I could get it'—would differ from Samwell? To measure the stature of Cook, however, one needs no recourse to legend or controversy; to compare his voyages,

not in the mass of their result but individually, with the achievement of other men who were deemed with justice to have made
contribution to geography, is its adequate realization. Chance
might enable the most ignorant man to discover islands, said
La Pérouse, but it belonged only to great men to leave nothing
more to be done regarding the coast they had found. Yet one
thinks of Cook, not only as him who would always be in the
eyes of that immortal Frenchman 'the first of navigators', or as
the scientist for whose safety the governments of France and
Spain took such honourable thought, but also as the tall smiling
figure who on the beach at Ship Cove, in Queen Charlotte's
Sound, threw trifles for naked Maori urchins to scramble for,
laughing and fearless, till his pockets were empty. For the rest,
the map of the Pacific is his ample panegyric.

# EPILOGUE

WHEN the *Resolution* and *Discovery* returned from that last four years' voyage they returned from an ocean known thenceforth in all its main features. It had been measured with an accuracy approximated in no way by the men who first furrowed its waters, so vast and so often inimical. Scarcely any region of its great expanse but had witnessed the sails of some navigator, outward bound perhaps in hope and expectation, perhaps making desperately with short supplies and ebbing faith towards the nearest port of civilized men. From decade to decade through two centuries and a half the possible boundaries of a great continent had been pushed back, while geographer after geographer asserted its existence, till Cook in two voyages of matchless skill and pertinacity shattered finally the age-old figment. Yet not finally; for a continent, though uninhabitable, there might still be behind that silent wall of ice from which Cook had retired, defeated but relieved, in 1774; and of that possibility Cook had made his definite thesis. The exploration of the Antarctic was no work for the eighteenth century. In place of the continent that was no more than a shadow of the mind, were islands almost beyond computation, and in 1780 there were few archipelagos of importance that had escaped discovery and identification. In essentials the modern map had assumed its form. True, those who had contributed to its elucidation returned with small report of gold and silver, of populous cities and splendid civilizations. The immediate greed of men was little served. At least the reality, however different, was hardly less absorbing; science was to gather a harvest in our day unexhausted still.

Although when Cook died the nature of the Pacific had been so brilliantly revealed, there were other voyages after his which added in sum greatly to the ascertained knowledge of the ocean;

and to the chief of these voyages before the end of Cook's century reference is due, brief but imperative. They were voyages that added to detail, verified, corrected; in doing so, they displayed a continued curiosity which was in the tradition of geographical discovery, a courage and endurance which were its characteristics not less; displayed, too, in one instance the tragedy which walks with lofty enterprise. This tragedy was that of Jean François Galoup de La Pérouse, he who with such deep-founded enthusiasm registered his admiration of Cook; and it was bound up with the final illumination of what had seemed to be a permanent mystery of the ocean, the identity of the Solomon Islands.

That group, so early discovered, so extravagantly rumoured, and so often sought in vain, had become the subject of scepticism by the very men who after two hundred years passed through it and fought its savage inhabitants. Indeed, the Solomons were lost in a haze that could not be dispelled without acute and comparative study of the records. And the most primary records did not exist—or rather, they were buried in the obscure archives to which Spain consigned her knowledge of discovery deemed unprofitable. Nor, till the voyages of Carteret and Bougainville, was there matter of comparison. The rumours of the quayside, however startling in their evocations of wealth, were in useful detail distressingly vague. Quiros, it will be remembered, in one of his more tightly reasoned dissertations, had concluded that Santa Cruz, the Solomons and New Guinea must all be close together; but it is not a matter for surprise that the Solomons at least should have been speedily and distantly removed. Dead reckoning had led Mendaña to put his Western Isles 1700 leagues from Peru; they were in reality 2,000 miles more distant. It was natural that by 1646 they should be incorporated into the Marquesas, that in the passage of time their supposed longitude should vary from 2,400 to 7,500 miles west of Peru and even their latitude from 7° to 19° S. It was natural that Carteret should sail five degrees west of the position attributed to them in his own day and, not meeting them, utter his unbelief. It was perhaps natural that even after French geographers had convincingly demonstrated a valid identification Dalrymple should refuse his credence to any Solomon Islands apart from New Britain, and that Cook should agree with him.

In 1613 the Spanish historian Figueroa had printed a short account of Mendaña's voyage. Till Europe began to prepare for the transit of Venus, its circulation was confined virtually to Spain, and then, in 1766, during the discussion of suitable sites for observation, Figueroa was translated. Then Carteret made his landfall; then came Bougainville, tentatively placing the group on his chart about five hundred miles north-west of Samoa; then in 1769 Surville, again unconscious of the re-discovery, anchoring in Port Praslin in the island of Ysabel, and touching during a lengthened stay at San Cristobal and its off-lying small islands, before making south into the Tasman Sea. Then in 1781 Maurelle, a Spaniard, sighted the Candelaria Shoals, or Roncador, off the islands' north-east coast. But none suspected the land of Mendaña, until in 1781 again a man of the study and not of the practice of navigation, the French geographer Buache, wrote his *Memoir on the Existence and Situation of Solomon's Islands*. The group, argued Buache, after careful examination of the evidence, must clearly lie between Santa Cruz and New Guinea. Now, in that part of the ocean, which had been traversed several times, the only large body of land was that discovered separately by Bougainville and Surville; this, then, must be the problematical archipelago. If in England unsatisfied geographers preferred New Britain, in France the identification won acceptance, and when La Pérouse set out on his voyage in 1785—a voyage to explore Pacific coasts and to gather information on the prospects alike of a whale fishery and of the fur trade—an additional part of his instructions was to verify the theory of Buache.

He sailed from Brest with two frigates, round the Horn to the coast of North America, part of which he explored with great thoroughness, and then towards the end of 1786 crossed the Pacific and refitted at Manila. In 1787 he examined the Asian coast as far north as Kamchatka; turned south to Samoa to re-

fresh, and then to Port Jackson in New South Wales, where the
first shiploads of convicts were laying the not very pleasant
foundations of British commonwealth in the Pacific. To the
English his appearance was a portent. Was the Anglo-French
rivalry, never still, to be continued on the shores of the south?
But the mission of La Pérouse was scientific, his personality and
his praise of Cook minimized English embarrassment, and when
in February 1788 he sailed for the Solomons he left a memory
which Australian historians willingly recall. He sailed, and
human eyes never gazed on him again. La Pérouse himself
became a mystery. It was not till thirty years later that the broken
remains of his frigates were found by the adventurer Dillon sunk
on the reef of Vanikoro, one of the Santa Cruz islands, and men
could mourn him in the full knowledge of his fate.

   In time the next discoveries of moment were British, and
they arose from British wrong-doing rather than from any
programme of exploration. Tasman had seen fleetingly and in
danger the northern coasts of Fiji; Cook on his second voyage
had sailed south of it. Now Bligh, who had sailed with Cook,
on his boat voyage to Timor after the *Bounty* mutiny in 1789,
passed right through the group and made some rough but quite
intelligible charts; he had already discovered Aitutaki, one of
the Cook islands, and went on from Fiji through the Banks
group, north of the New Hebrides. This was a remarkable
harvest. The mutineers themselves, on their way from Tahiti to
Pitcairn, discovered Rarotonga, the most important of the Cook
group. Contemporary with these unexpected results of the
bread-fruit voyage were those of which the first convict ships
were the agents, as they sailed home according to particular
instructions, after delivering their freight to Botany Bay.
Among the commanders of these, Captain Lever of the *Lady
Penrhyn* discovered two of the islands north-east of New
Zealand afterwards called the Kermadecs, and later Penrhyn
Island; while Captains Marshall and Gilbert in the *Scarborough*
and *Charlotte*, passing through a part of the ocean hitherto little
known, encountered those two large groups of islets which

now bear their names—individual atolls of which had been sighted by the Spanish seamen so long before in the sixteenth century. In 1789 Lieutenant Shortland in the *Alexander* took a different route round the north of New Guinea and coasted the shores of Guadalcanal and San Cristobal. Shortland in his turn failed to recognize these two among the Solomon Islands, and imagining they were a fresh discovery named them New Georgia. Minor additions to the map were made by other commanders, but for importance the observations of Marshall, Gilbert and Shortland stand certainly first.

Yet the French geographical effort continued, and French was the final identification of the Solomons by Bruni D'Entrecasteaux. The voyage of D'Entrecasteaux was fitted out in 1791 to search for La Pérouse; it also had objects of pure science, as was testified by the naturalists and hydrographers who accompanied the expedition. Two ships sailed, the *Recherche* and *Espérance*—in command of the latter was Huon de Kermadec, whose name like that of his senior is commemorated in island groups of the western Pacific. La Pérouse was not found, but both geography and natural history benefited. D'Entrecasteaux sailed round the Cape of Good Hope, called at Van Diemen's Land, from thence investigated the western side of New Caledonia, unseen by Cook, passed through the Solomons and the Admiralty Islands and circumnavigated Australia, sailing from its south-west point once again to Van Diemen's Land. Leaving Adventure Bay at the end of February 1793, he touched at New Zealand, and corrected slightly Cook's position for the North Cape; named the Kermadecs, visited the Friendly Islands and other groups and spent some time on the New Guinea coast. His name remains in the D'Entrecasteaux Islands discovered by him off that treacherous coast in 1792. The most important work of the voyage was undoubtedly the investigation of the Solomons, the recognition of many of the features Mendaña had described and the restoration as by right of the Spanish names, overlaid as they were by French and English, together with the exploration of that labyrinth of islands

stretching out from the east end of New Guinea, that Archipelago of the Louisiade which had been such a long-continued
agony to Bougainville. Kermadec died at New Caledonia in
May 1793, and D'Entrecasteaux himself at sea just after leaving
the coast of New Britain in August of the same year. The
war that had broken out between France and Holland was less
regardful of the rights of science than that earlier one which had
protected the safety of Cook—for reaching Java the expedition
was broken up and several of its chief members made prisoners.
Unfortunate in its close as this voyage was, it had finally vindi-
cated the memory of Mendaña and the logic of Buache; and
while it was in its earliest stages, another Frenchman was
examining with greater pains than had been hitherto expended,
so it seemed, another of Mendaña's discoveries, the Marquesas.
Cook had touched on their southern shores, for once without
looking closely into the whole group; in 1791 Etienne
Marchand, bound from Cape Horn to the North-west
American coast, examined the islands to the north and north-
westward of Santa Cristina. He then called at Hawaii, and after
his American visit returned home by way of the Ladrones and
the East Indies. He published an account of his voyage at the end
of the century, and not until ten years later did another seaman's
journal appear in print, from which it became plain that
Marchand had been anticipated in his discoveries, only a few
weeks earlier, by the American merchant captain Joseph
Ingraham, of the brigantine *Hope*, out of Boston, bound to the
same coast as Marchand, and like him pursuing the fur trade.

Among a multiplicity of further voyages two are notable for
their length and thoroughness, that of Alessandro Malaspina, an
Italian sailing under the flag of Spain, and that of Vancouver.
In original discovery the voyage of Malaspina did little, but
from a scientific point of view it has been judged the most
important ever to leave Spanish shores. Two ships, the
*Descubierta* and *Atrevida*, starting in the summer of 1789, went
round the Horn to Guayaquil in Peru; and thence to the
Galapagos, Panama and Acapulco. From Acapulco, Malaspina

sailed to Alaska to search like so many others for a strait leading
to Hudson Bay; unsuccessful, he returned in the autumn of
1791. He then crossed the Pacific and through 1792 carried out
a fresh survey of the Philippines; during the following year
cruised through the south-western part of the ocean, touching
on the coasts of New South Wales and New Zealand; proceeded
to a narrow examination of Tonga and its sister islands, and
crossing the Pacific again rounded the Horn and reached Spain
in September 1794. This great voyage was instrumental in the
consolidation of Spanish political and commercial interests in
the Pacific, so far as that was then possible—for the centuries
since Magellan had disallowed in no uncertain fashion the magnificent pretensions of the Treaty of Tordesillas; while the mass
of hydrographical and other scientific observation which was
its result was evidence of an enterprise and solidity of attainment still proudly Spanish. The almost equally long voyage of
Vancouver, with the *Discovery* and *Chatham*, between April
1791 and October 1795, is celebrated for its detailed examination of the coast of New Albion as far north as the Alaskan
peninsula—a coast so remarkably complicated that Vancouver's
systematic and painstaking survey ranks with the most distinguished work of the kind ever done. Its result was finally to
annihilate the possibility of a passage through the continent—a
work that fell worthily to one who had sailed with Cook, the
great dispeller of illusion. This main task of the expedition
began in 1792. Its prelude was a passage round the Cape of
Good Hope to the south-west corner of Australia and the first
survey of 300 miles of its coast eastward, the charting of a
group of rocky islets south of New Zealand called the Snares,
and the addition to the map of the Chatham Islands, east of that
country. And so Vancouver came from the south to New
Albion and the island that is his memorial.

These then were the most distinguished of the many voyages
that in the last twenty years of the century formed an appendix
to the original discovery of the age—an appendix not unworthy

in plan and result of the epoch it completed. They were voyages among many; where knowledge is illimitable its agents are not to be confined in number. During those two decades, during the decades of a new century, ship after ship set sail from ports as various as the interests of mankind and brought back its tale of success or failure, often of some new islet seen, some coral paradise, microscopical with its fringe of palms and circle of surf in the huge frame of the southern ocean. As those decades advanced the strange became familiar, the constellations of the south swung not above the sailor alone but above the colonist; de Brosses and Callander had their imperial fulfilment, not in the countries of their choice, in devious ways by them unguessed. It was men whose calling had led them to Australia itself who answered the last great questions of the Australian coast—Bass separated Van Diemen's Land from the greater island, Flinders resolved Dampier's doubts in the north. Into New Zealand came a civilization that transformed but did not always beautify, and in war as well as in peace, through long and melancholy campaigns, was Cook's analysis of the native mind proved full of truth. Rarely indeed did any Pacific island of consequence remain untouched by the commerce and the alien ideals of Europe, by the traffic of the labour agent and the planter, by a religion with a too limited gospel of salvation; and the inevitable fell on those far-stretched archipelagos with an ignoble violence that can cause good men little but regret.

In the story of the exploration by which the outlines of the ocean were revealed, at least, there is abundant nobility. To gaze back to the speculations of Ptolemy, to the dogmatisms and doubts of the medieval time, to the leaping enthusiasms and the pious temerities, so generous yet so narrowly national, of the Renaissance and its reaction, to the growing science and the extraordinary fulfilment of the seventeenth and eighteenth centuries, with their emergent humanity above their passionate economic and imperial ambition, is to follow in one department the expansion of the mind of man. It is to watch at once the growth of a tradition and its destruction, the counterplay of denial and affirmation, the enthronement of fact on fantasy. In that growth and destruction two men above all others stand out curiously opposed, after the first tremendous achievement of Magellan—Quiros and Cook. It has been argued that from the three great Spanish expeditions of the sixteenth and nascent seventeenth centuries the science of geography derived no advantage—all their discoveries had to be rediscovered, their narratives, so far as they were published, provided the world only with controversy and speculation. The judgment is from one aspect valid: it is possible to argue that Quiros was a vain enthusiast. No judgment at the same time could be more mistaken; for in after years no name was more in the minds of geographers and discoverers than his. From the descriptions of his faith men took their starting-point; in relation to the vision of his piety they collated their discoveries; in the demolition of the continent whose lineaments he had so confidently drawn was their final triumph. In that triumph the figure of Cook, so dissimilar, so equally the embodiment of his age, so much more the master of a regulated and secular enthusiasm, stands supreme. Nor was his fulfilment of the tradition altogether the denial of its faith, startlingly different as was the continent in which Cook, too, believed somewhat from the excited glories of the apostle. For as an apostle and a prophet one must reckon Quiros; in Cook's life is the consummation of the spirit of scientific navigation.

Yet one gazes on the infinite curve of the Pacific today, that ocean which washes continents and explodes its waters alike on tropic reefs and the encircling ice of both poles, not without memory of the ships of other voyagers nor their baffled hopes: in them, we may say, however they differed in accomplishment or intent, stirred a spirit which in some sort gives constancy and wholeness to the inconstant and fragmentary lives of men: their effort, too, was not without result, and in the enlargement of the knowledge with which men contemplate this globe they have their given place.

# BIBLIOGRAPHY

THE following short bibliography aims merely at listing (a) the principal printed primary authorities for the history of exploration in the Pacific, together with (b) collections of 'Voyages', etc., and (c) modern works most likely to be of use to the student. In (a) the letter H denotes a publication of the Hakluyt Society.

## (a) PRIMARY AUTHORITIES

Banks, [Sir] Joseph. *The Endeavour Journal of Joseph Banks*, edited by J. C. Beaglehole. 2 vols. Sydney, 1962.

Bougainville, Louis Antoine de. *Voyage autour du monde*. Paris, 1771. English translation by J. R. Forster, *A Voyage round the World*. London, 1772.

Byron, John. *Byron's Journal of his Circumnavigation, 1764–1766*, edited by Robert E. Gallagher. Cambridge, 1964 (H).

Carteret, Philip. *Philip Carteret's Voyage round the World, 1766–1769*, edited by Helen M. Wallis. 2 vols. Cambridge, 1965 (H).

Cook, James. *The Journals of Captain James Cook on his Voyages of Discovery*, edited by J. C. Beaglehole. 3 vols. Cambridge, 1955–6 (H).

Dampier, William. *Voyages*, edited by John Masefield. 2 vols. London, 1906. *A New Voyage round the World*, edited by N. M. Penzer. London, 1927.

Drake, Francis (the younger). *The World Encompassed*; with an appreciation by Sir Richard Carnac Temple. London, 1926.

Heeres, J. E. *The Part Borne by the Dutch in the Discovery of Australia*. London, 1899.

[Le Maire]. *The East and West Indian Mirror* (for 'Australian Navigations Discovered by Jacob Le Maire'), edited by J. A. J. de Villiers. London, 1906 (H).

[Magellan]. *Magellan's Voyage Around the World by Antonio Pigafetta Three Contemporary Accounts*, edited by Charles E. Nowell. Evanston, Illinois, 1962.

*The First Voyage Round the World by Magellan*, edited by Lord Stanley of Alderley. London, 1874 (H).

[Mendaña]. *The Discovery of the Solomon Islands*, edited by Lord Amherst of Hackney and Basil Thomson. 2 vols. London, 1901 (H).

Parkinson, Sydney. *A Journal of a Voyage to the South Seas*. London, 1773.

[Quiros]. *The Voyages of Pedro Fernandez de Quiros*, edited by Sir Clements Markham. 2 vols. London, 1904 (H).
*Austrialia del Espiritu Santo. Documents on the voyage of Quiros to the South Sea, 1605–6*, edited by the Rev. Celsus Kelly, O.F.M. Cambridge, 1965.

[Roggeveen]. *De Reis van Mr. Jacob Roggeveen*, edited by F. E. Baron Mulert. The Hague, 1919.

Tasman, Abel Janszoon. *Journal*, edited by J. E. Heeres. Amsterdam, 1898. *De Reizen van Abel Janszoon Tasman en Franchoys Jacobszoon Visscher . . . in 1642–3 en 1644*, edited by R. Posthumus Meyjes. The Hague, 1919.

[Torres]. *New Light on the Discovery of Australia*, edited by Henry N. Stevens. London, 1930 (H).

[Wallis]. *The Discovery of Tahiti. A Journal of the second voyage of H.M.S. Dolphin . . . written by her master, George Robertson*, edited by Hugh Carrington. London, 1948 (H).

## (b) 'VOYAGES', etc.

Brosses, Charles de. *Histoire des Navigations aux Terres Australes*. 2 vols. Paris, 1756.

Burney, James. *A Chronological History of the Discoveries in the South Sea or Pacific Ocean*. 5 vols. London, 1803–17. *A Chronological History of North-Eastern Voyages of Discovery*. London, 1819.

Callander, John. *Terra Australis Cognita*. 3 vols. Edinburgh, 1766–8.

Dalrymple, Alexander. *An Account of the Discoveries made in the South Pacifick Ocean previous to 1764*. London, 1767. *An Historical Collection of the several Voyages and Discoveries in the South Pacific Ocean*. 2 vols. London, 1770–71.

Fleurieu, C. P. C. de. *Découvertes des François, en 1768 et 1769, dans le sud-est de la Nouvelle Guinée*. Paris, 1790. *Discoveries of the*

*French in 1768 and 1769, to the South-East of New Guinea*. London, 1791.

Harris, John. *Navigantium atque Itinerantium Bibliotheca; or, A complete collection of voyages and travels*. London, 1705. Second edition edited by John Campbell. 2 vols. London, 1744–8.

Hawkesworth, John. *An Account of the Voyages . . . by Commodore Byron, Captain Wallis, Captain Carteret and Captain Cook*. 3 vols. London, 1773.


## (c) MODERN WORKS

Beaglehole, J. C. *The Discovery of New Zealand*. 2nd ed., London, 1961.

Beazley, C. R. *The Dawn of Modern Geography*. 3 vols. London, 1897–1906.

Carrington, Hugh. *Life of Captain Cook*. London, 1939.

Dahlgren, E. W. *The Discovery of the Hawaiian Islands*. Uppsala, 1917.

Dunmore, John. *French Explorers in the Pacific*. [Vol. I] *The Eighteenth Century*. Oxford, 1965.

Giblin, R. W. *The Early History of Tasmania. The Geographical Era 1642–1804*. London, 1928.

Guillemard, F. H. H. *The Life of Ferdinand Magellan*. London, 1890.

Heawood, Edward. *A History of Geographical Discovery in the Seventeenth and Eighteenth Centuries*. Cambridge, 1912.

Henderson, G. C. *The Discoverers of the Fiji Islands*. London, 1933.

Kitson, Arthur. *Captain James Cook*. London, 1907.

Martin-Allanic, Jean Etienne. *Bougainville navigateur et les découvertes de son temps*. 2 vols. Paris, 1964.

Newton, Arthur Percival (editor). *Travel and Travellers of the Middle Ages*. London, 1926.

Sharp, Andrew. *The Discovery of the Pacific Islands*. Oxford, 1960. *The Discovery of Australia*. Oxford, 1963.

Stokes, John F. G. *Hawaii's Discovery by Spaniards, Theories traced and refuted*; Papers of the Hawaiian Historical Society, No. 20. Honolulu, 1939.

Taylor, E. G. R. *Tudor Geography 1485–1583*. London, 1930.

Wilkinson, Clennell. *William Dampier*. London, 1929.

Williamson, James A. *The Observations of Sir Richard Hawkins.* Edited . . . with Introduction, Notes and Appendices. London, 1933. *Cook and the Opening of the Pacific.* London, 1946.

Wood, G. Arnold. *The Discovery of Australia.* London, 1922. *The Voyage of the Endeavour.* Melbourne, 1926.

Wroth, Lawrence C. *The Early Cartography of the Pacific.* Papers of the Bibliographical Society of America, Vol. 38, no. 2. New York, 1944.

# INDEX

MAPS

J.C. Beaglehole: The Exploration of the Pacific

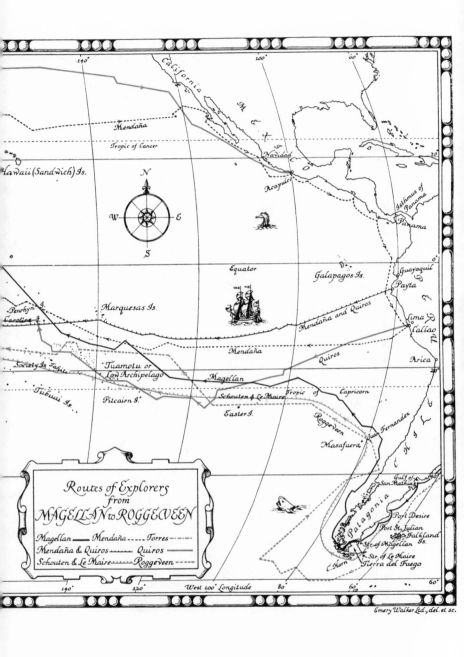

Routes of Explorers
from
MAGELLAN to ROGGEVEEN

| | | |
|---|---|---|
| Magellan ——— | Mendaña ..... | Torres —··—··— |
| Mendaña & Quiros ——— | Quiros ——— | |
| Schouten & Le Maire ————— | Roggeveen ————— | |

Emery Walker Ltd., del. et sc.

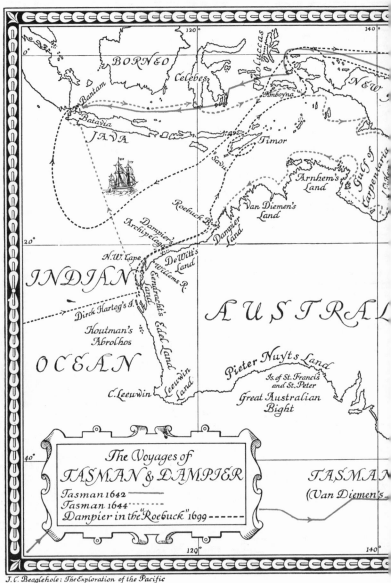

BORNEO

Celebes

Bantam

Batavia

JAVA

Moluccas

Amboyna

Timor

Seru

NEW

Gulf of Carpentaria

Arnhem's Land

Van Diemen's Land

Roebuck B.

Dampier's Archipelago

Dampier Land

DeWitt's Land

N.W. Cape

Willem's R.

Endracht's Land

INDIAN

Dirck Hartog's I.

Houtman's Abrolhos

Edel Land

Leeuwin Land

OCEAN

C. Leeuwin

AUSTRAL

Pieter Nuyts Land

Is. of St. Francis and St. Peter

Great Australian Bight

The Voyages of
TASMAN & DAMPIER
Tasman 1642 ———
Tasman 1644 ············
Dampier in the "Roebuck" 1699 ------

TASMAN
(Van Diemen's

160°

180°

Gilbert

*Equator* 0°

Islands

New Hanover

New Ireland

*Le Maire I.*

Solomon

Ontong Java

New
Britain

Dampier Str.

Is.

Sta. Cruz Is.

Ellice

Islands

New

Hebrides

Horne I.

Fiji Is.

Tonga
(Friendly)
Is.

New
Caledonia

Tongatapu

Eua

20°

Norfolk I.

Kermadec Is.

N

Three Kings I.
C. Maria van Diemen

W E

T A S M A N

Mt. Egmont

C. Farewell

S

40°

S E A

Cook Strait

Storm Bay

Southern Alps

Chatham Is.

160°

180°

Emery Walker Ltd., del. et sc.

CHINA

JAPAN

Macao

20°

Manila · Philippine Is.

Samar

Mindanao

Pelew Is.

Borneo

Celebes

Batavia

Java

Timor

Molaccas

New Guinea

Admiralty Is.

New Ireland

Green I.

Marchen I.

Solomon Is.

Louisiade Arch.

Torres Str.

Great Barrier Reef

Endeavour Str.

Tinian

Guam

Ladrone Is.

Wake I.

Caroline Islands

Marshall Is.

Gilbert Is.

Byron I.

Phœ

Ontong Java

Ellice

Is.

Toke

Santa Cruz Is.

Banks Is.

Horne Is.

Wallis

Espiritu Santo

New Hebrides

Fiji Is.

AUSTRALIA

20°

New Caledonia

Loyalty Is.

To

(Frie

Kerma

40°

Bass Strait

Tasmania

Tasman

Sea

New

Zealand

Chat

60°     80°          100°     East 120° Longitude     140°          160°          180°

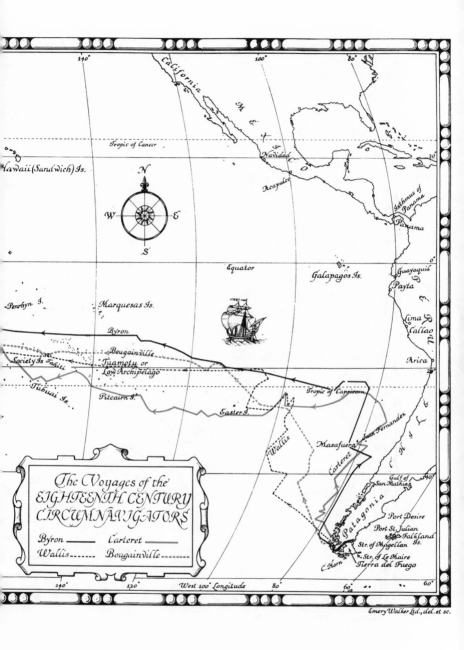

The Voyages of the EIGHTEENTH CENTURY CIRCUMNAVIGATORS

Byron ——  Carteret ——
Wallis ------  Bougainville -----

California

Mexico

Tropic of Cancer

Hawaii (Sandwich) Is.

Navidad

Acapulco

Isthmus of Panama

Panama

Equator

Galapagos Is.

Guayaquil

Payta

Penrhyn I.

Marquesas Is.

Lima
Callao

Byron

Bougainville

Arica

Society Is Tahiti

Tuamotu or
Low Archipelago

Tubuai Is.

Pitcairn I.

Tropic of Capricorn

Easter I.

Wallis

Masafuera

Juan Fernandez

Carteret

Gulf of
San Mathias

Patagonia

Port Desire

Port St. Julian

Falkland Is.

Str. of Magellan

C. Horn

Str. of Le Maire

Tierra del Fuego

140°    120°    West 100° Longitude    80°    60°    60°

Emery Walker Ltd., del. et sc.

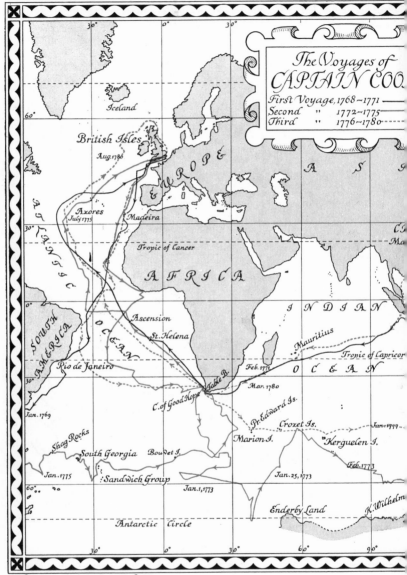

The Voyages of
*CAPTAIN COO*

*First Voyage, 1768–1771* ———
*Second* " *1772–1775* ———
*Third* " *1776–1780* - - - - -

30° 0° 30°

Iceland

British Isles
*Aug. 1780*

E U R O P E

A        S

Azores
*July 1775*        Madeira

30°

Tropic of Cancer

A F R I C A

I N D I A N

Ascension

St. Helena

Mauritius

Tropic of Capricor

Rio de Janeiro        Feb. 1771        O C E A N

Table B.

C. of Good Hope        Mar. 1780

Pr. Edward Is.

*Jan. 1769*

Shag Rocks        Croxet Is.        *Jan. 1777*

South Georgia        Bouvet J.        Marion J.        Kerguelen J.

*Jan. 1775*        Feb. 1773

Sandwich Group        Jan. 25, 1773

*Jan. 1, 1773*

60°

Enderby Land        K. Wilhelm

Antarctic        Circle

30°        0°        30°        60°        90°